The First Book of
Norton Utilities® 7

The First Book of
Norton Utilities® 7

Joseph Wikert
Revised by Lisa Bucki

alpha
books

A Division of Prentice Hall Computer Publishing
11711 North College, Carmel, Indiana 46032 USA

To "my boys," Steve and Bo, the best darn partners in crime a gal could hope for.

© 1993 by Alpha Books

**THIRD EDITION
FIRST PRINTING—1993**

All rights reserved. No part of this book shall be reproduced, stored in a retrieval system, or transmitted by any means, electronic, mechanical, photocopying, recording, or otherwise, without written permission from the publisher. No patent liability is assumed with respect to the use of the information contained herein. Although every precaution has been taken in the preparation of this book, the publisher and author assume no responsibility for errors or omissions. Neither is any liability assumed for damages resulting from the use of the information contained herein. For information, address SAMS, 11711 N. College Ave., Carmel, IN 46032.

International Standard Book Number: 1-56761-116-8
Library of Congress Catalog Card Number: 92-75150

95 94 93   8 7 6 5 4 3 2 1

Interpretation of the printing code: the rightmost number of the first series of numbers is the year of the book's printing; the rightmost number of the second series of numbers is the number of the book's printing. For example, a printing code of 93-1 shows that the first printing of the book occurred in 1993.

Screen reproductions in this book were created by means of the program Collage Plus from Inner Media, Inc., Hollis, NH.

Printed in the United States of America

Publisher:
Marie Butler-Knight

Associate Publisher
Lisa A. Bucki

Managing Editor:
Elizabeth Keaffaber

Acquisitions Manager:
Stephen R. Poland

Development Editor:
Faithe Wempen

Manuscript Editor:
Audra Gable

Cover Artist:
Held & Diedrich Design

Indexer:
Jeanne Clark

Production Team:
Diana Bigham, Katy Bodenmiller, Scott Cook, Tim Cox, Mark Enochs, Tom Loveman, Roger Morgan, Joe Ramon, Carrie Roth, Greg Simsic

Special thanks to C. Herbert Feltner for ensuring the technical accuracy of this book.

Contents

1　An Introduction to The Norton Utilities　3

　Summarizing the Utilities 4
　　BE: Batch Enhancer 4
　　CALIBRAT: Calibrate 5
　　DISKEDIT: Disk Editor 5
　　DISKMON: Disk Monitor 5
　　DISKREET: Diskreet 5
　　DISKTOOL: Disk Tools 5
　　DUPDISK: Duplicate Disk 6
　　FILEFIND: File Find 6
　　FILEFIX: File Fix 6
　　IMAGE: Image 6
　　NCACHE2: Norton Cache 7
　　NCC: Norton Control Center 7
　　NCD: Norton Change Directory 7
　　NDD: Norton Disk Doctor 7
　　NDIAGS: Norton Diagnostics 8
　　NORTON: The Norton Program 8
　　RESCUE: Rescue Disk 8
　　SFORMAT: Safe Format 8
　　SMARTCAN: SmartCan 9
　　SPEEDISK: Speed Disk 9
　　SYSINFO: System Information 9
　　UNERASE: UnErase 9
　　UNFORMAT: UnFormat 10
　　WIPEINFO: Wipe Information 10
　Accessing the Utilities with the Norton Program 10
　Using Menus and Dialog Boxes 14
　Getting Help 18
　　The Norton Advisor 18
　　Help Within a Utility 19
　　Utility Syntax Help 20
　Quitting a Utility 21

2 DOS and Utility Basics — 23

What Is DOS? 23
DOS Version Numbers 24
Understanding Microprocessors
(the "Brains" of Your PC) 25
Getting a Grip on PC Memory 26
    Comparing RAM and ROM 26
    How Much RAM? 27
    Looking at Other Memory Users—TSRs 28
Storing Your Information—Disks
and Disk Drives 29
    Portable Storage 29
    Storing Data Inside Your System
    on a Hard Disk 30
Getting Information About Your System
with SYSINFO 31
    The File Menu 33
        View CONFIG.SYS 33
        View AUTOEXEC.BAT 33
        View NDOS.INI 33
        View WIN.INI 34
        View SYSTEM.INI 34
        Print Report 34
    The System Menu 35
        System Summary 35
        Video Summary 35
        Hardware Interrupts and Software
          Interrupts 36
        Network Information 36
        CMOS Status 36
    The Disks Menu 37
    The Memory Menu 37
        Memory Usage Summary 37
        Expanded and Extended Memory
          Summaries 39
        Memory Block List 39
        TSR Programs 39
        Device Drivers 40

  The Benchmarks Menu 40
   CPU Speed 40
   Hard Disk Speed 41
   Overall Performance Index 41
   Network Performance Speed 42
 Norton Diagnostics 42
  The Diagnostics Menus 43
 NCC: Norton Control Center 45
  Cursor Size 46
  DOS Colors 46
  Palette Colors 48
  Video Mode 48
  Keyboard Speed 49
  Mouse Speed 51
  Serial Ports 52
  Watches 53
  Country Info 55
  Time and Date 55

3 File and Directory Basics   57

 Understanding Files 57
  Using Wild Card Characters
   in File Operations 58
 Directories and Tree Structures 58
 Managing Your Disks and Directories 60
  Making Directories 62
  Deleting Directories 63

4 Using Norton File Utilities   65

 Finding Files 66
  Searching for Text with FILEFIND 69
  Finding Text Using the Command Line 71
 Working with File Attributes 72
  Setting and Clearing File Attributes 72
  Modifying File Attributes
   from the Command Line 74
  Clearing All Attributes 75
  Filtering File Selections 75

Date/Time Stamps 76
    Setting Date/Time Stamps
      from the Command Line 78
    Using the Default Date and Time 78
Quickly Recovering an Erased File 79
    UNERASE: The Inside Story 81
    What To Do If UNERASE Fails 82
Preserving Deleted Files with SmartCan 83
    Recovering Files from the SMARTCAN 85
    Purging Files from the SMARTCAN 86
Repairing Special Files with FILEFIX 87

5 Managing Your Directories and Disks 91

NCD: Norton Change Directory 92
    The NCD Speed Search 93
    The NCD Function Keys 94
        F1—Getting Help 94
        F2—Rescanning Your Disk 94
        F3—Changing the Drive 95
        F6—Renaming a Directory 96
        F7—Making a Directory 96
        F8—Deleting a Directory 96
    Volume Label Maintenance 97
    Pruning and Grafting Directories 98
Recovering a Deleted Directory 100
    After Recovering a Directory 102
Changing the Order of Directories and Files 103
Finding Your Way Through the Disk Forest 106

6 Maintaining Hard and Floppy Disks 109

Understanding Disk Structures 109
    Bits, Bytes, Sectors, and Clusters 110
    Tracks and Cylinders 111
Disk Areas 112
    Boot Record 113
    Root Directory 113
    File Allocation Table 113
    Data Area 115

Obtaining Disk Information 115
   Disk Summary 116
   Disk Characteristics 118
   Partition Tables 118
Formatting Disks 119
   SFORMAT: The Safe Format Alternative 120
   SFORMAT Options 121
Preserving Important Disk Information 124
   Maintaining a Good "Image" 124
Recovering Data from an Accidentally
  Formatted Disk 126
   The Importance of IMAGE 128
Duplicating a Disk 130
Diagnosing and Correcting Disk Problems 132
   Surface Test Configuration 135
   Other Disk Doctor Options 137
   Undoing NDD Repairs 138

7 Introducing NDOS   141

Loading and Unloading NDOS 141
Getting Help 143
Using NDOS Commands 144
   Entering More Than One Command 145
   Repeating Commands 145
   Wild Cards 146
   Specifying Multiple Files 146
   Hot NDOS Commands 146

8 Enhancing Your Batch Files   151

Creating a Batch File 152
   A Simple Batch File 152
      The ECHO Command 154
      The REM Command 154
      The DIR Command 154
      The PAUSE Command 155
Batch File Parameters 155
Looping Within a Batch File 157
Conditional Execution (IF and GOTO) 158

Interactive Batch Files 160
BE: Batch Enhancer 161
    The CLS Subcommand 164
    The SA Subcommand 164
    The WINDOW Subcommand 166
    The ROWCOL Subcommand 167
    The ASK Subcommand 168
    The ERRORLEVEL Variable 168
    The BOX Subcommand 169
    The BEEP Subcommand 170
    The DELAY Subcommand 170
    Batch Enhancer Script Files 171
    Other Batch Enhancer Commands 174

9 Recovery Techniques   177

Miscellaneous Disk Tools 177
    Using DISKTOOL to Make a Disk Bootable 178
    Backtracking after a Disk RECOVERy 179
    Reviving a Defective Diskette 181
    Marking Clusters 181
    Creating a Rescue Diskette 182
Using the Disk Editor 184
    A Note on Hexadecimal Notation 186
    Working with the Hexadecimal/ASCII View 187
    Selecting Other Views and Objects 188
    Printing Your Selection 190
Manually UNERASEing Files 191

10 Security Techniques   197

Viruses and Disk Protection 197
Monitoring Disk Activity 198
    Disk Monitor Options 200
    Disk Light 201
    Parking Your Hard Disk 201
Protecting Sensitive Files 202
    Encrypting Files 202
    Encryption Options 205
    Decrypting Files 206

Removing a File Permanently with WIPEINFO 207
    WIPEINFO Configuration 208
    Wiping a Disk 210

11 Making Your System More Efficient   215

Using SPEEDISK 215
Using a Disk Cache 218
    NCACHE and Microsoft Windows 219
Using CALIBRAT 219

12 Using the Norton Backup   225

Be Safe—Back It Up! 225
Norton Backup Options 226
Installing and Configuring Backup 227
    Installing the Norton Backup 227
    Configuring the Norton Backup
      for Your System 231
        Program Level...231
        Video and Mouse Settings 231
        Backup Devices 232
        Configuration Tests 232
Working with the Norton Backup............................233
    Getting Help When You Need It 234
    Exiting the Program 235
The Basic Backup 236
    Selecting the Backup Drives 238
    Selecting the Backup Type 239
        Full Backup 239
        Incremental Backup 240
        Differential Backup 240
        Full Copy 240
        Incremental Copy 241
    Selecting Backup Options 241
        Verify Backup Data (Read and Compare) 242
        Compress Backup Data (Save Time) 242
        Password Protect Backup Sets.......................242
        Perform an Unattended Backup 242
        Retry Busy Network Files 242

      Generate a Backup Report 242
      Norton Disk Doctor Scan Before Backup 243
      Audible Prompts (Beep) 243
      Protect Active Backup Sets 243
      Keep Old Backup Catalogs on Hard Disk 243
      Quit After Backup 243
   Selecting Files to Back Up 243
      The Display Option 245
   Starting the Basic Backup 246
Comparing Your Backup Files to the Originals 249
The Basic Restore 250
   Selecting the Drives to Restore to and From 253
   What Is a Catalog? 253
   Selecting Catalog Files 255
   Retrieving and Rebuilding a Catalog 256
   Selecting Restore Options 257
   Selecting Files to Restore 258
   Starting the Basic Restore 259
Using Macros with the Norton Backup 260
   Loading a Setup File 261
   Recording a Backup Macro 261
   Playing a Macro 263

13 Protecting Your System with The Norton AntiVirus   267

What Are Viruses? 267
Introducing The Norton AntiVirus 268
Hard Disk Installation 269
   Running Install 269
   Running The Norton AntiVirus
      with Windows 271
Running Virus Intercept 272
Running Virus Clinic 274
   Moving Around 275
   Configuring The Norton AntiVirus 277
   Scanning 280
   What to Do with the Scan Results 283
Virus Definitions 284
Leaving the Virus Clinic 285

A Installation and Configuration 287

Using the Emergency Disks 287
Installing The Norton Utilities 288
Configuration 292
Setting Up The Norton Utilities to Run
  with Windows 297

B Command Line Utilities 301

Directory Sort (DS.EXE) 302
File Attributes (FA.EXE) 303
File Date (FD.EXE) 304
File Locate (FL.EXE) 305
File Size (FS.EXE) 306
Line Print (LP.EXE) 307
Text Search (TS.EXE) 308

Index 311

Introduction

Congratulations on your purchase of one of the fine software packages from Symantec! This book explains how to use the following Norton products:

- The Norton Utilities Version 7.0
- Norton Backup Version 2.0
- The Norton AntiVirus Version 2.1

If you're just starting out with any of these popular products, you'll appreciate the way topics are covered in *The First Book of The Norton Utilities 7*. This book takes you by the hand and leads you step by step through all the fundamental features of each software package. As a more knowledgeable user, you will appreciate the way important operations are summarized with quick steps in this book.

Conventions Used in This Book

As you read through *The First Book of The Norton Utilities 7* you'll notice certain conventions we've used to make the book easier for you to use.

- Actions that you take (for example, pressing a key, selecting a menu, or choosing an option) will appear in color.

- Text that you should type is shown in `bold color computer type like this`.
- Keys that you press are shown as keycaps, such as ⏎Enter and Tab⇥.
- Many commands are activated by pressing two or more keys at the same time. These key presses or selections are separated by a plus sign (+) in the text. For example, "Press Alt+F1" means that you should hold down the Alt key while you press F1, and then release both at once. (You don't type the plus sign.)
- As a keyboard shortcut, commands often have a selection letter which appears underlined on-screen. In this book, the selection letter is printed in boldface for easy recognition (for example, **F**ile).

QUICK STEPS Look for this icon for Quick Steps that tell you how to perform important tasks in The Norton Utilities. Quick Steps and the page numbers on which they appear are listed on the inside front cover of this book.

FYI IDEAS **FYIdea:** Practical ideas for using The Norton Utilities are outlined throughout this book.

TIP: Helpful tips and shortcuts are included in Tip boxes.

NOTE: Important information that should be noted when using The Norton Utilities is included in Note boxes.

> **CAUTION**
>
> These notes warn you of potential pitfalls and problems which you should avoid when using The Norton Utilities.

This book also uses the following shorthand terms for common mouse operations:

- *Point* means to place the mouse pointer over an object on-screen.

- *Click* means to point to an object and click the left mouse button. Unless told otherwise, you should always use the left mouse button.

- *Double-click* means to point to an object and press the left mouse button twice rapidly.

Acknowledgments

First Edition

I would like to thank Kraig Lane with Peter Norton Computing, Inc., for all his assistance throughout the development of *The First Book of The Norton Utilities*. Thanks also to Richard Swadley, Marie Butler-Knight, Joe Kraynak, and Herb Feltner for all their contributions to this book.—Joe Wikert

Second and Third Editions

My sincere appreciation goes to Marie Butler-Knight and Steve Poland for offering me another opportunity to tickle my computer keys for fun and profit. The fine editorial staff of Alpha Books also deserves a warm thank you for their dedicated efforts to fine-tune this manuscript. Faithe Wempen, development editor; Audra Gable, copy editor; and Liz Keaffaber, managing editor, all can be credited for the quality of this book. And, finally, to my family and friends who patiently put up with excuses like "Can't do it, I've got to write!" for well over a month, I offer both thanks and a warning: "Watch out, because I'm back in circulation."—Lisa Bucki

Trademarks

All terms mentioned in this book that are known to be trademarks or service marks are listed below. In addition, terms suspected of being trademarks or service marks have been appropriately capitalized. Alpha Books cannot attest to the accuracy of this information. Use of a term in this book should not be regarded as affecting the validity of any trademark or service mark.

Clipper is a registered trademark of Nantucket, Inc.

COMPAQ is a registered trademark of COMPAQ Computer Corporation.

CompuServe is a registered trademark of CompuServe Incorporated.

dBASE, dBASE II, dBASE III, dBASE IV, and MultiMate are registered trademarks of Ashton-Tate.

dBXL is a trademark of WordTech Systems, Inc.

DESQview is a trademark of Quarterdeck Office Systems.

FoxBASE is a registered trademark of Fox Software, Inc.

IBM, IBM PC ST, and PS/2 are registered trademarks of International Business Machines Corporation.

Lotus, Symphony, and 1-2-3 are registered trademarks of Lotus Development Corporation.

MCI Logo and MCI Mail are registered service marks of MCI Communications Corporation.

Mosaic Twin is a registered trademark of Mosaic Software, Inc.

MS Word, MS-DOS, MS Works, MS Windows Write, and Excel are trademarks of Microsoft Corporation.

The Norton Utilities, Norton Disk Doctor, WipeFile, Wipe Disk, and UnErase are registered trademarks and Speed Disk, Disk Monitor, Calibrate, Diskreet, and WipeInfo are trademarks of Peter Norton Computing, Incorporated.

PC Paintbrush is a registered trademark of ZSoft Corporation.

Quattro and Paradox are registered trademarks of Borland International, Inc.

R:Base is a registered trademark of Microrim, Inc.

Reflex is a registered trademark of Borland/Analytica, Inc.

Software Carousel is a registered trademark of Paperback Software International.

WordPerfect is a registered trademark of WordPerfect Corporation.

WordStar Pro and WordStar 2000 are registered trademarks of WordStar International, Inc.

Words & Figures is a registered trademark of Lifetree Software, Inc.

XyWrite is a registered trademark of XYQUEST, Inc.

In This Chapter

What the utilities are and what they do

Utility integration

How to get help

This first chapter explains how The Norton Utilities can simplify your life as a PC user. It briefly discusses each utility in general, then takes a close look at the Norton program, which lets you access The Utilities via menus. If you need to install The Norton Utilities on your system, see Appendix A, "Installation and Configuration," for complete instructions.

This chapter reviews these fundamentals of The Norton Utilities:

- If your computer runs DOS, it will also run The Norton Utilities.
- The NORTON program is a handy tool that provides information about (and easy access to) all the other utilities.
- The Norton Utilities offer two different types of on-screen help: help within a utility (using F1) and utility syntax help (using the ? parameter).

Running NORTON to Access the Utilities

1. Type the command **NORTON** at the DOS prompt (usually C> or C:\>).
2. Press [↵Enter]. This starts the main NORTON program.

Chapter

1

An Introduction to The Norton Utilities

As a PC user you may have encountered situations where DOS was not as helpful as you might expect. For example, what if you want to delete a file and make it unrecoverable? As far as DOS is concerned, it's easy to retrieve a file if you haven't saved anything else to the same disk. There is no DOS command to securely delete a file. Fortunately, as an owner of The Norton Utilities, you now have access to tools for solving this and many other DOS-related shortcomings.

The programs included in The Norton Utilities can help you

- Recover files and data when problems occur, and help head off similar losses of data.

- Improve the speed and memory usage of your system.

- Secure against data loss or having data altered or viewed by unauthorized users.
- Complete common computing tasks more efficiently and effectively.

The Norton Utilities will run on any IBM PC or 100% compatible PC running DOS 2.0 or higher with a minimum of 512K of available RAM. The Utilities support the popular display configurations including Hercules, CGA, EGA, VGA, and Super VGA. A hard disk is required.

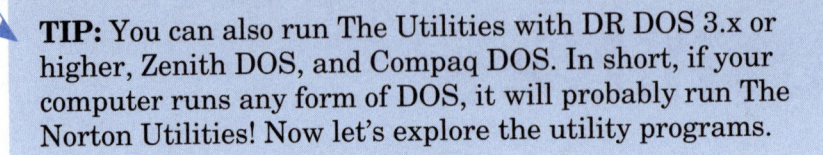

> **TIP:** You can also run The Utilities with DR DOS 3.x or higher, Zenith DOS, and Compaq DOS. In short, if your computer runs any form of DOS, it will probably run The Norton Utilities! Now let's explore the utility programs.

Summarizing the Utilities

The inside back cover of this book lists all the Norton utilities and tells where to look in this book for a detailed explanation of each of them. Following are descriptions of some of the utilities you're most likely to use in your day-to-day operations.

BE: Batch Enhancer

The BE utility adds a great deal of flexibility to the already powerful DOS batch file feature. If you are tired of dull and dreary batch files, you will enjoy using BE to enhance them with color, pop-up windows, sound, and more. Features such as the GOTO, JUMP, and EXIT commands give you more control over batch file execution. Other commands enable you to work with the system clock, reboot your system, or check the status of certain keys. Perhaps the most important benefit of BE, however, is that it lets you easily create interactive menu-driven batch files.

CALIBRAT: Calibrate

The CALIBRAT utility performs several tests on your PC's hard disk. This powerful utility also has the ability to rewrite the data on your hard disk to improve the disk's efficiency and performance.

DISKEDIT: Disk Editor

The DISKEDIT utility enables you to locate, view, and edit virtually all areas of a disk, including RAM, and print selections of the information you're viewing. You can also use DISKEDIT to view important DOS system files, the layout of DOS disks, or even non-DOS or badly damaged disks.

DISKMON: Disk Monitor

The DISKMON utility lets you monitor all disk activity on your system and can prevent computer viruses from invading your system.

DISKREET: Diskreet

Use the DISKREET utility to prevent others from viewing the contents of your personal/private files. DISKREET encodes files with password protection so only you can decode and understand them.

DISKTOOL: Disk Tools

Norton's DISKTOOL utility is actually several tools in one. DISKTOOL lets you perform several disk-related functions, including making a disk bootable, reviving a defective diskette, and saving/restoring important system configuration information.

DUPDISK: Duplicate Disk

You can use the DUPDISK utility to make an exact copy of a disk onto a disk of the same size and capacity (3 1/2", 1.4MB or 720K; 5 1/4", 1.2MB or 360K). DUPDISK uses your computer's expanded or extended memory (part of the random access memory—RAM—on some systems) to store the data you're copying, elimating the need to repeatedly swap disks in and out of a drive. You also can make more than one copy of a disk once its contents are read into RAM. (See Chapter 2 for more on RAM.)

FILEFIND: File Find

As its name implies, the FILEFIND utility helps you find files that may be located anywhere on your disk, but that's only part of FILEFIND's functionality. DOS maintains a set of file attributes and date/time stamps for every file on a disk. In addition to other useful operations, FILEFIND can easily modify a file's attributes and date/time stamps.

FILEFIX: File Fix

FILEFIX is an intelligent file repair tool that can fix damaged Lotus 1-2-3, Symphony, Excel, Quattro Pro, dBASE, and WordPerfect files. FILEFIX builds a new copy of the damaged file, recovering as much data as possible.

IMAGE: Image

Use IMAGE to prepare for an inadvertent file erasure or disk format. IMAGE writes important disk information to a special file that Norton's file recovery utilities (UNERASE and UNFORMAT) use. Image is similar to the MIRROR program that comes with DOS 5 and 6.

NCACHE2: Norton Cache

The Norton Cache utility expedites disk operations by maintaining frequently accessed disk data in expanded or extended memory. This cache utility is easily tailored for any PC configuration. NCACHE2 is also compatible with Windows 3.x. (To run NCACHE2, you need DOS 3.0 or higher and 640K of conventional memory. See Chapter 2 for more on memory.)

NCC: Norton Control Center

The NCC utility provides a centralized function for setting and adjusting everything from DOS's display colors to your keyboard's repeat rate. This utility also allows you to configure up to four serial ports, set your PC's time and date, and more.

NCD: Norton Change Directory

This utility is Norton's answer to DOS's cryptic CHDIR (CD) command, which changes the active directory. It is easy to forget where a subdirectory is located, especially when you have subdirectories off of subdirectories (for example, C:\UTILITY\SHELLS\NU). NCD offers a graphical representation, or tree structure, of your disk's directory layout as well as a speed search option to locate a specific entry quickly. You can easily "prune and graft" to move a directory and its contents (including subdirectories) to a new location.

NDD: Norton Disk Doctor

The NDD utility can diagnose and even correct many common disk problems. NDD is the first utility you should consult when you encounter problems with unreadable and damaged files. You can also try running Disk Doctor for other problems, such as memory problems, which could be file problems in disguise.

NDIAGS: Norton Diagnostics

This new feature in version 7.0 of The Norton Utilities lets you diagnose hardware problems. You can check the operation of components such as the system board, ports, and video display. Use this utility to minimize the time you spend troubleshooting.

NORTON: The Norton Program

Later in this chapter, you will see how the NORTON utility provides a menu from which all the other Norton utilities may be executed. NORTON doesn't just provide access to the other utilities; it also provides detailed help (including syntax for each utility) and help with common DOS and application errors (including the utility that may solve the problem) through the Help feature and The Norton Advisor Help menu command.

RESCUE: Rescue Disk

In some cases, such as when a file allocation table is damaged, you need to use emergency measures to restore your system to operation. The RESCUE utility enables you to create a rescue disk holding critical information such as system files and file allocation tables, and then to recopy that information to a disk when damage has occurred.

SFORMAT: Safe Format

SFORMAT is a powerful utility that provides a safe and fast means to format hard and floppy disks. As noted in Appendix A, which covers installation, you can (and should) let the Installation program replace DOS's FORMAT with Norton's SFORMAT. SFORMAT offers an easy-to-use menu feature for selecting different format modes.

SMARTCAN: SmartCan

This utility is a powerful tool that prevents deleted file data from being overwritten so that files can be recovered long after they are deleted. Copies of deleted files are hidden in a special holding area, from which they can be retrieved on command.

SPEEDISK: Speed Disk

Disks develop inefficient unused areas, or become *fragmented*, as a result of creating, modifying, and deleting files. Fragmented hard disks are a common cause of poor PC performance. Use SPEEDISK to unfragment and optimize your hard disk with one of several different optimization methods.

SYSINFO: System Information

The System Information utility is perhaps best known for calculating common benchmarks for PC performance comparison. This utility also provides PC configuration details, including microprocessor, memory, video, and disk drive information.

UNERASE: UnErase

This cornerstone of The Norton Utilities allows you to quickly and easily recover accidentally deleted files. The sooner you run UNERASE after deleting a file, the better your chances are of complete data recovery. UNERASE is superior to DOS' UNDELETE command in a couple of ways. First, you can use UNERASE to retrieve the deleted file from the SMARTCAN utility, which stores deleted files (as many as it can hold in the disk space you specified) so that they cannot be overwritten by other files you save and copy. Secondly, UNERASE lets you manually rebuild deleted files, so you can recover files that would be unrecoverable with UNDELETE.

UNFORMAT: UnFormat

UNFORMAT is a lifesaver for the "Oops, I just formatted the wrong disk!" syndrome. UNFORMAT recovers as many files as possible from an accidentally formatted disk. Be sure to use the IMAGE utility (discussed earlier) regularly to assist UNFORMAT in its recovery process.

WIPEINFO: Wipe Information

With all of Norton's wonderful data recovery utilities (for example, UNFORMAT and UNERASE), you may be wondering how to permanently remove data from a disk. Norton's WIPEINFO utility overwrites all data in a file or disk so that it cannot be recovered; this is an important utility to use when working with confidential files, particularly on a network. Use WIPEINFO with extreme caution though, because even the most powerful Norton utility cannot recover data from a disk after you run WIPEINFO.

Accessing the Utilities with the Norton Program

Now that you've been briefly introduced to the most important Norton utilities, let's take a closer look at NORTON, the utility integration tool that provides a friendly interface to all the other utilities.

Quick Steps: Running NORTON to Access the Utilities

1. Type **NORTON** at the DOS prompt (usually C> or C:\>).

2. Press ⏎Enter   The NORTON utility starts (see Figure 1.1).

An Introduction to The Norton Utilities

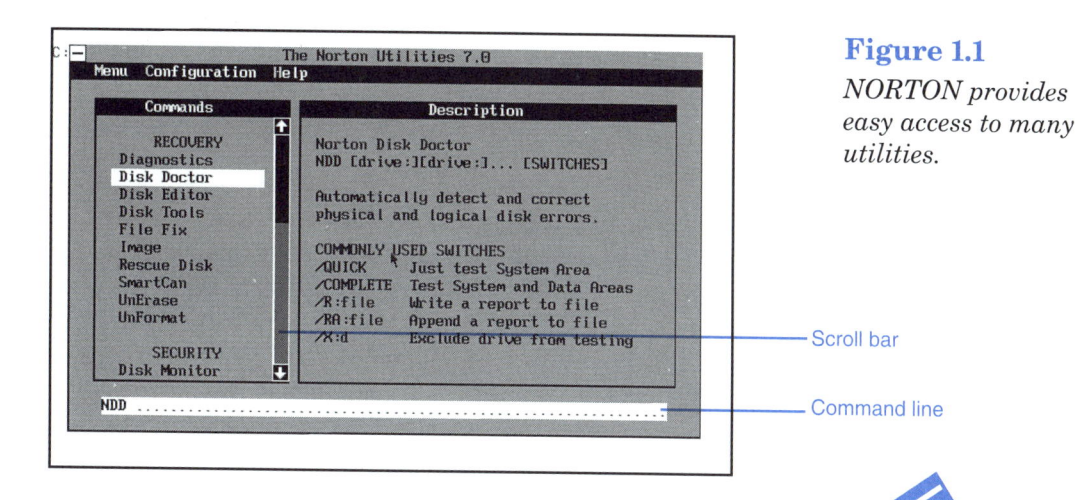

Figure 1.1
NORTON provides easy access to many utilities.

TIP: If the message `Bad command or file name` is displayed, you may have incorrectly installed The Norton Utilities. The configuration portion of the Installation program can (and should) be used to place the Norton directory in your AUTOEXEC.BAT file's PATH statement (for example, PATH=C:\NU). For this change to the AUTOEXEC.BAT file to take effect, you must reboot your PC after installation. For more information, see Appendix A.

The screen in Figure 1.1 is divided into three sections. The left side of Figure 1.1 shows a list of several of the Norton utilities split into categories, such as RECOVERY and SECURITY. Press the down arrow key or click with the mouse to highlight the Disk Doctor entry. The right side of the screen now provides a description of the Norton Disk Doctor (NDD) utility, including syntax and usage. The bottom line of Figure 1.1 contains the letters NDD and a blinking cursor. Press the down arrow key a few times or click on other utility names and notice three things:

- Each time you press the down arrow key, the next utility name in the list on the left side of the screen is highlighted.

Chapter 1

- A description of the newly highlighted utility on the left side of the screen is shown on the right side of the screen.

- The bottom line of the screen changes to show the program name of the highlighted utility.

For example, the screen in Figure 1.2 shows what is displayed when you highlight System Info. (NOTE: The list of utilities on the left side of the screen in Figure 1.1 scrolls up/down when you reach the bottom/top of the exposed portion of the list. The System Information (SYSINFO) utility appears near the end of the tools list.) Note that when you select System Info from the NORTON screen, the command for starting it, SYSINFO, appears in the command line. You can add switches to this command line that will be active when you start the highlighted program.

> **TIP:** Notice that the Commands list in Figure 1.1 has a *scroll bar* along the right side. Using the mouse, click on the up and down arrows at the ends of this and any other scroll bar in The Norton Utilities to move through the list.

Figure 1.2

System Info appears in the Commands list. Highlighting it provides a description of its syntax.

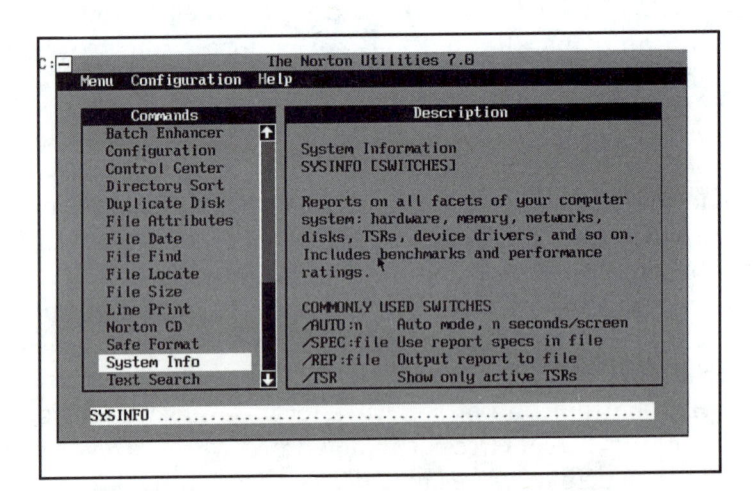

You can run any of the other utilities within NORTON by selecting it, entering any necessary parameters, then pressing `Enter`. Or, you can double-click on the utility name in the list to run the utility.

An Introduction to The Norton Utilities

Select System Info (as shown in Figure 1.2) and press ↵Enter to run SYSINFO and display the System Summary screen in Figure 1.3. You will examine SYSINFO specifics in Chapter 2, so for now, press Esc to return to the screen in Figure 1.2.

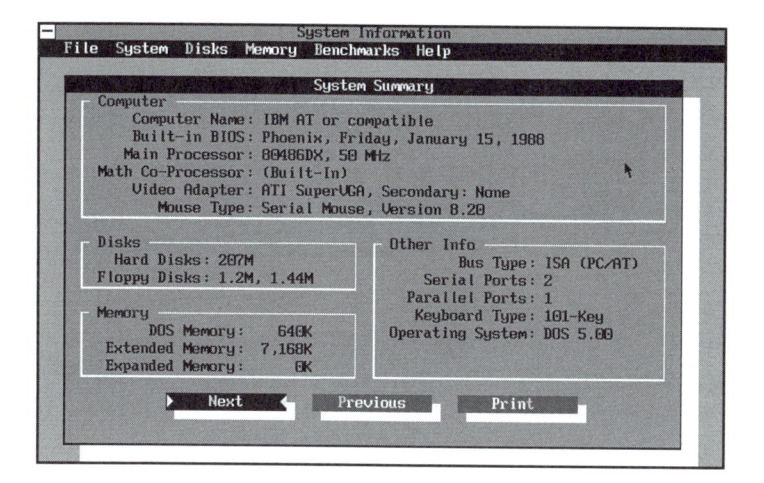

```
┌─ System Information ─────────────────────────┐
│ File System Disks Memory Benchmarks Help     │
│         ┌──────── System Summary ────────┐   │
│         │ Computer                       │   │
│         │   Computer Name: IBM AT or compatible
│         │   Built-in BIOS: Phoenix, Friday, January 15, 1988
│         │   Main Processor: 80486DX, 50 MHz
│         │   Math Co-Processor: (Built-In)
│         │   Video Adapter: ATI SuperVGA, Secondary: None
│         │   Mouse Type: Serial Mouse, Version 8.20
│         │
│         │ ┌─ Disks ──────────┐ ┌─ Other Info ────────────┐
│         │ │ Hard Disks: 207M │ │ Bus Type: ISA (PC/AT)   │
│         │ │ Floppy Disks: 1.2M, 1.44M │ Serial Ports: 2  │
│         │ │                  │ │ Parallel Ports: 1       │
│         │ ┌─ Memory ─────────┐ │ Keyboard Type: 101-Key  │
│         │ │   DOS Memory:   640K │ Operating System: DOS 5.00
│         │ │   Extended Memory: 7,168K
│         │ │   Expanded Memory:    0K
│         │
│         │   ▶ Next ◀   Previous   Print
└──────────────────────────────────────────────┘
```

Figure 1.3
The System Summary screen is the first System Information screen displayed.

You did not specify any parameters when you ran SYSINFO. As you can see in Figure 1.2, the syntax for SYSINFO is

    SYSINFO [switches]

where the *switches* are either /AUTO:n, /SPEC:file, /REP:file, or /TSR as described in the Description panel. Now let's run SYSINFO with a /TSR parameter by selecting System Info on the NORTON screen (Figure 1.2) and typing /TSR on the command line as shown in Figure 1.4.

NOTE: The /TSR parameter tells SYSINFO to display a list of the TSR (terminate-and-stay-resident in memory) programs running on your system.

Figure 1.4
NORTON provides a command line on which to enter parameters.

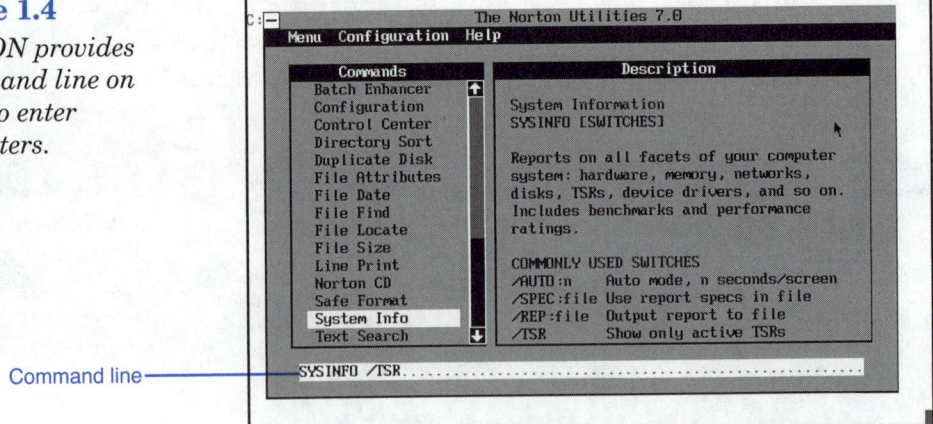

Notice that the /TSR parameter appears at the bottom of the SYSINFO screen as you type it in. The bottom line of the NORTON screen is a pseudo-DOS command line. It will display and allow you to edit the highlighted utility's name and parameters. Now you can press ↵Enter to run SYSINFO with the /TSR parameter. Press Esc to return to the NORTON utility.

Using Menus and Dialog Boxes

Most of the Norton utilities include pull-down menus that offer access to additional utility features and settings. When the NORTON screen in Figure 1.1 is displayed, press F10 and the down arrow to pull down the NORTON **M**enu menu (Figure 1.5). (NOTE: If your PC is configured with a mouse, you can pull down a menu by positioning the mouse cursor over the menu name—for example, **M**enu—and clicking.)

An Introduction to The Norton Utilities   15

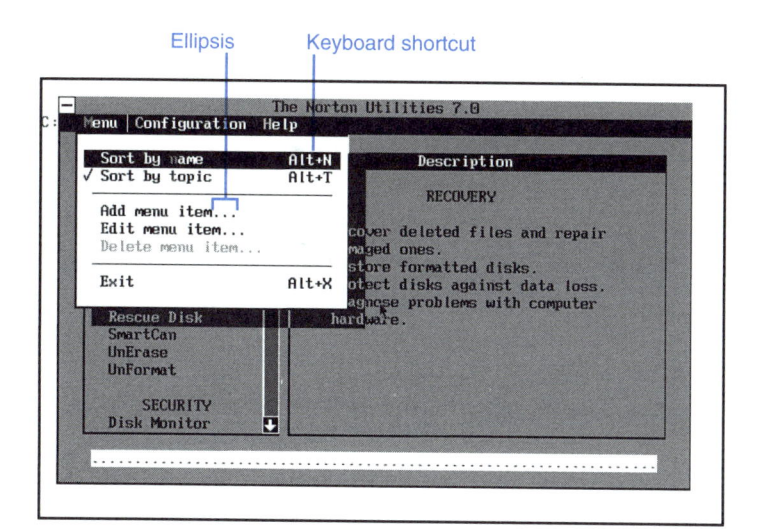

Figure 1.5
The Menu menu is one of three pull-down menus available to customize the program.

> **NOTE:** The following are common mouse operations:
> *Point* means to place the mouse pointer over an object on-screen.
> *Click* means to point to an object and click the left mouse button. Unless told otherwise, you should always use the left mouse button.
> *Double-click* means to point to an object and press the left mouse button twice rapidly.

Some menu commands include keyboard shortcuts that you can use to select the command without using the menu. The ellipsis (...) following some command names means that selecting that command displays a dialog box in which you specify additional choices.

With the **M**enu menu displayed, press the right arrow key or click on Configuration with the mouse to pull down the **C**onfiguration menu. The first option, **V**ideo and mouse..., is highlighted. Press ⏎Enter or click on the Video and mouse... option to see the dialog box in Figure 1.6.

Figure 1.6

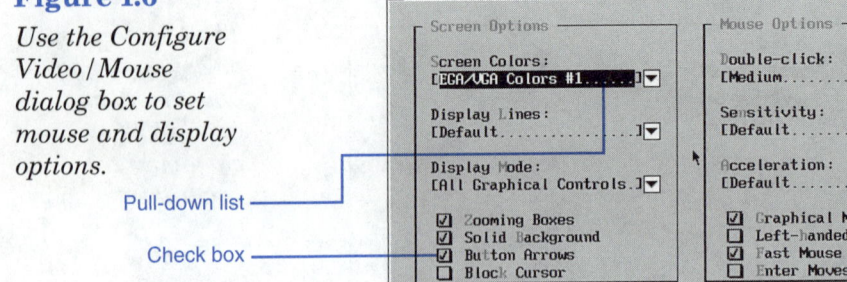

Use the Configure Video/Mouse dialog box to set mouse and display options.

— Pull-down list
— Check box
— Command button

> **TIP:** You can also press the highlighted (and capitalized) letter in a command choice to select it.

The dialog box shown in Figure 1.6 lets you set up The Norton Utilities for your PC's video and mouse configuration. It contains many of the components that appear in a typical dialog box.

> **NOTE:** Your Norton screens (especially the ones that contain dialog boxes) may look different from the ones in this book, depending on the Graphics Option you select when you configure The Norton Utilities during installation or with NUCONFIG. For this book, I've selected EGA/VGA Colors #1 for the **S**creen Colors, the Default Display **L**ines setting, and All Graphical Controls as the Display **M**ode. See Appendix A for more information.

The Norton dialog boxes have check boxes, radio buttons, text boxes, and command buttons. Following are highlights of how to move among and select dialog box options.

An Introduction to The Norton Utilities

- Select an option by pressing the highlighted letter in its name (or press `Alt` plus the higlighted letter, as in `Alt`+`F`) or by clicking on it with the mouse.

- Or, use `Tab`, `↑`, `↓`, `←`, or `→` to move the cursor among the options, then perform a second step to select the option:

  When the cursor is in a check box, press `Enter` to select that option.

  Move to a text box and type your entry.

  Move to a command button and press `Enter` to perform the command.

- You can select only one option button at a time.

- Select the Cancel command button to close a dialog box without invoking its choices.

In addition, dialog boxes may have lists and pull-down lists (that have a down arrow beside them). Use these techniques to make selections from such lists:

- Move to a list and use the up and down arrows to highlight your choice. (You can also use the scroll bar to highlight your choice.) Then press `Enter` to make your selection. Or, you can select a list item by clicking on it.

- Move to the list and press `Alt`+`↓` or click on the arrow beside the list to display the list. Make your selection as you would from a regular dialog box list.

> **NOTE:** Much of this book will give the keystroke method of selecting commands. If you have a mouse, you may find it easier to continue pointing and clicking or double-clicking to make selections.

Getting Help

The Norton Utilities offer two different types of on-screen help: help within a utility and utility syntax help.

The Norton Advisor

The NORTON Help system includes a command called The Norton Advisor, which offers easy-to-read suggestions for solving common hard and floppy disk problems and problems which result in DOS and CHKDSK error messages or error messages from the application programs on your system. For example, if you pull down the **Help** menu, choose The Norton Advisor, and select Application error messages, the screen shown in Figure 1.7 appears. The screen lists the program type and the error messages. Highlight the error message you're getting, then select the Go To command button for an explanation of what might be wrong and a suggested course of action (using one of the Norton utilities, if appropriate).

Figure 1.7
The Advisor provides help for application error messages.

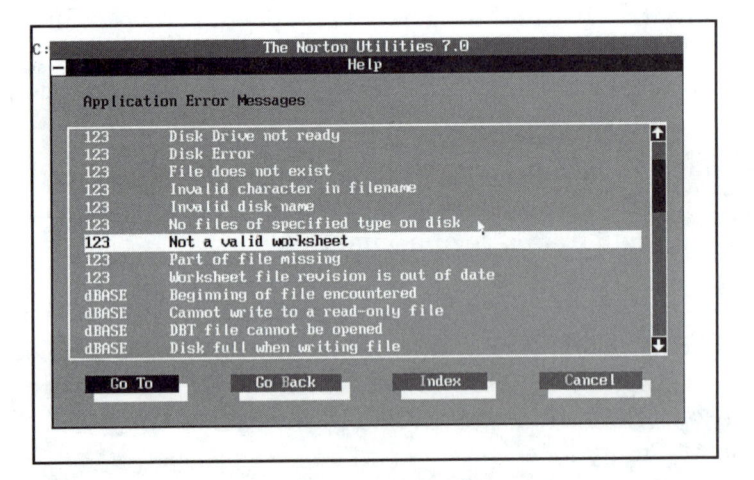

The last choice in the first screen of Advisor, Search..., enables you to check for error messages by entering part of the message or key words from the message. Choosing Search displays the dialog box shown in Figure 1.8. The *cursor* (a blinking underline or box) appears in a *text box*, where you can type the full or partial error message. After you do so, press [Alt]+[I] (or click with the mouse) to select the **I**nclude Application Error Messages check box if you would like to search for application error messages, as well. Then select Start Search to perform the search. When Search finds the message, it will present you with information about the problem and a probable solution.

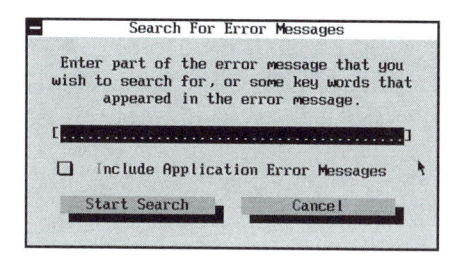

Figure 1.8
The Search For Error Messages dialog box.

Help Within a Utility

The Help screen in Figure 1.9 is displayed if you press [F1] while the NORTON screen is displayed (Figure 1.1).

The screen in Figure 1.9 describes many of the NORTON features we already discussed. Use the up or down arrow keys to scroll through the Help screen and learn more about the NORTON utility. Click on any highlighted topic for more information about it. Most of the Norton utilities display a help screen when you press F1. These help screens provide information about how to use the utility, special keys, and other important points. If you require help within a utility and you don't feel like reaching for the documentation, press [F1], and you might find what you need!

Figure 1.9
NORTON's Help screens provide general information about the program, as well as specific help for each utility.

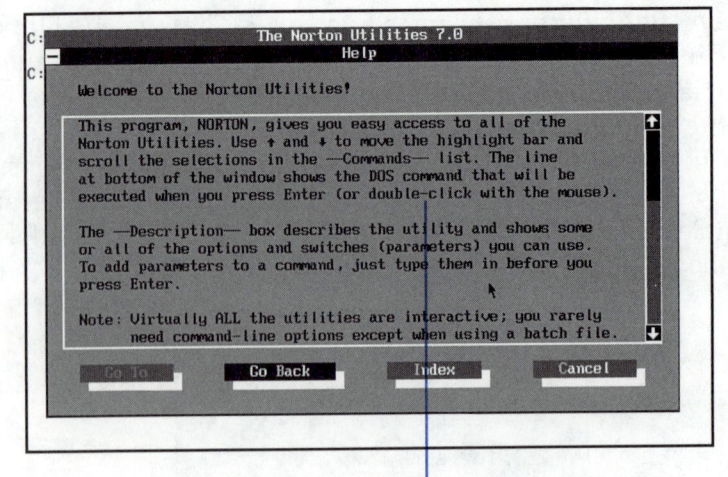

```
C:                    The Norton Utilities 7.0
                              Help
C:
     Welcome to the Norton Utilities!

     This program, NORTON, gives you easy access to all of the
     Norton Utilities. Use ↑ and ↓ to move the highlight bar and
     scroll the selections in the —Commands— list. The line
     at bottom of the window shows the DOS command that will be
     executed when you press Enter (or double-click with the mouse).

     The —Description— box describes the utility and shows some
     or all of the options and switches (parameters) you can use.
     To add parameters to a command, just type them in before you
     press Enter.

     Note: Virtually ALL the utilities are interactive; you rarely
           need command-line options except when using a batch file.

        Go To         Go Back          Index           Cancel
```

Click on a highlighted term for more information about it.

Utility Syntax Help

It's convenient to have help within a utility via the F1 key. But what if you're using a utility directly from the DOS prompt and you want help? All you need to do is type in the utility name with a question mark switch and press ↵Enter. For example, if you want to see SYSINFO's syntax, type **SYSINFO /?** and press ↵Enter, and Norton shows you the syntax as in Figure 1.10.

Figure 1.10
When you type /? after a command, NORTON shows you the proper syntax for the command.

```
System Information  Copyright 1993 by Symantec Corporation

Display system configuration information, and performance statistics.

SYSINFO [/AUTO:n] [/N] [/NOHDM] [/SOUND]
SYSINFO /DEMO
SYSINFO /REP:file1 [/SPEC:file2]
SYSINFO /TSR
SYSINFO [drive:] /SUMMARY
SYSINFO [drive:] /DI

    /AUTO:n        Automatically cycle through all information screens
                   (delay n seconds between screens).
    /N             Suppress Memory Scan.
    /NOHDM         Do not attempt to detect hard drive model.
    /SOUND         Beep between CPU tests.
    /DEMO          Cycle through benchmark tests only.
    /REP:file1     Print a report to the specified file.
    /SPEC:file2    Use the specified report settings.
    /TSR           Print list of TSR programs.
    drive          Drive on which information is desired.
    /SUMMARY       Print SysInfo summary screen.
    /DI            Print information on current or specified drive.

C:\NORTON>
```

An Introduction to The Norton Utilities

The help information in Figure 1.10 might look familiar to you. Similar information was displayed in the NORTON utility for SYSINFO (see Figure 1.2). The /? help feature is handy when you want to quickly see a utility's syntax without running NORTON or thumbing through documentation.

Quitting a Utility

There are several methods of quitting any utility, including the main Norton program. To close or quit a utility, choose one of the following methods.

- Choose the **File Exit** command by clicking on **File** or pressing **Alt**+**F**, then clicking on **Exit** or pressing **X**.

- Double-click the close box shown in the upper left corner of the window, which looks like this: ▬

- Press **Esc**.

In This Chapter

Understanding DOS and PC hardware

Obtaining configuration data with SYSINFO

Testing your hardware with NDIAGS

Configuring PC attributes with NCC

This chapter introduces you to three special utilities, System Information (SYSINFO), Norton Diagnostics (NDIAGS) and Norton Control Center (NCC), which provide operations that are either difficult or impossible to perform via DOS. You also will learn about DOS and a few of the important hardre components within your PC.

Starting a Utility from the DOS Prompt

1. At the DOS prompt, type the command to start the utility, for example:

   - **SYSINFO** for Sdystem Information
   - **NDIAGS** for Norton Diagnostics
   - **NCC** for Norton Control Center.

2. Press ⏎Enter. The first screen of the utility appears.

Chapter 2

DOS and Utility Basics

This chapter explains some DOS and PC hardware fundamentals. You will need to understand these concepts before you can appreciate all the information The Norton Utilities can provide.

What Is DOS?

Your PC's hardware does not directly understand the commands you type at your keyboard. When you enter the command DIR C:*.*, an interface translates the command so that your PC's hardware can understand it. The primary interface between you and your hardware is a program called the **D**isk **O**perating **S**ystem, or DOS, for short.

DOS serves two purposes. First, DOS keeps the computer "awake" and ready to perform. Its command processor (COMMAND.COM) receives and interprets the commands you type, turning your words into action. As you'll learn in Chapter 7, The Norton Utilities comes with its own command processor, NDOS, that you can use as a replacement for COMMAND.COM. NDOS works just like COMMAND.COM, but gives you some additional features and flexibility.

Second, DOS's tool collection allows you to copy, delete, and rename files, format disks, view directories, and the like. Many of DOS's commands can be cryptic and cumbersome to use, though. The Norton Utilities is less cryptic and cumbersome, which is one of the reasons The Norton Utilities is so popular.

DOS Version Numbers

Several different versions of DOS have been distributed since the original DOS for the IBM PC. To see which version of DOS your PC is running, type **VER** at the DOS prompt (which looks like C:> or C:\>) and press ↵Enter. The VER command is another of DOS' many built-in tools. When I run DOS' VER command, it indicates my PC is running MS-DOS version 5.0. The "MS" in MS-DOS stands for Microsoft, the company that develops and distributes the DOS package I use.

Versions of DOS 4.x and higher offer some important improvements, such as the ability to use very large hard disk partitions. (Hard disk partitions are discussed later in this chapter in the PC Disks section.) DOS 4.x and above also offers a "shell," which substitutes a graphic command interface for the traditional DOS command line (entering commands at a prompt).

DOS versions 5.x and 6.x offer even more features. The Norton Utilities supports DOS 5.0 and 6.0's task-switching, deletion-tracking, format recovery, and LOADHIGH (loads and runs specified programs in upper memory) features. If you use DOS 5.0 or 6.0, when you installed The Norton Utilities on your system, you also had the option of adding help about the utilities to the DOS help information.

Regardless of the version, DOS relies on many different components of your PC to do its job. Let's take a look at what I feel is the most important of these components, the microprocessor.

Understanding Microprocessors (the "Brains" of Your PC)

Every PC contains a chip called the Central Processing Unit, or CPU. The CPU controls virtually all processing within the computer. As is true with DOS, several different models of microprocessors have been used in PCs since the IBM PC was introduced.

The CPU holds circuitry that translates all the instructions you enter via the keyboard or mouse. Two important factors determine the efficiency with which your processor operates: the data bus size, which is measured in bits (explained in the next section), and its speed.

> **NOTE:** A microprocessor's speed is expressed in megahertz, or MHz, for short. (Each MHz consists of a million vibrations per second; therefore, 2 MHz is 2 million vibrations per second, and so on.) The original IBM PC's microprocessor ran at 4.77 MHz. Today you can purchase an 80486-based PC running at 25, 33, or even 50 MHz.

Table 2.1 summarizes the bus size and speeds of the CPU chips on computers offered during the last few years.

Chip name	Bus size	Speed
8086	8-bit	4.77Mhz
		10MHz
80286	16-bit	8MHz
		16MHz
80386SX	16-bit	20MHz
		33MHz

Table 2.1
CPU chip bus size and speeds

continues

Table 2.1
Continued

Chip name	Bus size	Speed
80386	32-bit	20MHz
		33MHz
80486	32-bit	33MHz
		50MHz
		66MHz

With this microprocessor knowledge under your belt, let's now take a look at the types of memory your PC uses to store and manipulate data.

Getting a Grip on PC Memory

PC memory consists of silicon chips that store data. The smallest piece of data a chip can store is called a **bi**nary dig**it**, or bit. A binary digit is either a one or a zero; no other values are allowed. A bit is very similar to a light switch, which also has two possible states: on or off. When a bit holds a value of one, we say that the bit is *on*. Alternatively, a bit that is *off* holds a value of zero.

The amount of memory in your PC is expressed in *bytes*; 1 byte is made up of 8 bits. Large amounts of memory are expressed in kilobytes (K) or megabytes (MB). One kilobyte of memory equals 1,024 bytes. For example, if your PC has 640K of memory, it can work with or store up to 640 x 1,024 (655,360) bytes. Each megabyte of memory equals 1,024 kilobytes (1,024 x 1,024), or 1,048,576 bytes.

There are actually two different types of memory in your PC: RAM and ROM.

Comparing RAM and ROM

RAM is short for Random-Access Memory, which means your PC can access different RAM locations without having to traverse every location in between. Actually, your PC can access both RAM and ROM in a random manner, so this is not what differentiates the two.

ROM is an acronym for Read-Only Memory. Your PC can read from ROM memory, but it cannot write to ROM. The primary difference between RAM and ROM is that data can be read from and/or written to RAM; the information held in ROM is fixed and cannot be overwritten.

RAM is sometimes referred to as *volatile memory*. That is, the information stored in RAM is lost when you turn your PC off. In contrast, the contents of ROM are not lost or changed when you turn off your computer. Most ROM chips contain important programs that control fundamental device operations on your PC (for example, disk drive reads/writes).

How Much RAM?

When someone says a PC has 2MB of memory, they are referring to the amount of RAM. Your PC uses RAM to hold your applications programs and their data while the programs are active. Many microprocessors can handle up to 32MB of memory.

When DOS was first developed, the programmers didn't conceive of anyone using more than 640K of RAM, so they designed DOS so 640K was the maximum. To this day, even though you can put many megabytes of RAM into a PC, DOS can't access more than 640K of it directly. That 640K is called *base memory*.

However, as time went by, increasingly sophisticated applications required more than 640K, so tricky DOS programmers developed ways to circumvent the 640K limitation. They built their programs to use the additional chunks of memory indirectly. Suddenly, it became useful to put more than 640K of memory into PCs—many megabytes more. This additional memory became known as either *extended* or *expanded* memory, depending on its type.

Most applications available today, particulary applications that run through Microsoft Windows, require at least 2MB of memory to operate. For instance, Quarterdeck's DESQview program allows you to run several applications simultaneously (multitasking) using extended or expanded memory.

> **TIP:** PC prices have fallen rapidly in the last year, while applications have become more complex—memory- and speed-intensive. If you're in the market for a new PC, buy an 80486-based system that runs at a clock speed of at least 50MHz and has at least 8MB of memory. If you can afford to buy an even faster machine with more memory, do it! Buying the best-equipped system you can afford will enable you to run the latest software products and extend the amount of time you have to enjoy your PC before it becomes outdated.

Looking at Other Memory Users—TSRs

TSR is an acronym for Terminate-and-Stay-Resident. Once a TSR program has been loaded, it becomes almost invisible until you press a special key to use it. This special key or key combination is also called a *hot key*.

TSR programs are executed from the DOS command line like any other program. Once you load a TSR program, it requires a portion of DOS's 640K of accessible RAM to remain resident. Although each TSR program may take up only a few kilobytes of RAM, the 640K pool may be significantly reduced when several TSR programs are loaded. That is when you will start running into problems executing non-TSR programs that require almost all of DOS' 640K of memory.

Fortunately, there are several commercially available utilities that allow you to place your TSR programs in expanded or extended memory rather than base memory. Some TSR programs offer this option as a standard feature so you do not need to purchase a special utility to free up base RAM space. Recent versions of DOS also let you load programs in expanded and extended memory.

Storing Your Information —Disks and Disk Drives

Now let's take a look at another PC storage medium—disks. When you use your PC to store information that you want to retrieve later, the PC writes that information magnetically onto the surface of a *disk*. In contrast to RAM, your PC can read the information it has written to a disk any time in the future. Because disks hold data more permanently, they are often referred to as *storage*.

> **CAUTION**
>
> Don't confuse RAM with disk storage space. If someone says, "Your computer needs more memory to run this program," you need more RAM. If someone says, "You don't have enough space to copy these files," you need more disk space.

Portable Storage

The small, square plastic disks you insert into a drive slot in the front of your computer are called *floppy diskettes*. (Even though the smaller-sized ones have rigid plastic cases, they contain a round, flexible, magnetically-coated disk.) Several brands and models of floppy diskettes are on the market. Table 2.2 gives storage information for the four most popular floppy diskette types. Check a disk label if you're not sure what density it is.

Table 2.2
Floppy Disk Specifications

Disk Size	Type	Storage Capacity
5 1/4"	Double-sided, double-density	360K
5 1/4"	Double-sided, high-density	1.2MB
3 1/2"	Double-sided, double-density	720K
3 1/2"	Double-sided, high-density	1.44MB

Drives on older PCs (called low- or double-density drives) may only be capable of reading double-density floppy diskettes. Newer, high-density drives can read both double- and high-density diskettes.

> **CAUTION** If you use a high-density drive to format a double-density diskette, you must tell your PC to format the disk as double-density. Chapter 6 describes The Norton Utility, SFORMAT, which lets you tell your system how to format disks.

Storing Data Inside Your System on a Hard Disk

In the early days of PCs, data storage was limited to slow, low-density floppy disks. Nowadays, most PCs come equipped with an internal hard disk, which stores data magnetically just as floppy disks do. The original PC hard disks stored from 5 to 30MB of data. Today's hard disks are much faster than those earlier models and offer up to several hundred megabytes of storage in one unit.

If you are using DOS 2.x or 3.x, you are limited to a maximum hard disk partition size of 32MB. When you partition a hard disk via DOS' FDISK command, you are telling DOS how to configure the hard disk as one or more *logical drives*. Although you have only one physical hard disk in your PC, you can have DOS treat it as several logical disk drives (for example, C:, D:, and E:). For example, if you have a 100MB hard disk, you could use FDISK to partition it as follows:

Logical Drive	Size (in megabytes)
C:	32
D:	32
E:	32
F:	4

Versions 4.0 and above of DOS allow unlimited logical disk partition sizes. The 100MB disk just described can be set up via FDISK as one 100MB partition.

Disks and disk formats are fairly complex subjects, and we have only scratched the surface of the subject so far. More advanced disk concepts, as well as the disk-based Norton utilities, are covered in Chapters 5 and 6.

Getting Information About Your System with SYSINFO

We briefly discussed SYSINFO (the System Information utility) in Chapter 1, and you saw how it can be invoked from the main NORTON program. Now let's use our newly found DOS and hardware knowledge to see exactly what SYSINFO reports. You can also invoke SYSINFO directly from the DOS prompt as shown in the following Quick Steps.

Chapter 2

QUICK STEPS

Starting SYSINFO from the DOS Prompt

1. At the DOS prompt, type `SYSINFO` and press `Enter`.

   The System Summary screen is displayed (Figure 2.1).

2. Press `Enter`.

   The Video Summary screen is displayed.

3. Press `Enter`.

   The Hardware Interrupts screen is displayed.

4. Keep pressing `Enter` to browse through the rest of SYSINFO's screens.

5. When you want to leave SYSINFO, press `Esc`, double-click on the close box in the upper left corner of the screen, or choose File Exit.

   SYSINFO returns you to the DOS prompt.

Figure 2.1
The System Summary screen contains general system information.

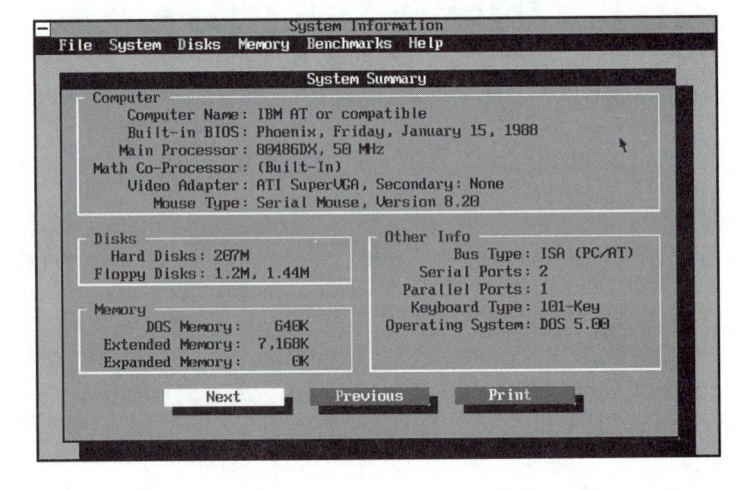

```
┌─ System Information ─────────────────────────────────┐
│ File  System  Disks  Memory  Benchmarks  Help        │
├──────────────── System Summary ──────────────────────┤
│ ┌─ Computer ─────────────────────────────────────┐   │
│ │     Computer Name: IBM AT or compatible        │   │
│ │      Built-in BIOS: Phoenix, Friday, January 15, 1988 │
│ │     Main Processor: 80486DX, 50 MHz            │   │
│ │  Math Co-Processor: (Built-In)                 │   │
│ │       Video Adapter: ATI SuperVGA, Secondary: None │
│ │         Mouse Type: Serial Mouse, Version 8.20 │   │
│ └────────────────────────────────────────────────┘   │
│ ┌─ Disks ──────────────┐ ┌─ Other Info ──────────┐   │
│ │   Hard Disks: 207M    │ │    Bus Type: ISA (PC/AT) │
│ │ Floppy Disks: 1.2M, 1.44M │ │ Serial Ports: 2   │   │
│ └──────────────────────┘ │ Parallel Ports: 1     │   │
│ ┌─ Memory ─────────────┐ │ Keyboard Type: 101-Key │   │
│ │    DOS Memory: 640K   │ │ Operating System: DOS 5.00 │
│ │ Extended Memory: 7,168K│ └───────────────────────┘   │
│ │ Expanded Memory:    0K│                             │
│ └──────────────────────┘                             │
│         [  Next  ]  [ Previous ]  [  Print  ]        │
└──────────────────────────────────────────────────────┘
```

The SYSINFO menus provide five types of information: **F**ile, **S**ystem, **D**isks, **M**emory, and **B**enchmarks. (You also can access **H**elp.) If you keep pressing Enter to view the next screen, all the **S**ystem menu screens are displayed first, followed by all the **D**isks menu screens, and so on. If you don't want to display all the SYSINFO screens, you can quickly jump from one SYSINFO screen to any other one by choosing the SYSINFO command you want from the pull-down menus.

The File Menu

The **F**ile menu allows you to view several files that perform special functions for your system and print a SYSINFO report.

View CONFIG.SYS

CONFIG.SYS is an important file, containing configuration information for special devices or device drivers used with your PC. (*Device drivers* are applications that allow DOS to recognize and interface with special hardware devices such as a mouse.) The View **C**ONFIG.SYS option on the **F**ile menu lets you look at the contents of your CONFIG.SYS file.

View AUTOEXEC.BAT

AUTOEXEC.BAT is a special type of file called a *batch file*. (Batch files are thoroughly discussed in Chapter 8, "Enhancing Your Batch Files.") AUTOEXEC.BAT contains the set of commands that are executed every time you turn on or reboot your PC. The View **A**UTOEXEC.BAT option on the **F**ile menu lets you look at the contents of your AUTOEXEC.BAT file.

View NDOS.INI

NDOS.INI contains configuration information for NDOS, the Norton command interpreter you can use in place of DOS' COMMAND.COM. The View **N**DOS.INI command on the **F**ile menu lets you look at this file, but not edit it.

View WIN.INI

If you have Microsoft Windows on your system, you're probably aware that the WIN.INI file determines numerous aspects of how Windows appears on-screen, controls fonts available to Windows, contains information about Windows applications, and more. This **F**ile menu command lets you view the contents of WIN.INI.

View SYSTEM.INI

Another file Windows reads when it starts is SYSTEM.INI. This file controls Windows sound and video (screen) drivers, among other aspects of the Windows operating environment. And, of course, the View **SYSTEM.INI** command on the **F**ile menu lets you take a look at this file.

Print Report

If you would like a printout of all of SYSINFO's statistics, you can select the Print Report option from the File menu. This displays the Report Topics screen shown in Figure 2.2.

The Report Topics screen lets you construct customized SYSINFO reports by choosing which SYSINFO screens to print. You can even specify a report header and/or special notes you want to appear at the bottom of the report. The SYSINFO report can be sent directly to your printer or written to a file. You also can **S**ave your settings and **L**oad them again later.

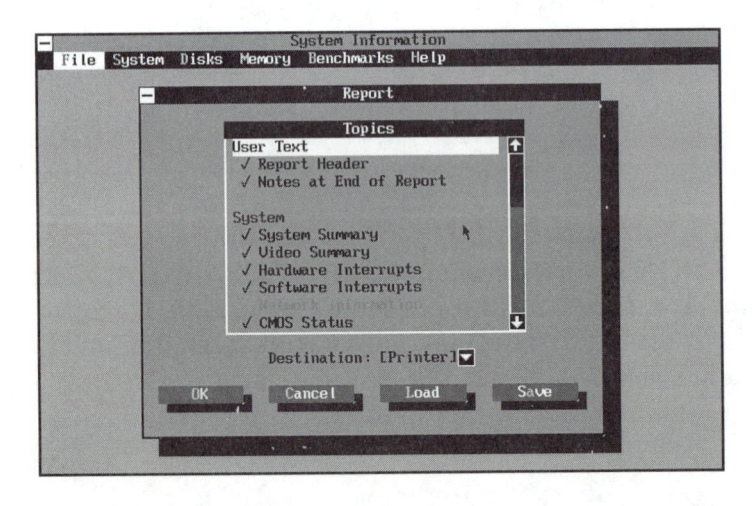

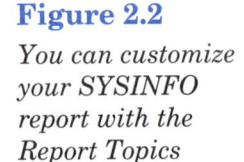

Figure 2.2

You can customize your SYSINFO report with the Report Topics screen.

The System Menu

The System menu consists of six selections: **S**ystem Summary, **V**ideo Summary, **H**ardware Interrupts, Software **I**nterrupts, **N**etwork Information, and **C**MOS Status.

System Summary

The System Summary screen (Figure 2.1) provides details about your computer system, including disk/memory size and other interesting facts. The screen is split into four areas: Computer, Disks, Memory, and Other Info. Most of the information displayed is self-explanatory, but you should note a couple of important items.

The second line in the Computer section, Built-in BIOS:, indicates the date of my PC's Basic Input/Output System (BIOS) ROM. The BIOS provides an interface to your PC's hardware for input/output activities. The BIOS date could be important if you are having problems running certain programs on your PC. Check with your PC dealer to determine if your BIOS is out-of-date and needs to be upgraded.

The System Summary screen is also an excellent reference for quickly determining a PC's configuration. For example, in Figure 2.1, you can see that my PC is an 80486-based model with a 207MB hard disk and 1.2MB and 1.44MB floppy disk drives. Further, I have a SuperVGA video card, a mouse, and a 101-key keyboard.

Video Summary

The **V**ideo Summary screen (Figure 2.3) shows information about your PC's video configuration. This information includes details about your PC's display adapter, character specifics, and video memory.

Figure 2.3

The Video Summary screen reports your PC's video configuration.

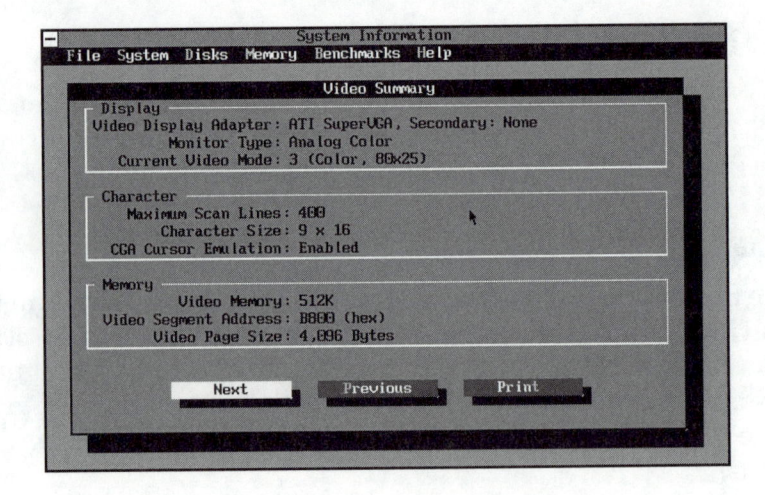

```
┌─────────────────── System Information ───────────────────┐
│ File System Disks Memory Benchmarks Help                 │
│  ┌──────────────── Video Summary ──────────────────────┐ │
│  │ ┌─Display─────────────────────────────────────────┐ │ │
│  │ │ Video Display Adapter: ATI SuperVGA, Secondary: None│ │
│  │ │         Monitor Type: Analog Color              │ │ │
│  │ │    Current Video Mode: 3 (Color, 80x25)         │ │ │
│  │ └─────────────────────────────────────────────────┘ │ │
│  │ ┌─Character───────────────────────────────────────┐ │ │
│  │ │     Maximum Scan Lines: 400                     │ │ │
│  │ │         Character Size: 9 x 16                  │ │ │
│  │ │    CGA Cursor Emulation: Enabled                │ │ │
│  │ └─────────────────────────────────────────────────┘ │ │
│  │ ┌─Memory──────────────────────────────────────────┐ │ │
│  │ │          Video Memory: 512K                     │ │ │
│  │ │   Video Segment Address: B800 (hex)             │ │ │
│  │ │       Video Page Size: 4,096 Bytes              │ │ │
│  │ └─────────────────────────────────────────────────┘ │ │
│  │                                                      │ │
│  │        [ Next ]      [ Previous ]     [ Print ]     │ │
│  └─────────────────────────────────────────────────────┘ │
└──────────────────────────────────────────────────────────┘
```

Hardware Interrupts and Software Interrupts

The next two SYSINFO screens provide information about hardware and software interrupts. An interrupt causes the microprocessor to stop what it is currently doing and perform some special task. The interrupt information provided on these screens is useful for programmers writing sophisticated applications and identifying the sources of memory conflicts.

Network Information

The Network Information screen is accessible only if your PC is connected to a Novell network. This screen reports miscellaneous network and network-user details.

CMOS Status

The last SYSINFO screen in the **S**ystem category, the CMOS Values screen, provides specifics about your PC's memory and hard/floppy disk drives and appears when you select **C**MOS Status.

CMOS is an abbreviation for Complementary Metal-Oxide Semiconductor. CMOS RAM chips require less power than non-CMOS RAM chips, so that the small battery within your PC is enough to preserve their contents even after the computer is turned off. Your PC's hardware configuration information is stored in CMOS memory.

The CMOS Values screen shows the contents of this memory in a readable form. If any invalid or incorrect results are shown in the CMOS Status portion of the CMOS Values screen, you should consult your PC owner's manual and/or run the SETUP utility that accompanied your PC.

> **NOTE:** SETUP is not a Norton utility. It is a hardware configuration utility that should have been delivered with your PC. If you cannot find your system's SETUP utility, contact your PC dealer.

The Disks Menu

For information about the SYSINFO **D**isks menu, refer to Chapter 6, "Maintaining Your Hard Disk Drive."

The Memory Menu

The Memory menu contains six selections: Memory **U**sage Summary, **E**xpanded Memory (EMS), E**x**tended Memory (XMS), Memory **B**lock List, **T**SR Programs, and **D**evice Drivers.

Memory Usage Summary

The screen in Figure 2.4 is displayed when you select the Memory **U**sage Summary option from the **M**emory menu.

Figure 2.4

The Memory Summary screen shows how your PC's memory is being used.

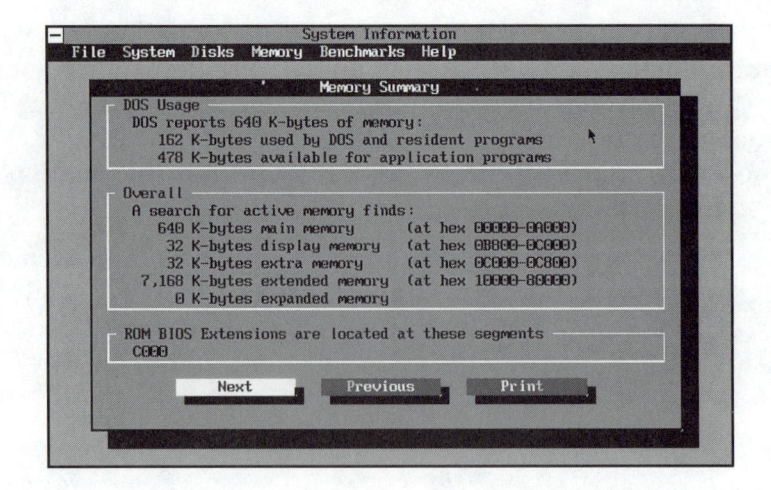

```
┌─ System Information ────────────────────────────┐
│ File  System  Disks  Memory  Benchmarks  Help   │
├─────────────── Memory Summary ──────────────────┤
│ ┌─ DOS Usage ───────────────────────────────┐   │
│ │ DOS reports 640 K-bytes of memory:        │   │
│ │   162 K-bytes used by DOS and resident programs │
│ │   478 K-bytes available for application programs│
│ └───────────────────────────────────────────┘   │
│ ┌─ Overall ─────────────────────────────────┐   │
│ │ A search for active memory finds:         │   │
│ │   640 K-bytes main memory     (at hex 00000-0A000) │
│ │    32 K-bytes display memory  (at hex 0B000-0C000) │
│ │    32 K-bytes extra memory    (at hex 0C000-0C800) │
│ │ 7,168 K-bytes extended memory (at hex 10000-80000) │
│ │     0 K-bytes expanded memory             │   │
│ └───────────────────────────────────────────┘   │
│ ┌─ ROM BIOS Extensions are located at these segments ─┐ │
│ │ C000                                       │   │
│ └───────────────────────────────────────────┘   │
│        [  Next  ]   [ Previous ]   [  Print  ]  │
└─────────────────────────────────────────────────┘
```

The Memory Summary screen in Figure 2.4 displays information about the various types of memory in your PC. This memory information is reported in three categories: DOS Usage, Overall, and ROM BIOS Extensions.

The DOS Usage section in Figure 2.4 shows the amount of memory used by and accessible to DOS. The total amount of memory reported by DOS is then split into two areas: memory used by DOS and resident programs (for example, TSR programs) and memory available for application programs.

In the Overall section of Figure 2.4, SYSINFO reports the total size and location of five memory areas: main memory, display memory, extra memory, extended memory, and expanded memory.

The total amount of *main memory* is generally equal to the amount of DOS (base) memory already reported. (One exception to this rule is if you are using an application switcher like SoftLogic Solutions' Software Carousel, which lets you keep several applications loaded in memory simultaneously.)

The amount of *display memory* reported by SYSINFO depends on what type of video adapter (CGA, EGA, VGA, and so on) you are using.

If you have memory available above the base 640K and below 1M, it will be listed as *extra memory*.

The amount of *expanded/extended memory* should reflect the total expanded or extended memory installed on your PC.

The ROM BIOS Extensions section in Figure 2.4 indicates the memory locations of any ROM BIOS extensions (for example, special add-on boards).

Expanded and Extended Memory Summaries

The Expanded Memory Summary screen is available only if you've added an expanded memory board to your system that lets it use memory beyond 640K, or if you've used one of several software options (such as EMM386) to convert extended memory to expanded memory. When available, select **E**xpanded Memory (EMS) from the **M**emory menu to display the summary of how much expanded memory is available, how it's allocated, and how it's managed.

Extended Memory (available on 80286, 80386, and 80486 PC compatibles) is memory above 1 MB used by DOS and the internal system. When you select the **Ex**tended Memory (XMS) choice from the **M**emory menu, the summary screen that appears tells you how much extended memory is available and gives you details about how it's allocated.

Memory Block List

The DOS Memory Blocks screen is displayed when you select the Memory **B**lock List option from the **M**emory menu. This screen displays information about DOS memory allocation, including the memory Address, Size, Owner, and Type (data, environment, or program).

TSR Programs

The TSR Programs screen shown in Figure 2.5 lists information about any active TSR applications.

Figure 2.5
All active TSR programs are listed on the TSR Programs screen.

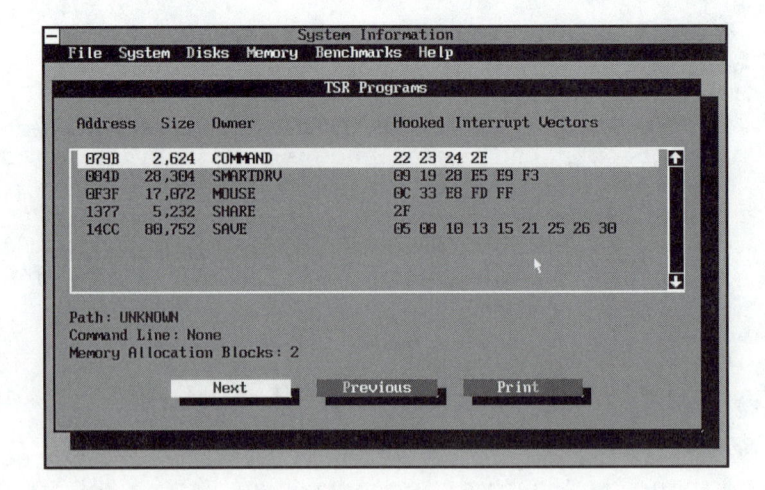

Device Drivers

The Device Drivers screen lists memory locations, names, and descriptions for all device drivers currently loaded in your PC.

The Benchmarks Menu

Norton's System Information is well known for its benchmark (PC performance comparison) reporting.

The **B**enchmarks menu offers four comparison selections: **C**PU Speed, **H**ard Disk Speed, **O**verall Performance Index, and **N**etwork Performance Speed.

CPU Speed

The CPU Speed screen (Figure 2.6) shows the CPU benchmark results of the PC being tested, along with the results of three other computers: a Compaq 486/33 MHz, an IBM AT 286/8 MHz, and an IBM PC XT 88/4.77 MHz.

The CPU speed information shown in Figure 2.6 is fairly easy to interpret. The IBM PC XT 88/4.77 MHz computer listed is an IBM PC XT with an 8088 microprocessor running at 4.77 MHz. SYSINFO's benchmark calculations show a comparison of the PC being tested to the IBM PC XT.

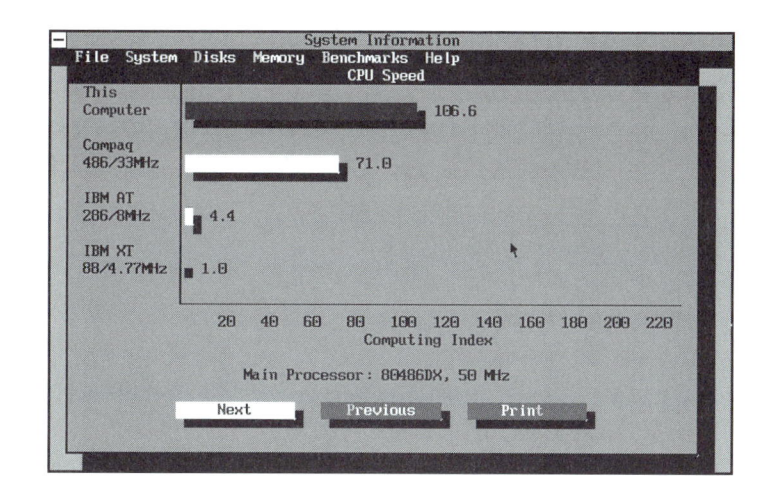

Figure 2.6
Microprocessor benchmark results are reported on the CPU Speed screen.

Figure 2.6 reports a 1.0 CPU rating for the IBM PC XT 88/4.77 MHz computer and a 4.4 rating for the IBM AT 286/8 MHz computer. So according to SYSINFO, the IBM AT's (286/8 MHz) microprocessor is 4.4 times as fast as the IBM PC XT's (88/4.77 MHz) microprocessor. Further, the Compaq's (486/33 MHz) microprocessor is 71.0 times as fast as the IBM PC XT's (88/4.77 MHz) microprocessor.

The CPU rating for this computer, shown at the top of Figure 2.6, is for my PC. As you can see, the SYSINFO CPU speed rating for my PC is 106.6. The bottom of Figure 2.6 also shows that my PC has an 80486DX microprocessor running at 50 MHz.

Hard Disk Speed

The SYSINFO **H**ard Disk Speed screen compares the performance of your PC's hard disk with a Compaq 486 disk, an IBM AT disk, and an IBM PC XT disk. The Disk Speed screen also reports other technical disk statistics, including average seek time, track-to-track seek time, and data transfer rate.

Overall Performance Index

The performance values reported in the CPU Speed and Disk Speed screens are averaged and presented in the Overall Performance Index screen.

Network Performance Speed

The Network Performance Speed screen is the last screen displayed in the SYSINFO Benchmarks area. This screen reports network read/write throughput values if your PC is connected to a Novell network.

Norton Diagnostics

One of the features that's new to version 7 of The Norton Utilities is the Norton Diagnostics (NDIAGS) utility. This program lets you test your system's hardware so you can diagnose problems.

Start Norton Diagnostics by typing **NDIAGS** at the DOS prompt and pressing Enter. You also can start it by choosing Diagnostics from the RECOVERY section of the Commands list at the left side of the main Norton program screen. Press Enter to proceed past the introductory screens that appear, and you'll see the main diagnostics screen (see Figure 2.7).

Figure 2.7

The opening screen of the Norton Diagostics program resembles the System Information screen, but displays different menu names.

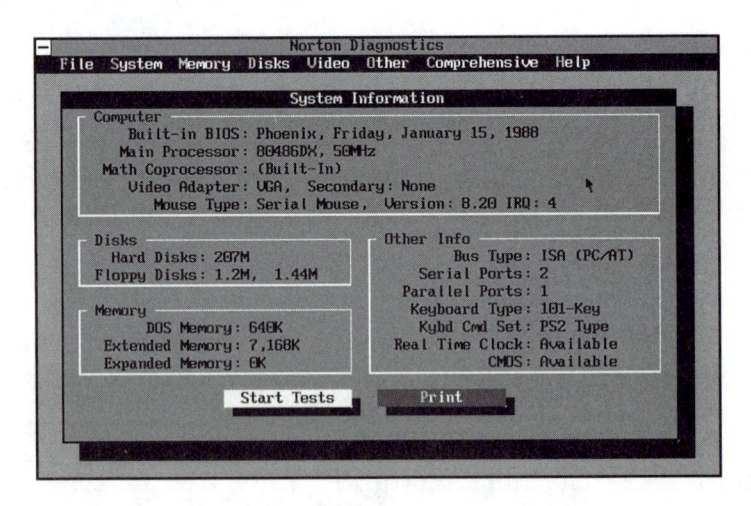

DOS and Utility Basics

> **TIP:** You'll also see an introductory information screen each time you start a diagnostic test. You can turn off these screens by turning on the Disable Intro. Messages check box anywhere it appears, or by using the File Options command.

To start any diagnostic test, simply choose its name from the menu where it appears. Some tests may ask you to respond to various prompts to progress. You also can choose to Cancel a test at any time. After Diagnostics finishes a test, it displays a screen with the test results and three choices. Choose Next Test to perform the next test listed on the menu you chose, Repeat Test to rerun the test just performed, or Print to output the test results to your printer. The following paragraphs describe the Norton Diagnostics menus and the tests you can select.

The Diagnostics Menus

The File menu lets you view and change some aspects of the current Hardware Configuration, such as the type of keyboard that's installed. The Options choice lets you turn off Loopback Plugs testing and the NDIAGS introductory screens. Also use this menu to create a diagnostic Report or to Exit diagnostics.

> **NOTE:** Loopbacks routes data that your system generates—say, from a serial port—back through the system for testing. This action simulates common operations that happen within your system, and allows more accurate, realistic testing.

Use the System menu to recheck system Information, perform a System Board Test, check the operation of your Serial Ports (1–4), Parallel Ports (1–4), and check the CMOS Status.

The **M**emory menu provides options for you to perform a **B**ase Memory Test, E**xt**ended Memory Test, and **E**xpanded Memory Test. Diagnostics checks memory operation by storing certain test patterns in memory, then verifying the patterns. Figure 2.8 shows the Base Memory Test Screen.

Figure 2.8

The results of running the Base Memory Test.

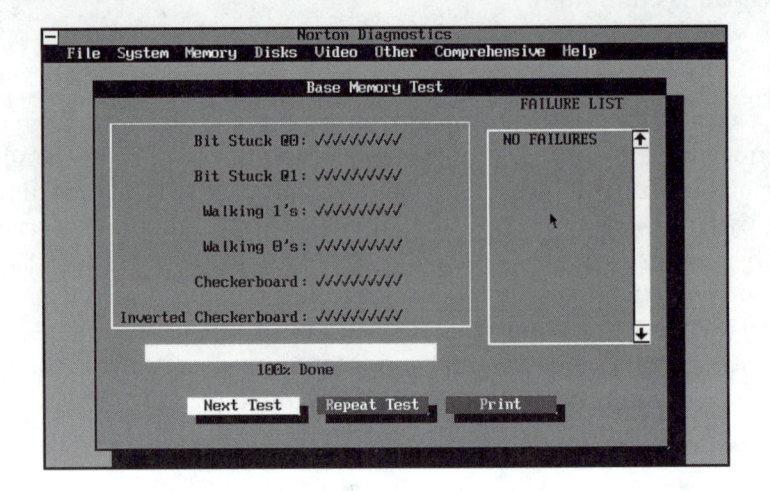

Use the **D**isks menu to check how well your system can position its read/write heads, rotate the disks, and detect write protection. This menu lets you check up to two installed hard disks and two installed floppy disk drives.

You can check your display **M**emory, M**o**de, **G**rid, and **C**olor using the tests offered on the **V**ideo menu. Some of these tests ask you to confirm that the screen looks OK by pressing Y as various screens appear.

The **O**ther menu lets you choose to perform a **M**ouse Test, **S**peaker Test, **K**eyboard Press Test, and Keyboard **L**ights Test.

Finally, the **C**omprehensive menu offers thorough Floppy Disk **A** and Floppy Disk **B** tests which check your system's ability to read and write floppies. You also can **R**un CALIBRAT, the utility that optimizes hard disk performance (see Chapter 11), and perform a **M**emory Test. The 16550A (**1**–**4**) options let you test First-In-First-Out (FIFO) serial ports on COM 1 through 4. (These options will only be available is your COM ports are equipped with FIFO capabilities.)

DOS and Utility Basics   45

NCC: Norton Control Center

The other utility we discuss in this chapter allows you to control and configure several attributes of your PC. The Norton Control Center (NCC) provides an easy interface for configuring display, keyboard, mouse, serial port, and other functions. You can start this utility from the Norton Program by choosing Control Center from the TOOLS options in the Commands list. Or you can start it from the DOS prompt using the following Quick Steps.

Running Norton Control Center (NCC)

1. At the DOS prompt, type **NCC**.

2. Press ↵Enter.   The Norton Control Center screen is displayed (Figure 2.9).

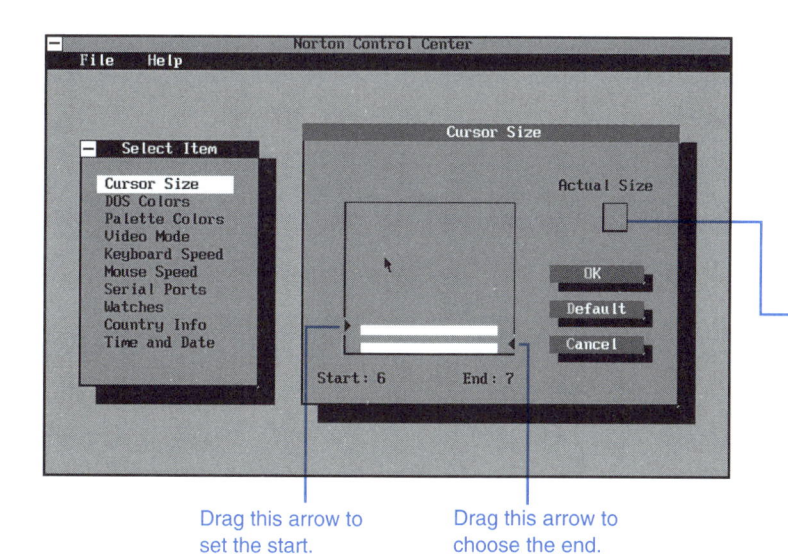

Figure 2.9
Norton Control Center screen provides access to ten customizable items.

—The currently selected shape appears here.

Drag this arrow to set the start.

Drag this arrow to choose the end.

As you can see in Figure 2.9, the Norton Control Center provides access to ten different items: **C**ursor Size, **D**OS Colors, **P**alette Colors, **V**ideo Mode, **K**eyboard Speed, **M**ouse Speed, **S**erial Ports, **W**atches, Country **I**nfo, and **T**ime and Date.

Cursor Size

Through the NCC interface (Figure 2.9), you can modify your cursor's appearance. You configure your cursor size by specifying two values: where the cursor starts and where it ends. The range of possible start/end values depends on your video adapter (CGA, EGA, and so on). The values on my VGA range from 0 to 7.

Quick Steps: Setting the Cursor Size

1. Press `C` or click in the Cursor Size window.

   This selects the Cursor Size window (see Figure 2.9).

2. Press `↑` or `↓` to move the cursor to the desired Start position and press `Tab`. Or drag the arrowhead along the left side of the box with the mouse.

   This sets the starting position of the cursor.

3. Press `↑` or `↓` to move the cursor to the desired end position and press `Enter`. Or drag the arrowhead on the right side of the box to the desired end position and click OK.

   This sets the cursor size and reactivates the Select Item window (Figure 2.9).

DOS Colors

NCC's DOS Colors option allows you to set the text color, background attributes, and border color for DOS screens.

DOS and Utility Basics 47

Setting the DOS Colors

QUICK STEPS

1. Use the arrow keys or click with the mouse to highlight the **DOS Colors** selection and press `↵Enter`. Or press `D`.

   This selects the DOS Colors option and displays the screen shown in Figure 2.10.

2. Press `↑` or `↓` to select the desired text color or click on it with the mouse. Use the mouse with the scroll arrows along the right side of the box to see more choices.

3. Press `Tab` or click to move to the Border Color box.

4. Use the arrow keys or click to select a Border color.

5. Press `↵Enter` or click OK.

   This ends the DOS Color selection process and reactivates the Select Item window.

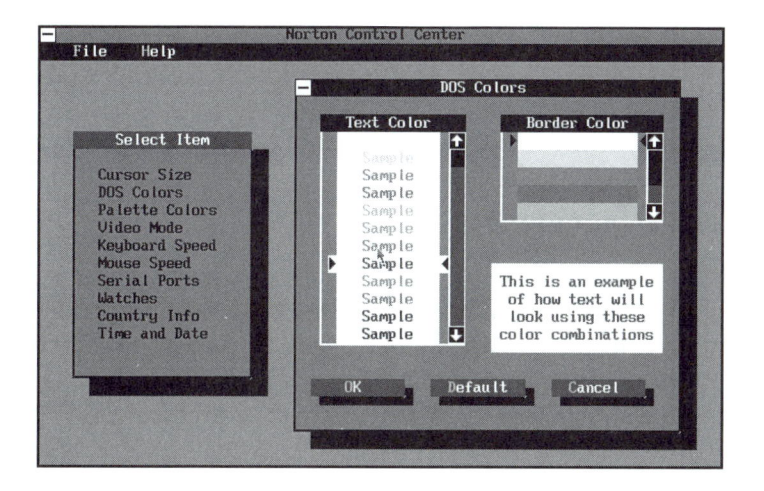

Figure 2.10
You can change your DOS color settings with the DOS Colors screen.

Palette Colors

If your PC is equipped with either an EGA, VGA, or SuperVGA monitor, you can use the Palette Colors selection to specify the 16 colors available for display use.

QUICK STEPS: Setting the Palette Colors

1. Use the arrow keys or click with the mouse to highlight the **Palette Colors** selection and press `Enter`. Or press `P`.

   This selects the Palette Colors option and displays the screen shown in Figure 2.11.

2. Use the arrow keys to select the desired palette color or click on the color you want.

   This scrolls through the 16 palette colors used in the Norton screens.

3. Press `A` or click on the **Change** button.

   The Change Color dialog box is displayed.

4. Select the desired color, and press `Enter` or click OK.

   This selects the new palette color.

5. Press `Enter` or click OK.

   This ends the Palette Color selection process and reactivates the Select Item window.

Video Mode

The Video Mode feature allows you to select which video mode to use if your monitor supports more than one mode. As you experiment with different display modes, you'll find that the compressed characters used in a compact mode (for example, 50 line EGA display) are sometimes difficult to read; therefore, most people stay with the default 25 Lines mode. Choose **Video Mode** from the Select Item list, and choose the options shown in Figure 2.12.

DOS and Utility Basics   49

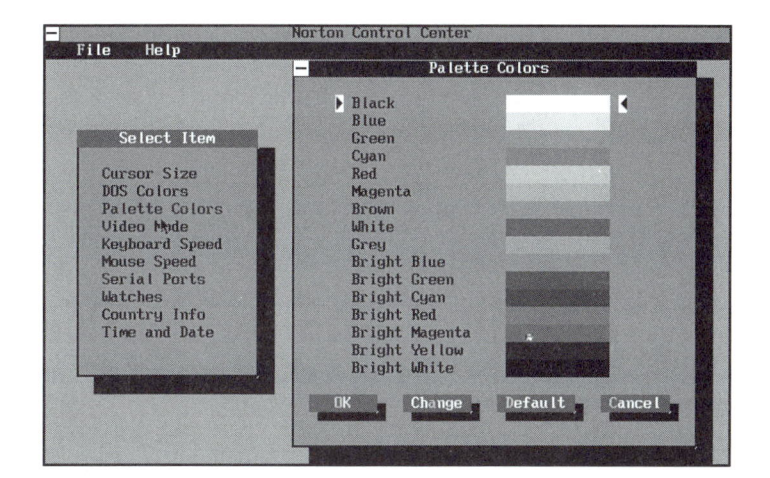

Figure 2.11
The Palette Colors screen lets you customize your colors.

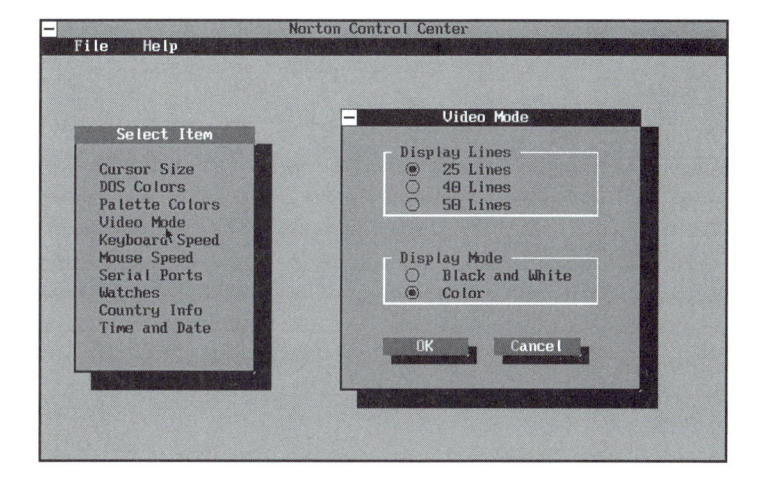

Figure 2.12
You can set up your monitor to operate in any of its available modes using the Video Mode screen.

Keyboard Speed

If your PC's microprocessor is an 80286, 80386, or 80486, you can use the Keyboard Speed utility to alter two keyboard characteristics: *keyboard repeat rate* and the *delay before auto repeat*. The keyboard repeat rate is the number of times a depressed key will repeat per second. The delay before auto repeat is the amount of time to wait after you press and hold down a key before it will automatically repeat.

QUICK STEPS

Setting the Keyboard Speed

1. Use the arrow keys or click with the mouse to highlight the Keyboard Speed selection and press [Enter]. Or press [K].

   This selects the Keyboard Speed option and displays the screen shown in Figure 2.13.

2. Use [←] and [→] or the mouse to move the keyboard repeat rate indicator to the desired setting.

3. Press [Tab] or click the delay slider on the display bar.

   The cursor moves to the repeat selection area of the screen.

4. Use [←] and [→] or the mouse to move the delay before auto repeat indicator to the desired setting.

5. Press [Enter] or click OK when you are satisfied with the keyboard rate settings.

   This ends the Keyboard Speed selection process and reactivates the Select Item window.

TIP: Press [Alt]+[A] or click the **F**ast button to choose the fastest keyboard repeat rate and delay before auto repeat rate.

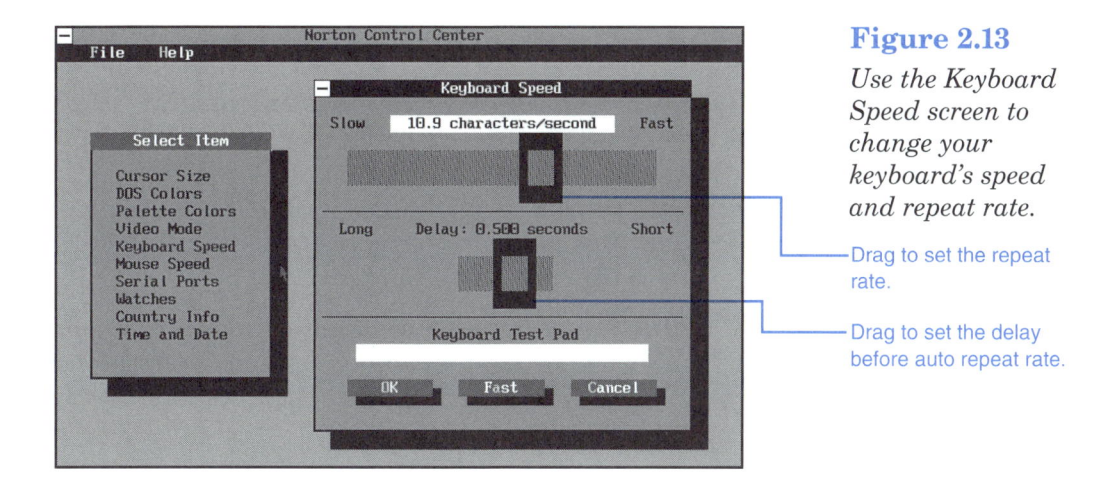

DOS and Utility Basics

Figure 2.13
Use the Keyboard Speed screen to change your keyboard's speed and repeat rate.

Drag to set the repeat rate.

Drag to set the delay before auto repeat rate.

Mouse Speed

If your PC is configured with a mouse, you can use NCC to set the mouse's sensitivity value. A high sensitivity value causes slight mouse movement to result in broad cursor movement. On the other hand, a low sensitivity value causes substantial mouse movement to result in slight cursor movement. Choose Mouse Speed from the Select Item list, then use the left and right arrow keys or the mouse to move the sensitivity slide shown in Figure 2.14.

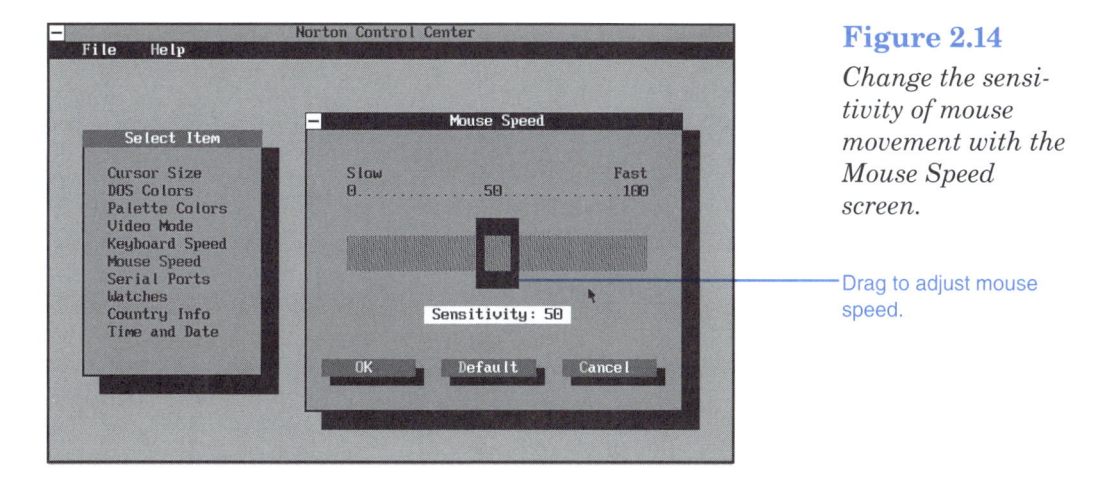

Figure 2.14
Change the sensitivity of mouse movement with the Mouse Speed screen.

Drag to adjust mouse speed.

Serial Ports

A *port* is an outlet on your PC that provides a plug-in interface for various peripheral devices (such as a mouse, modem, or printer). Your PC probably has several different ports, including serial and parallel ports. Typical serial devices include a mouse, modem, or serial printer. A parallel printer is generally the only device you would ever see connected to a parallel port.

NCC allows you to specify communications protocol for each of your PC's serial ports. This communications protocol includes: baud rate, parity, number of data bits, and number of stop bits.

QUICK STEPS

Configuring Serial Ports

1. Use the arrow keys or click with the mouse to highlight the Serial Ports selection and press [Enter]. Or press [S].

   This selects the Serial Ports option and displays the screen shown in Figure 2.15.

2. Press the up or down arrow keys or click to select a communications port (COM1, COM2, etc.) to configure.

3. Press [Tab] or click to move to the Baud selection area.

4. Use the arrow keys plus [Spacebar] or click to select a different baud rate.

5. Press [Tab] or click to move to the Stop Bits selection area.

6. Use the arrow keys plus [Spacebar] or click to select a different stop bits value.

DOS and Utility Basics 53

7. Press Tab↹ or click to move to the Parity selection area.

8. Use the arrow keys plus Spacebar or click to select a different parity.

9. Press Tab↹ or click to move to the Data Bits selection area.

10. Use the arrow keys plus Spacebar or click to select a different data bits value.

11. Press ↵Enter or click OK.   This ends the Serial Ports selection process and reactivates the Select Item window.

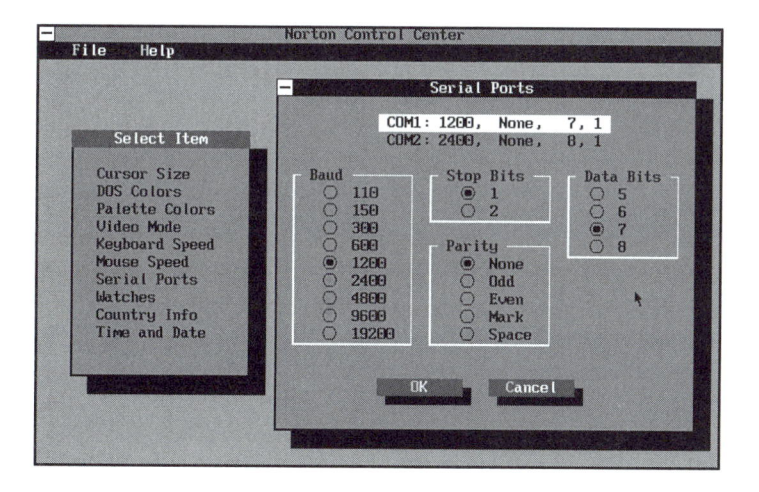

Figure 2.15
The Serial Ports screen displays and lets you modify the current serial port configuration.

Watches

Your PC has an internal clock that keeps track of the current time and date. The DOS TIME and DATE commands allow you to display and/or set the clock's time and date. The Norton Utilities

Chapter 2

takes timekeeping one step further. The NCC utility offers four independent stopwatches for tracking elapsed times. These stopwatches allow you to easily determine how long it took a program to run, a batch file to execute, and other similar duties.

QUICK STEPS — Using the Stopwatches

1. Use the arrow keys or click with the mouse to highlight the **W**atches selection and press `Enter`. Or press `W`.

   This selects the Watches option and displays the watches screen.

2. Select the desired watch by clicking on it or using the arrow keys plus `Spacebar`.

3. Press `Enter` to select the **S**tart and press `Enter` again to **P**ause. Or choose **R**eset.

   This starts, pauses, or resets the selected watch.

4. Click on **OK** or press `Alt`+`O`.

   This reactivates the left panel.

The Norton stopwatches also offer another, more useful method of tracking time. You can run NCC with a command line parameter to start or stop a specific watch without having to go through all the NCC menus and screens. When you type the command `NCC /START:1` and press `Enter`, NCC resets and starts stopwatch #1.

If you then type the command `NCC /STOP:1` and press `Enter`, you can see how much time has elapsed since you started the stopwatch.

Country Info

The Country Info selection in NCC allows you to configure your PC for use in foreign countries. With Country Info you can set up the following formats: Time, Date, Currency, List, and Numbers. For more informatin on using the Control Center to configure this option, see your Norton Utilities *User's Guide*.

Time and Date

The NCC Time and Date selection offers a visually pleasing alternative to DOS' TIME and DATE functions.

Setting the System Time and Date

1. With the arrow keys or the mouse, highlight the Time and Date selection and press `Enter`. Or press `T`.

    This selects the Time and Date option and displays the screen.

2. Enter the current month, day, and year in numeric format (for example, 09 13 93 for September 13, 1993).

    If you want to set the system time only, skip this step by pressing `Tab` three times.

3. Enter the current hour, minute, and second (for example, 08 23 59).

4. Enter either A or P (for A.M. or P.M.).

5. Press `Enter` or click OK.

    This ends the Time and Date selection process.

In This Chapter

Understanding file names and directories

Working with directories and tree structures

Maintaining your directories

Starting Norton Change Directory

- Type **NCD** and press ⏎Enter. Or, choose Norton CD from the Commands list of The Norton Utilities 7.0 screen. The currently active directory is highlighted.

Searching for a Directory on the NCD Tree

1. Start NCD.
2. Press ← to move the cursor to the beginning of the tree. The root directory is highlighted.
3. Start typing the name of the directory. As you type, the highlight bar moves to the directory that matches the characters you've typed so far until it reaches the directory that matches your latest entry.

Chapter 3

File and Directory Basics

The last chapter introduced you to a few facts about your computer's memory. This chapter begins looking at something you may already be a bit more familiar with—the files you create with your computer. Then we'll take a look at the DOS directory tree structure.

Understanding Files

Whether it's program instructions or data you've entered, information is collected by DOS in *files* that are stored on hard or floppy disks. Each file has its own unique name which distinguishes it from other files.

DOS sets some rules for the names you can give to your files. Each file name is made of a *base name* of up to eight characters, plus an optional *extension* of up to three characters. Use a period to separate the base name and the extension. Some programs automatically assign extensions to the files you create. For example, Microsoft Word assigns the extension .DOC to the document files you create with it. The .ASC or .TXT extensions often designate plain text (ASCII) files.

DOS is pretty flexible in letting you create base names. However, there are some characters you can't use:

" . / \ [ ] : * < > | + ; , ? spacebar

The file name is important, because DOS and your programs use the file name to recall the data stored in the file when you want to work on it again later. Using DOS commands and some of the Utilities, you can list, search for, rename, and repair files.

Using Wild Card Characters in File Operations

To perform an operation on a file, you specify its name when you issue the command. Sometimes you may want a command to affect a whole group of files, not just one. Or, you may need to find a file when you can't quite remember its name. Using *wild card characters* can help you in both situations.

You can use a question mark (?) in place of any character in a file name. For example, if you want to use the DIR command to find your quarterly sales report files, you could type `DIR QTR-?.XLS` and press `Enter`. DOS would list files named QTR-1.XLS, QTR-2.XLS, QTR-3.XLS, and QTR-4.XLS.

The wild card can stand for any group of characters. For example, you could use DIR A?.XLS to list all Excel spreadsheet files that begin with the letter A.

Directories and Tree Structures

Modern hard disk drives are capable of storing hundreds of megabytes of data and hundreds of files. DOS allows you to break a disk down into smaller, more manageable areas known as directories and subdirectories. As you may already know, a disk is similar to a filing cabinet because they both are used to store data. We can take that analogy one step further and say that a disk directory is comparable to a folder within the filing cabinet. Like a folder holds papers, a directory holds files. A subdirectory is merely a directory within a directory, or a folder within a folder.

A special directory, called the *root directory*, exists on all disks (for example, C:\). All other directories on a disk are either a direct or indirect descendent of the root directory. For example, in the path name C:\TEMP, TEMP is a first-level directory from the root C:. In the path name C:\TEMP\WORK, WORK is a subdirectory from the first-level directory C:\TEMP. Figure 3.1 shows the relationship between the root directory and other directories/subdirectries.

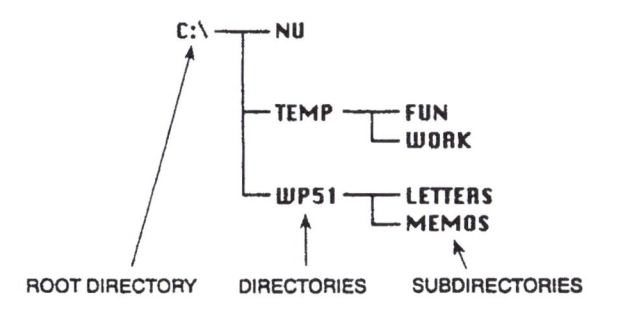

```
C:\ ——— NU
         ├── TEMP ──┬── FUN
         │          └── WORK
         └── WP51 ──┬── LETTERS
                    └── MEMOS
ROOT DIRECTORY   DIRECTORIES   SUBDIRECTORIES
```

Figure 3.1

Directories on a disk form a tree structure, with multiple branches and levels.

In Figure 3.1, there are three directories off the root: TEMP, NU, and WP51. Further, the TEMP and WP51 directories have subdirectories associated with them. Figure 3.1 is a graphical representation of DOS' directory tree structure—each descendent directory is shown as a branch off its parent directory. Unlike a real tree, however, the root of a DOS directory tree is at the *top* of the diagram.

The DOS MD and RD commands are used to make and remove directories, respectively. For example, the TEMP directory shown in Figure 3.1 can be created with the command MD C:\TEMP. And, if the MEMOS directory in Figure 3.1 is empty (that is it contains no files or subdirectories), it may be removed with the command RD C:\WP51\MEMOS.

Once you have created a few directories on your disk, how do you move from one directory to another? The DOS CD command is the basic vehicle for jumping from one directory to another. For example, the command CD C:\TEMP\WORK changes the active directory to C:\TEMP\WORK.

> **TIP:** Use DOS's PROMPT command to include the active directory in the DOS prompt. The command PROMPT PG changes the command prompt from C> to C:\> when in the root directory. The advantage of using this type of prompt is more apparent when another directory or subdirectory is active. For example, when the C:\TEMP\WORK directory is active, the DOS prompt becomes C:\TEMP\WORK>. You can add PROMPT PG to your AUTOEXEC.BAT file to make this feature automatic. (For more on AUTOEXEC.BAT, see "View AUTOEXEC.BAT" in Chapter 2. Chapter 4 gives more information on editing batch files like AUTOEXEC.BAT.)

Managing Your Disks and Directories

Gaining control over your files is an important first step in keeping your hard disk organized and uncluttered. But to do a complete job, you need to be able to manipulate your directory structure; that is, you need to be able to create new directories and remove directories that are no longer in use. One of the Norton Utilities, Norton Change Directory (NCD), gives you this control.

You can use NCD to display the structure of your disk in the form of a directory tree (see Figure 3.2). Because of this simplified display, you can attach new directories and lop off empty ones by simply highlighting the directory and entering the appropriate command.

File and Directory Basics

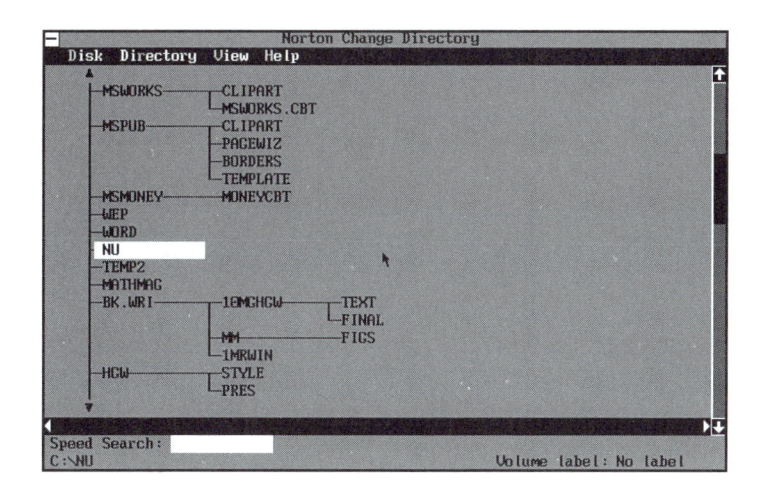

Figure 3.2
The NCD tree provides a graphic representation of your directory structure.

You can move the highlight bar to any directory by using the cursor keys or by clicking on the directory with the mouse. If you press ⏎Enter, this display disappears, and the directory you highlighted becomes the active directory. You can even search for a directory on the directory tree.

Searching for a Directory on the NCD Tree

1. Start NCD from the DOS prompt by typing **NCD** and pressing ⏎Enter. Or, choose Norton CD from the Commands list of The Norton Utilities 7.0 screen.

   The currently active directory is highlighted

2. Press ← to move the cursor to the beginning of the tree.

   The root directory is highlighted.

continues

> *continued*
>
> **3.** Start typing the name of the directory.
>
> As you type, the highlight bar moves to the directory that matches the characters you've typed so far until it reaches the directory that matches your latest entry.

The menu bar at the top of the screen offers the following additional commands:

Disk **R**escan Disk   Whenever you add or delete a directory, your change may not appear in the directory tree. Choose this command or press F2 to have the Commander update the directory structure to display the changes.

Di**r**ectory **R**ename   Choose this command or press F6 to rename the highlighted directory. A dialog box will appear asking you to enter the new name.

Di**r**ectory **M**ake   Move the highlight to the directory for which you want to create a subdirectory. Then press F7 or choose this command. You'll be asked to enter a name for the subdirectory. Type the name and press ↵Enter. You now have a new subdirectory.

Di**r**ectory **D**elete   To delete a directory, choose this command or press F8.

Disk E**x**it   Press Alt+X or choose the E**x**it command to close this window and return to your panels.

Making Directories

You can create a new directory in the NCD Tree display. Move the highlight bar over the directory under which you want the new directory. Then choose the **M**ake command from the Di**r**ectory menu or press F7. In either case, a dialog box appears, asking you to enter a name for the directory. You can enter a name of up to eight characters plus a three character extension. Press ↵Enter, and the new directory is created and highlighted.

Deleting Directories

Deleting directories is even easier than making them. Make sure the directory is empty unless you want to delete the files it contains. Highlight the directory you want to delete. Then choose the **Delete** command from the **Directory** menu or press F8. If the directory you're deleting contains any files, NCD displays a dialog box asking you to confirm your choice. Press Y or click **Y**es to delete, or choose **N**o if you change your mind.

> **NOTE:** Chapter 5 includes more on using NCD. That chapter tells you how to move directories using the Prune & Graft feature.

In This Chapter

Using FILEFIND to simplify file operations

Quickly recovering an erased file

Preserving deleted files

Repairing special files

Listing Files Using FILEFIND

1. At the DOS prompt, type **FILEFIND** and press Enter.
2. Type a file specification in the File Name: field (for example, C:*.*).
3. If needed, press Alt+D or click on Current directory only. Press Enter.
4. Press Enter or click OK to acknowledge the search completion message.

Recovering Deleted Files

1. Type **CD** and the name of the directory where the deleted file resided (for example, CD C:\WORK) and press Enter.
2. Type **UNERASE** and press Enter.
3. Highlight the file you wish to recover (for example, ?axmemo.txt).
4. Press U or click the UnErase button.
5. Type the first character of the deleted file's name (for example, T).

Chapter

4

Using Norton File Utilities

This chapter explains many of The Norton Utilities' features that compensate for DOS's file-handling shortcomings. One of these utilities, FILEFIND, is quite useful for many of your everyday PC tasks.

Lotus 1-2-3, Quattro Pro, Excel, WordPerfect, Symphony, and dBASE users will be pleased to know that version 7.0 of The Norton Utilities offers a FILEFIX utility that is intelligent enough to know how to repair damaged data files for these popular business applications.

But for most PC users, no one Norton utility may be as important as UNERASE, which can resurrect previously deleted files. When teamed up with the SmartCan utility, UNERASE provides the capability to recover files long after they have been deleted.

Finding Files

Norton's FILEFIND utility lets you search for a misplaced file on one or more disks with only one command—regardless of how many directories your disks contain. You can search for files on the entire disk, in the current directory, or in the current directory and its subdirectories. These Quick Steps explain how to run a basic FILEFIND procedure.

Quick Steps: Displaying Files Using FILEFIND

1. At the DOS prompt, type `FILEFIND` and press Enter. — This starts the FILEFIND utility and displays the File Find screen shown in Figure 4.1.

2. Type a file specification in the File Name: field (for example, C:*.*).

3. If needed, press Alt+D or click on Current directory only. Press Enter. — This tells FILEFIND to start looking for all files in C:.

4. If you want to stop the list as it scrolls, select the Stop command button. Use the Find command button to resume scrolling. — When the desired files are found, a search completion message appears.

5. Press Enter or click OK to acknowledge the search completion message. — This displays the list of files that match the search criteria (Figure 4.2).

Using Norton File Utilities

Figure 4.1
The File Find screen provides access to several file-handling tools.

- Radio buttons
- Command buttons
- Text boxes
- List box

Figure 4.2
FILEFIND displays a list of files matching the search criteria.

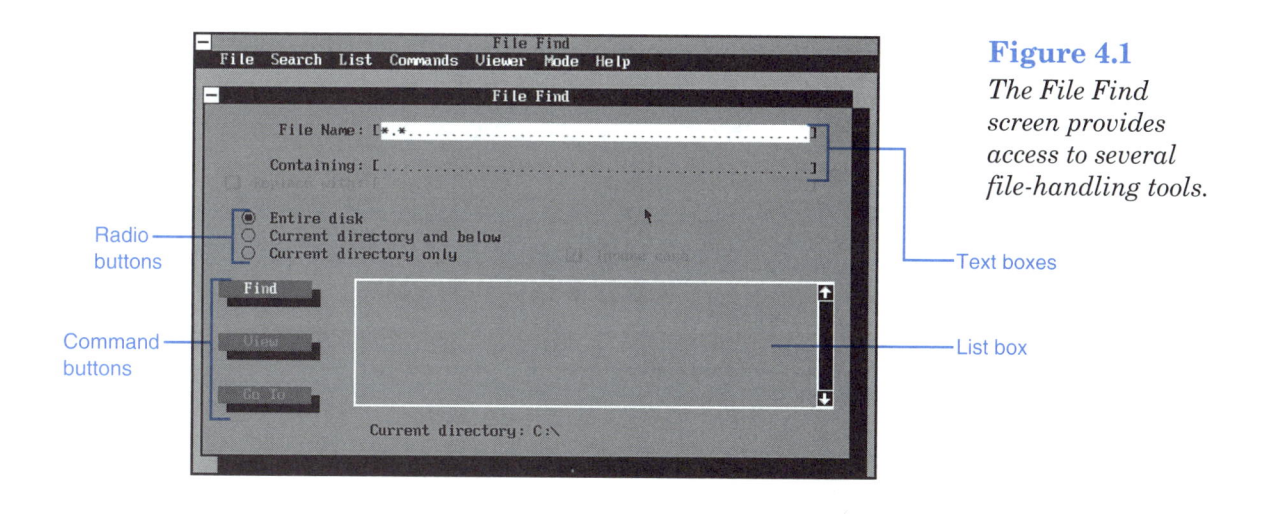

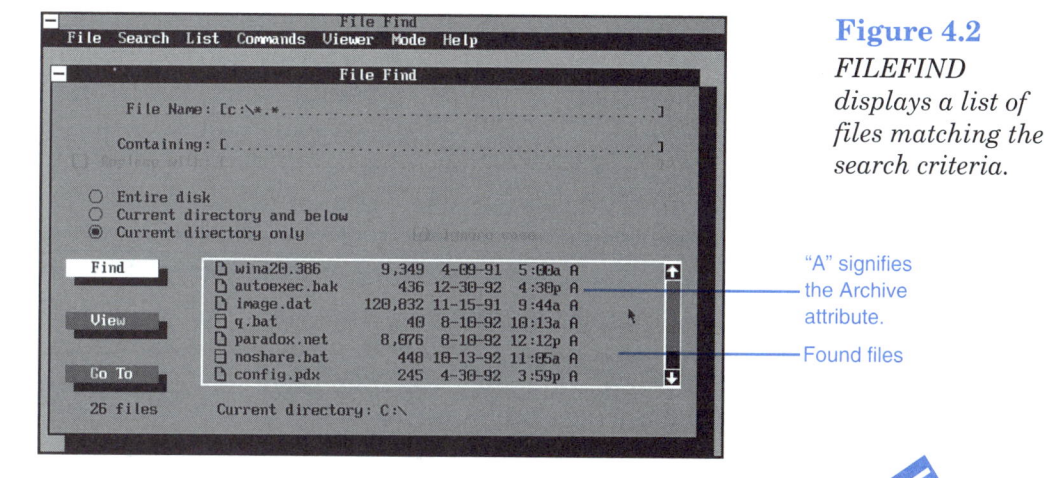

- "A" signifies the Archive attribute.
- Found files

> **NOTE:** The File Find screen works just like a dialog box. See Chapter 1 for more information on working with screens like this.

The FILEFIND listing in Figure 4.2 shows all files in the root directory of drive C:. The contents of this box can be scrolled by using either the up and down arrow keys or the mouse scroll bar along the right side of the box.

Chapter 4

You can also simultaneously start FILEFIND from the DOS prompt and enter a file specification for speed. Following are the Quick Steps that show you how to do both.

Quick Steps: Searching for a File with FILEFIND

1. Type the command **FILEFIND** followed by the name of the file you want to locate (for example, FILEFIND MYSTUFF.DOC).

2. Press ↵Enter.   This starts the FILEFIND utility and searches for the specified file.

3. Choose **OK** when the search is complete.

The screen in Figure 4.3 shows the result of searching for MYSTUFF.DOC on my hard disk. As you can see in Figure 4.3, FILEFIND has determined that MYSTUFF.DOC is located in my MEMOS\SERIOUS subdirectory.

Figure 4.3

I can use FILEFIND to locate the file MYSTUFF.DOC no matter where it is on my disk.

Results of search

Using Norton File Utilities

The FILEFIND utility searches through all directories and subdirectories on the currently active drive. You can use the wild-card character * with a colon (that is *:) to force FILEFIND to search for the specified file on all drives. For example, the command FILEFIND *:MYSTUFF.DOC instructs FILEFIND to look for MYSTUFF.DOC on all hard and floppy drives. This feature is especially handy if your hard disk is split into more than one logical partition and you wish to search the entire physical disk (for example, C:, D:, and E:).

> **NOTE:** Don't worry about not having a disk in your floppy drive when using the *: feature. If FILEFIND does not find a disk in a floppy drive when *: is used, it simply continues with the next drive.

FILEFIND supports the DOS wild-card characters * and ? for full or partial file name specifications. So if you cannot recall the full name of a misplaced file, you can still use FILEFIND to locate it (for example, FILEFIND MY*.DOC or FILEFIND CHAPT?.BK).

Searching for Text with FILEFIND

The FILEFIND utility does a fine job of locating misplaced files. Even if you know only part of the misplaced file's name, you can use FILEFIND to locate it. But what if you are looking for a file that contains information about a trip you recently took to California? Was the file named TRIP.RPT or CALIFOR.TRP? You have no idea what name you gave the trip report file, but you do know the file contains the string "trip report." FILEFIND can look inside each file on the disk and tell you which files contain your specific text string.

Searching for a Text String with FILEFIND

1. Type **FILEFIND** and press `Enter`.

   This starts the FILEFIND utility and displays the screen shown in Figure 4.1.

2. Press `Tab`, enter the text string you want to locate (for example, Lisa A. Bucki), and press `Enter` or click on **Find**.

   This initiates a search for the text string "Lisa A. Bucki" and displays a search completion message when finished.

3. Press `Enter` or click **OK** to acknowledge the search completion message.

   This displays a list of files containing the specified text string (Figure 4.4).

4. Use the arrow keys or the mouse to highlight a file shown in the list, and choose **View**.

   This displays the viewer screen, which shows the contents of the selected file and highlights the search text.

5. Press `F6` or choose **Viewer Next Match** to see if there are any other occurrences of the specified text string in the file being viewed.

   This highlights the next occurrence of the specified text string or displays a message if there are no more occurrences in the file.

Press `Esc` or choose **Close** when the viewer screen is displayed if you want to return to the list. You can then highlight a different file and press `Enter` to view it.

The list screen in Figure 4.4 shows file name, size, and date for all files containing the specified text string. The number of occurrences of the specified text string is also indicated after the time. For example, in Figure 4.4 we can see that the string "Lisa A. Bucki" occurs once in the file MYSTUFF.DOC.

Using Norton File Utilities

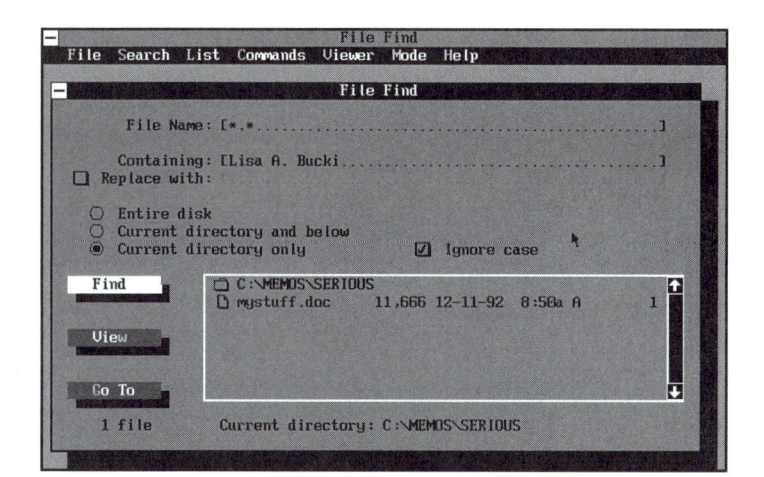

Figure 4.4
List of files containing a specified text string.

> **TIP:** By default, FILEFIND is not case sensitive, so the steps above would find the string "lisa a. bucki," "LISA A. BUCKI," or even "lIsa A. bUcki." Although I almost never use it, FILEFIND does offer a case sensitivity option, /CS. If we had used the /CS option in the Quick Steps example, FILEFIND would locate files containing only the lower-case string "lisa a. bucki."

Finding Text Using the Command Line

The text search feature of FILEFIND is a fast and powerful tool. The Quick Steps described earlier show how to run FILEFIND interactively. Once you are comfortable with FILEFIND, you may want to specify all parameters on the command line to save time.

The command FILEFIND C:*.* "Lisa A. Bucki" /S provides the same results as the earlier Quick Steps. The /S option tells FILEFIND to search through all subdirectories. Notice that the text string *Lisa A. Bucki* is enclosed in quotes here. When running FILEFIND from the command line, you must place the text string in quotes if it contains spaces. Without the quotes (that is, FILEFIND C:*.* Lisa A. Bucki /S), FILEFIND searches for the string *Lisa* and ignores the rest.

Working with File Attributes

DOS maintains special status information for each file on a disk. This information indicates the state of several important file attributes, including read-only, archive, system, and hidden (see Table 4.1). Norton's FILEFIND lets you display, set, or clear any of the four file attributes, including those inaccessible to ATTRIB. A file attribute is either on or off. FILEFIND displays an identifier for each attribute that is on (see Figure 4.2).

Table 4.1
File Attribute Definitions

Attribute	Meaning
Archive	Indicates file has not been backed up
Hidden	Indicates file is not visible via the DOS DIR command
Read-only	Indicates file cannot be modified
System	Indicates operating system (DOS) file

Setting and Clearing File Attributes

You can use File Find to set or clear any of the four file attributes. For example, let's clear the archive attribute for all files in C:'s root directory. (See Chapter 3 for more information about root directories.) The Change Attributes dialog box is displayed when you select the Set **A**ttributes option in the **C**ommands menu (Figure 4.5).

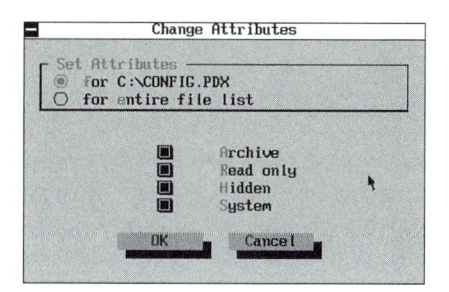

Using Norton File Utilities

Figure 4.5
The Change Attributes dialog box lets you assign one or more of the four file attributes to any file.

Press the Spacebar or click to select the for entire file list option in the Set Attributes portion of the Change Attributes dialog box. Then press Alt + A or click on the **Archive** attribute check box to turn it on (Figure 4.6). You may have to click on it or use Alt + A a couple of times to turn on the check box. Note that when the Change Attributes dialog box appears, all the check boxes appear as solid boxes until you change them to the on or off status. This clarifies for you which attributes are unchanged.

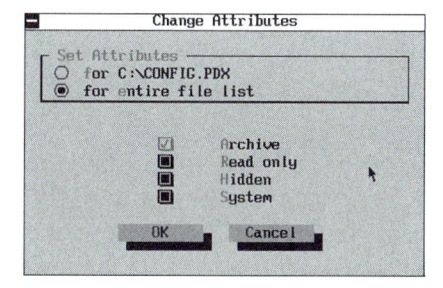

Figure 4.6
You can clear an attribute from a file by turning off the check box beside it.

Press Enter or click **OK** to initiate the file attribute change. When FILEFIND is finished changing the attributes, the summary box in Figure 4.7 is displayed, which shows how many files were affected and which attributes were set or cleaned.

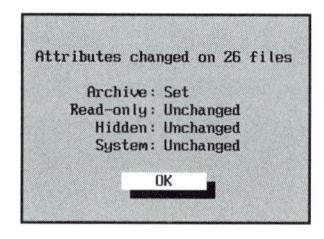

Figure 4.7
FILEFIND displays a summary of the changes made.

Modifying File Attributes from the Command Line

FILEFIND also lets you set file attributes directly from the DOS command line if you desire. This technique is a time-saver and lets you avoid all the menu and dialog box selections discussed previously. When you type FILEFIND from the command prompt, it finds the specified files and displays them in the FILEFIND screen. Table 4.2 shows the four file attributes and their corresponding FILEFIND command line identifiers.

Table 4.2
FILEFIND Identifiers

File Attribute	Identifier
Archive	/A
Hidden	/HID
Read-only	/R
System	/SYS

To find a file with a certain attribute from the command line, use the appropriate switch, as in FILEFIND *.* /HID, which finds hidden files. Use a plus sign (+) after the file attribute identifier to turn on an attribute. For example, the command FILEFIND C:\TEST.TXT /HID+ turns on the hidden attribute for the file TEST.TXT in the root directory. Place a minus sign (–) after a file attribute identifier to turn off an attribute. For example, FILEFIND C:\TEST.TXT /R- turns off TEST.TXT's read-only attribute.

You can use combinations of identifiers to set or clear several attributes with one command. For example, the command FILEFIND C:\TEST.TXT /A+/HID+/R- turns on the archive and hidden attributes and turns off the read-only attribute.

> **CAUTION** By default, File Find searches the entire disk. To work with a single directory from the command line, include the directory in your file specification, as in FILEFIND \NU*.EXE, or use the File Attributes (FA) utility described in Appendix B.

Clearing All Attributes

Although the command FILEFIND *.* /A-/HID-/R-/SYS- clears attributes for all files in the current directory, FILEFIND offers the /CLEAR option as a shortcut alternative. Therefore, FILEFIND *.* /CLEAR is equivalent to FILEFIND *.* /A-/HID-/R-/SYS- but is much easier to type.

> **TIP:** The DOS DEL command cannot find hidden/system files and will not delete read-only files. I use FILEFIND with the /CLEAR option to turn off the hidden and read-only attributes so I can delete an entire directory with DEL. Also, FILEFIND can be used with Norton's WIPEINFO utility (discussed later in this chapter) to remove files in directories/subdirectories quickly and easily.

Filtering File Selections

In the previous examples, you have seen how to use the * wild-card character to select specific files for FILEFIND. DOS's ? wild-card character may be used for more restrictive file selections as well. But what if you want to hide *all* archived files in a directory? No combination of * and ? will accomplish this. In this situation, you need to use file attribute identifiers as file filters.

The command FILEFIND C:*.* /HID lists all hidden files in drive C. The /HID identifier in this command acts as an additional file filter for the C:*.* specification. We can use this feature to set or clear file attributes based on the values of other file attributes. For example, here is the command to hide all archived files: FILEFIND C:*.* /A/HID+. Since the file selection (C:*.*) is modified by the archive filter (/A), this command turns on the hidden attribute for archive files only.

Date/Time Stamps

The date/time stamps shown in a DIR or FILEFIND listing typically indicate when a file was created or last modified. DOS does not offer a command to easily modify a file's date/time stamps, but fortunately, The Norton Utilities do.

> **NOTE:** DOS's COPY command does not change a file's date/time stamps. For example, the command COPY TEST.TXT TESTBACK.TXT creates a new file TESTBACK.TXT with the same date/time stamps as TEST.TXT.

The versatile FILEFIND utility provides an easy way to set a file's date/time stamps. The following Quick Steps show an example of setting date/time stamps using FILEFIND.

Quick Steps: Setting a File's Date/Time Stamps

1. At the DOS prompt, type `FILEFIND` and press Enter.

   This starts the FILEFIND utility and displays the screen shown in Figure 4.1.

2. Type a file specification in the File Name: field (for example, C:\AUTOEXEC.BAT) and press Enter.

   FILEFIND locates the specified file and displays a search completion message.

3. Press Enter or click **OK** to acknowledge the search completion message.

   FILEFIND then displays the list of files that match the search criteria.

Using Norton File Utilities

4. Select the **Commands** menu, then select **Set Date/Time**.

    The Set Date/Time dialog box shown in Figure 4.8 is displayed.

5. Press `Alt`+`T` or simply click on the **Set Time To** check box.

6. Press `Tab` or click on the text box to the right of the Set **T**ime To check box. Enter the current time (for example, 2:00 PM).

7. Press `Alt`+`D` or click on the Set **D**ate To check box.

8. Press `Tab`, enter the current date (for example, 3-30-93), and press `Enter`.

    FILEFIND changes the date/time stamps for the AUTOEXEC.BAT file to the values you specified. A completion message is displayed when the date/time change is made.

9. Press `Enter` or click **OK**.

    This returns you to the FileFind screen.

Figure 4.8

Specify the file's new date and time using the Set Date/Time dialog box.

Setting Date/Time Stamps from the Command Line

Use the /D and /T options with FILEFIND to set file date/time stamps from the command line. For example, the command

```
FILEFIND C:\AUTOEXEC.BAT /D03-30-93 /T14:20:00
```

sets the date/time stamps for the AUTOEXEC.BAT file to 3-30-93 2:20 PM.

> **CAUTION** FILEFIND lets you set dates only from 1980 on.

The preceding example showed you how FILEFIND can set both the date and time, but you can also use this utility to set just one of those values (for example, FILEFIND C:\AUTOEXEC.BAT /D03-30-93 or FILEFIND C:\AUTOEXEC.BAT /T14:20:00). In addition, you can use the DOS wild-card characters in FILEFIND's file specification (for example, FILEFIND C:\NU*.*/T14:20:00).

When setting date/time stamps with FILEFIND from the command line, the date and time formats are mm-dd-yy and hh:mm:ss, respectively. The time value is expressed in 24-hour clock format, so 15:20:00 is 3:20 PM. And you can omit leading zeroes, so /D3-3-93 is the same as /D03-03-93.

Using the Default Date and Time

One of the most useful applications for FILEFIND is to have it set a file's date/time stamp to the current date/time. This is accomplished via the /NOW option (for example, FILEFIND C:*.* /NOW). Use DOS's DATE and TIME commands to make sure your PC's internal date and time are correct before using this option.

Quickly Recovering an Erased File

So far, you have learned about several functions you can perform with File Find. It allows you to list files and change file attributes. But for my money, no one file-based utility is as important as Norton's UNERASE.

> **CAUTION**
>
> If you want to recover deleted files from your hard disk and you haven't installed The Norton Utilities, *do not* install the utilities now! The Norton installation program copies all the utilities to your hard disk and may overwrite the deleted files you want to recover. Instead, insert the Norton Emergency Disk #1 into your A: (or B:) drive and substitute A:UNERASE (or B:UNERASE) for UNERASE in the Quick Steps that follow.

The UNERASE utility gives you the ability to easily recover previously deleted files from your hard or floppy disks.

> **NOTE:** When DOS deletes a file, it still remembers all but the first character of the deleted file's name. UNERASE displays a question mark (?) as the first character of a deleted file's name. As part of the UNERASE procedure, you must provide the real first character of the deleted file's name.

Chapter 4

Recovering Deleted Files

1. At the DOS prompt, type CD and the name of the directory where the deleted file resided (for example, CD C:\WORK) and press Enter.

2. Type UNERASE and press Enter. — This starts the UNERASE utility and displays the screen shown in Figure 4.9.

3. Press the up or down arrow key or click to highlight the file you want to recover (for example, ?axmemo.txt).

4. Press U or click on the UnErase button. — This displays the first character dialog box shown in Figure 4.10.

5. Type the first character of the deleted file's name (for example, T). — This recovers the deleted file.

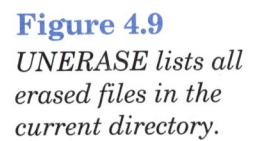

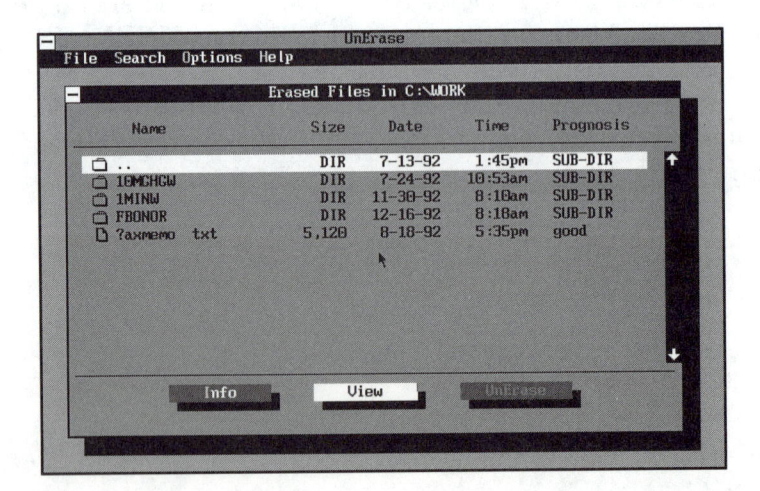

Figure 4.9
UNERASE lists all erased files in the current directory.

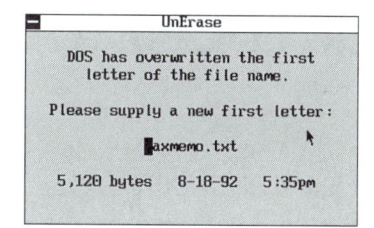

Figure 4.10
Specify the first character of the deleted file's name in the first character dialog box.

UNERASE: The Inside Story

One of the DOS DEL command's nicest features is that it does not destroy a file's contents; rather, DEL tells DOS to make the specified file's disk space available for other storage. For example, let's say the file C:\WORK\TAXMEMO.TXT is 950 bytes large and therefore occupies only one cluster on a hard disk on which each cluster consists of 2,048 bytes. Let's also say that cluster #20 is where C:\WORK\TAXMEMO.TXT resides.

The command DEL C:\WORK\TAXMEMO.TXT does not affect cluster #20. All the data in C:\WORK\TAXMEMO.TXT still resides on the disk, at cluster #20, even after I use DEL to remove the file. The only thing DEL does is inform DOS that the cluster(s) occupied by the deleted file(s) is now available for use by other files. Although the contents of C:\WORK\TAXMEMO.TXT still exist on the disk, it is now unprotected by DOS and could be overwritten the next time something is copied to the disk.

The UNERASE utility is fairly effective at recovering deleted files because it knows how to analyze unused clusters. Keep in mind that every time you copy a file, save a file from a word processor, or perform a similar operation, you run the risk of overwriting the unprotected data of a deleted file. Therefore, the chances of recovering an accidentally deleted file are best if you run UNERASE immediately after the deletion.

What To Do If UNERASE Fails . . .

The Prognosis column in Figure 4.9 indicates whether UNERASE thinks it can recover the specified files. A "good" prognosis means that UNERASE can probably resurrect the file with no manual intervention. However, a file with a "poor" prognosis may be more difficult to recover. Regardless of the prognosis listed, you should first try the Quick Steps for Recovering Deleted Files to recover the deleted file. The message shown in Figure 4.11 is displayed if UNERASE cannot recover the specified file.

Figure 4.11
Sometimes UNERASE may not be able to recover a file.

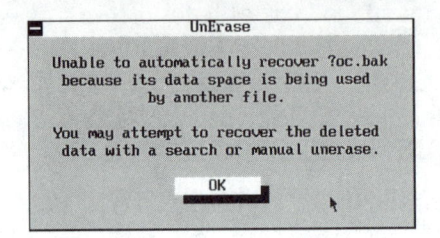

There are many reasons why UNERASE may be unable to recover certain files automatically, and most of them can be circumvented manually. So if you encounter a problem while automatically recovering a file with UNERASE, don't give up hope! UNERASE offers a manual recovery feature that you may be able to use to reconstruct the deleted file. This advanced feature is covered in Chapter 9.

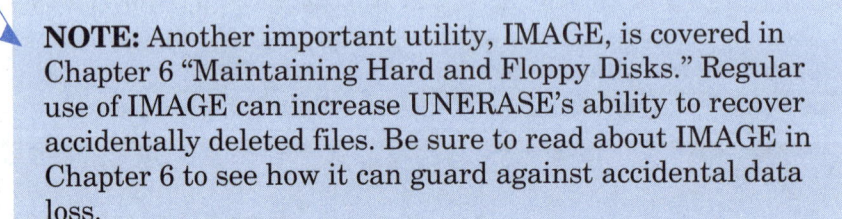

> **NOTE:** Another important utility, IMAGE, is covered in Chapter 6 "Maintaining Hard and Floppy Disks." Regular use of IMAGE can increase UNERASE's ability to recover accidentally deleted files. Be sure to read about IMAGE in Chapter 6 to see how it can guard against accidental data loss.

Now let's discuss the SmartCan utility, which can be instrumental in allowing an automatic UNERASE of older deleted files.

Preserving Deleted Files with SmartCan

Although Norton's UNERASE utility can often recover recently deleted files, it is not always 100% successful. By itself, UNERASE can fully recover only those deleted files that have not been overwritten by other files. Since you never know when a copy command is going to overwrite a deleted file, you might consider using the SmartCan utility to extend the life of deleted files. SmartCan is a TSR utility that can prevent deleted file data from being overwritten so that files may be recovered long after they are deleted.

Using SmartCan to Protect Deleted File Data

1. At the DOS prompt, type **SMARTCAN** and press [Enter]. — This starts the SmartCan utility and displays the initial screen shown in Figure 4.12.

2. Press [Alt]+[E] or click on **E**nable SmartCan. — This turns on the SmartCan utility.

3. Press [Alt]+[D] or click **D**rives. — The Drives dialog box is displayed.

4. Use [Tab] and [Spacebar] or click to specify which drives you want to protect, then press [Enter] or click on **OK**. — This selects drives to protect and updates the initial screen. Notice that the number of drives selected in this step is now indicated in the Drives: field next to the Choose drives dialog box.

continues

Chapter 4

continued

5. Make your selections in the Files to Protect area of the dialog box.

6. Press `Alt`+`U` or click on **Purge Files Held over [] Days** to turn it on or off. To change the number of days, press `Tab` or click on the text box, then type a number.

7. Press `Alt`+`H` or click on **Hold at Most [] KB of Erased Files** to turn it on or off. Press `Tab` and enter the maximum amount of deleted file data you wish to retain.

   For example, you might enter 1000, which is 1000K or approximately 1 MB.

8. Press `Enter` or click **OK**.

   This concludes SmartCan configuration. Remember that SmartCan is a TSR utility, so it is still resident in memory and ready to preserve data each time you delete a file.

Figure 4.12
The initial SmartCan screen lets you configure the utility for your PC.

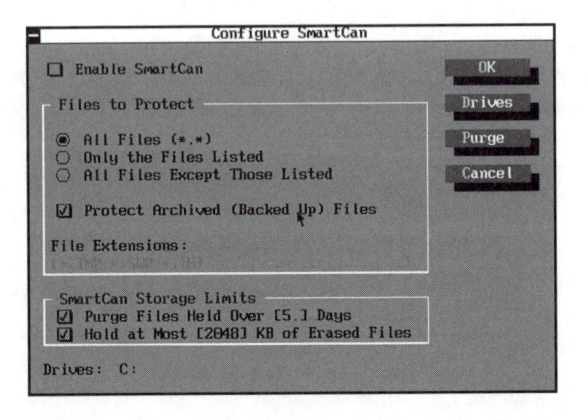

After you complete these Quick Steps, the SmartCan utility is configured and loaded as a TSR program. Each time you delete a file, SmartCan places the contents of the deleted file in a special directory called SMARTCAN. To ensure that SmartCan has been properly loaded, use DOS's DIR command to see if a SMARTCAN directory exists on each drive you specified in Step 3 of the preceding Quick Steps.

Unless you change the default SmartCan parameter settings, the SMARTCAN directory will retain files up to 5 days after they are deleted. No more than 2 MB of deleted files will be maintained in the SMARTCAN directory. When this size limit is reached, SmartCan will begin to delete, or purge, the oldest files in the SMARTCAN directory to make room for newly deleted files. You may wish to adjust this size limit based upon the size of your hard disk, how much space is available on your hard disk, how often you delete files, and so on.

When you turn your PC off today and turn it back on tomorrow, you don't need to go through the Quick Steps to restart SmartCan. SmartCan stores your configuration information in a file called SMARTCAN.INI in the NU directory. To restart SmartCan with your configuration information, use the /ON option and run EP /ON from the DOS command line.

SmartCan also offers an option that uninstalls the utility. The command EP /OFF disables the utility and removes it from memory. Another command line option, /STATUS, lets you check the current condition of the ERASE PROTECT utility. If you enter the command EP /STATUS, ERASE PROTECT indicates whether it is enabled or disabled and shows the current configuration settings.

Recovering Files from the SMARTCAN

Norton's UNERASE utility is used to recover deleted files that SmartCan has saved in the SMARTCAN directory. The UNERASE utility checks to see if a SMARTCAN directory exists on the active drive. If this special directory does exist, UNERASE uses the information in the .SAV and SMARTCAN.MAP files to quickly and easily recover any deleted files that have been retained.

Purging Files from the SMARTCAN

Once a file has been deleted, it may remain in the SMARTCAN directory for several days, depending upon your SmartCan configuration. Don't expect the deleted file's name to show up in a directory listing of SMARTCAN, however. When you delete a file, SmartCan places it in the SMARTCAN directory and gives it a special file name. The deleted files retained in the SMARTCAN directory have a .SAV extension but the rest of their file names are fairly meaningless. A special file in the SMARTCAN directory called EP.MAP is SmartCan's cross reference between these meaningless file names and the original file names.

When you are certain that you want to delete a file and completely remove it from your disk, you can use SmartCan's purge feature to erase it. When you select the **P**urge command button in Figure 4.12, the Purge Deleted Files screen in Figure 4.13 is displayed.

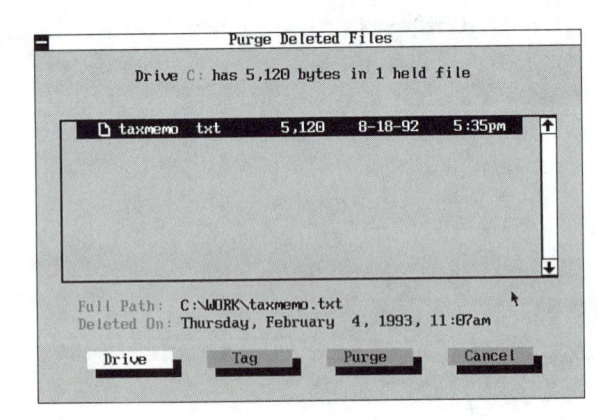

Figure 4.13

The Purge Deleted Files screen shows a list of all deleted files that may be purged.

The Purge Deleted Files screen shows a list of the files currently in the SMARTCAN directory. You can use the up and down arrow keys to scroll through this list and use `Spacebar` to mark a highlighted file for deletion. Or, you can double-click to choose a file. After you have marked all the files you wish to purge from the SMARTCAN directory, click on the **P**urge button or press `Alt`+`P` to erase the files. Remember that once a file has been purged from the SMARTCAN directory there is no guarantee that you will be able to recover it with UNERASE.

> **TIP:** A quick way to specify multiple files to purge is using the **T**ag button. Select **T**ag, type a file specification, then press `Enter` or click **OK**.

Repairing Special Files with FILEFIX

If you use Lotus 1-2-3, Quattro Pro, Excel, Symphony, dBASE, Clipper or WordPerfect files, you will be happy to know that The Norton Utilities includes a tool to help you repair corrupt data files for these popular business applications. A data file can become corrupted for one of several reasons including a malfunctioning disk or a software bug.

If you are having problems with a data file that's in any of the formats I mentioned, you should consider letting FILEFIX try to repair the damage. FILEFIX creates a new, undamaged version of the data file and leaves the original damaged file intact. The following Quick Steps explain how to repair an Excel data file, but the steps are similar for other types of files.

Quick Steps: Repairing an Excel Data File

1. At the DOS prompt, type `FILEFIX` and press Enter. — This starts the FILEFIX utility and displays the File FileFix screen shown in Figure 4.14.

2. Use ↓ to highlight Excel and press Enter or double-click on Excel.

3. Use the **D**irectories list to move to the directory that holds the file you want to repair. Press Alt+D or click to go to the list. Use the arrow keys plus Enter or double-click to select the directory you want. — A list of the files of that type in the specified directory appears in the Files list.

4. Press Alt+L or click in the Files list. Use the up and down arrow keys or click on a file to highlight it.

5. Press Enter or click **OK**. — The Repair Excel File screen is displayed.

6. Press Alt+B or click on **B**egin to accept the default fixed file name.

7. Select one of the report selection boxes. — The recovery process begins. Based on your selection, FILEFIX either prints a report, writes a report to a file (you specify a report file name on a subsequent screen), or skips the report process.

8. A message appears when File Fix is done. Press ⏎Enter or click OK.

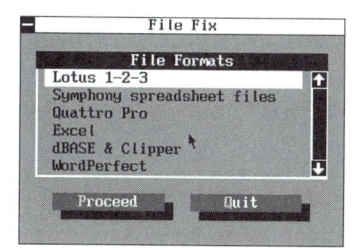

Figure 4.14
Select the type of damaged file with the FILEFIX type selection screen.

The FILEFIX utility has the intelligence to know what may be wrong with a damaged data file. Because FILEFIX knows the internal structure of these data file types, it can make an educated guess at how to repair the damage. After you use FILEFIX to repair a data file, you should immediately test the repaired data file to see if the damage has been corrected. Do *not* delete the original damaged data file until you are satisfied with the contents of the repaired data file created by FILEFIX.

In This Chapter

Using Norton Change Directory to simplify directory operations

Using Prune & Graft

Recovering a deleted directory

Sorting directories and files

Finding your way through the disk forest.

Changing Directories with Norton Change Directory (NCD)

1. At the DOS prompt, type **NCD** and press `Enter`.
2. Highlight the destination directory and press `Enter`.

Pruning & Grafting Directories

1. At the main NCD screen, press `Alt`+`G` or choose **Di**rectory **P**rune & Graft.
2. Highlight the name of the directory you want to move.
3. Choose **P**rune.
4. Specify the new location for the directory and its contents.
5. Choose **G**raft.
6. Use steps 2 through 5 to move other directories, if you wish.
7. To end the Prune & Graft operation, select the **C**lose button.

Recovering Deleted Directories with UNERASE

1. Use the NCD utility to move to the parent of the deleted directory. Press `Esc`.
2. Type the command **UNERASE** and press `Enter`.
3. Highlight the directory you wish to recover, then press `U` or click on the **U**nErase command button.
4. Type the first character of the deleted directory's name.

Chapter 5

Managing Your Directories and Disks

This important chapter revisits a couple of The Norton Utilities that help you manage your disks. The disk-based utilities covered in this chapter will help you with everything from working with directories and subdirectories to locating text strings.

Then we discuss the Norton Change Directory (NCD) utility, which offers a visual alternative to several of the DOS directory commands. You learn how to organize your disk with the Prune & Graft feature of NCD and the Directory Sort utility. Finally, we cover two important features of the FILEFIND utility that help you locate files and text strings on your disks.

NCD: Norton Change Directory

Although the DOS CD command is adequate for moving about from directory to directory, the Norton Change Directory (NCD) utility offers a graphical approach to directory navigation.

Quick Steps: Changing Directories with Norton Change Directory (NCD)

1. At the DOS prompt, type NCD and press Enter.

   This starts the NCD utility and displays a directory tree structure like the one shown in Figure 5.1.

2. Use the arrow keys or click to highlight the destination directory (for example, WINDOW), and press Enter.

   The destination directory becomes the active directory, and the NCD utility is terminated.

Figure 5.1

The NCD utility provides many useful directory tools.

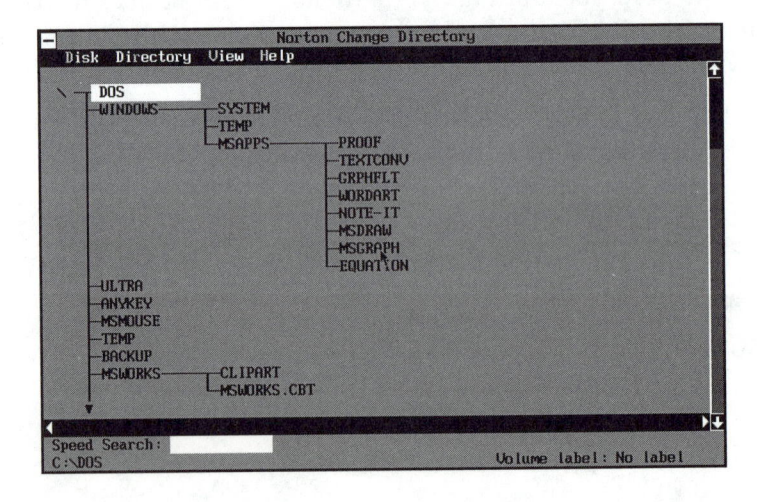

The screen in Figure 5.1 shows the directory tree structure, arranging it in vertical columns. In other words, the root directory is in the far left column, and the first level of directories appears in the next column to the right. In Figure 5.1, DOS is the current directory; NCD denotes the current directory with an inverse block around it.

As you learned in the Quick Steps, you can use the arrow keys or mouse to move from one directory to another with NCD. In general, the up and down arrow keys will move vertically through the tree, and the left and right arrow keys will move horizontally. You can also use the Home and End keys to jump to the top (root) and bottom (lowest directory/subdirectory) of the tree, respectively. The PgUp and PgDn keys are handy for quickly moving up and down through the tree a screenful at a time.

Although the selection block moves from one directory to another when you press the arrow keys, the active directory is not changed until you press ↵Enter (as shown in step 2 of the Quick Steps). You can press Esc at any time within NCD to quit the utility and return to DOS without changing directories.

The NCD Speed Search

A Speed Search box appears in the bottom left portion of the NCD screen in Figure 5.1. The Speed Search feature allows you to quickly jump from one directory to another without having to search for your destination with the arrow keys. For example, to move the highlight to the WINDOWS directory on my drive (the first directory listed that begins with W), press W and the selection block moves to WINDOWS (Figure 5.2).

Now press ↵Enter to make WINDOWS the active directory. The Norton Speed Search feature is very simple to use: just keep typing the letters of the name you want to locate until you find a match. Depending on how you name your directories, Speed Search needs from one to eight keystrokes to locate the desired directory.

Figure 5.2
Using Speed Search with NCD

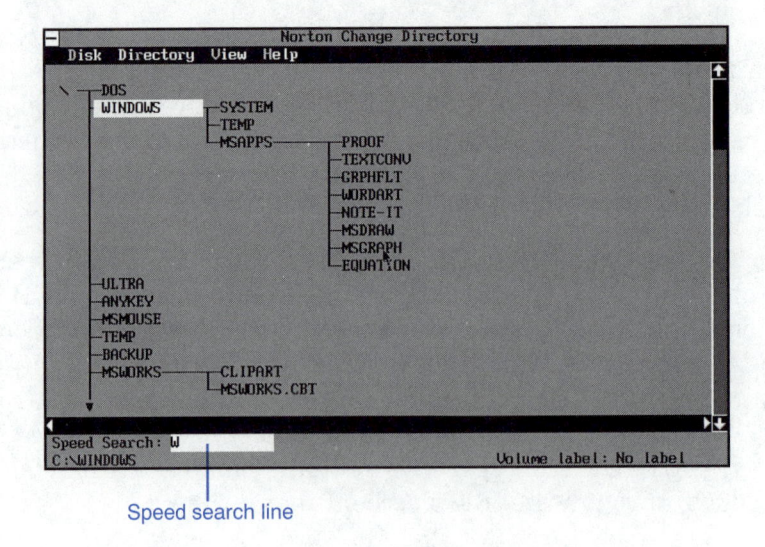

Speed search line

The NCD Function Keys

The NCD utility isn't just a visual replacement for DOS's CD command; NCD offers several other features as well, which are accessible through the **D**isk, Di**r**ectory, and **V**iew menus. I find it easier to use these other features via function keys rather than the pull-down menus. NCD supports eight function keys: F1, F2, F3, and F6 through F10.

F1—Getting Help

Pressing F1 provides helpful information about the NCD utility (Figure 5.3). When you're through with Help, choose Cancel to return to what you were doing.

F2—Rescanning Your Disk

The first time you run NCD, it scans your disk to create a list of the directories/subdirectories. This information is stored in a file called TREEINFO.NCD in the root directory. Each subsequent time you run NCD, it uses the TREEINFO.NCD file to generate the directory tree on your monitor.

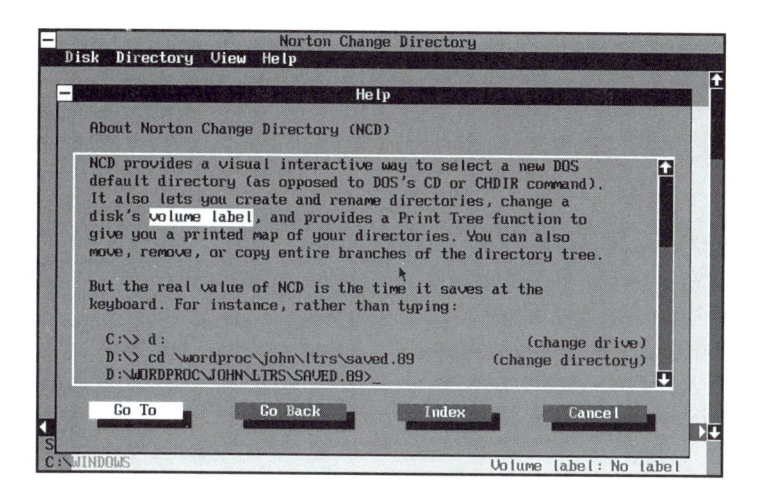

Figure 5.3
Pressing F1 accesses the Help screen.

Unfortunately, DOS directory commands do not keep TREEINFO.NCD up to date. So if you create or remove directories with MD or RD after the TREEINFO.NCD file is created, NCD may report erroneous directory information. If you suspect the TREEINFO.NCD file is out of sync with your disk's directory structure, press [F2] to rescan the disk and update TREEINFO.NCD. Or choose the **D**isk **R**escan Disk command.

F3—Changing the Drive

Press [F3] or use the **D**isk **C**hange Disk command to switch from one disk drive to another within NCD. When you press F3, the screen in Figure 5.4, which lists all the valid drive selections, is displayed.

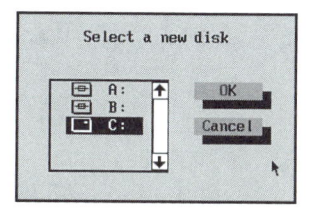

Figure 5.4
The NCD drive selection box lets you change the active drive.

Use the arrow keys or click the mouse to move the selection block to the desired drive, then press ⏎Enter or click **OK**. Or just type the drive letter (for example, C) and NCD immediately switches to that drive.

F6—Renaming a Directory

The rename key (F6) or the Di**r**ectory **R**ename command gives you the ability to rename a directory or subdirectory. You can't rename a directory using DOS, making this feature one of the nicer ones offered in The Norton Utilities. Move the selection block to the directory/subdirectory you wish to rename, and press F6 (Figure 5.5).

Figure 5.5

Pressing F6 or choosing Directory Rename lets you rename a directory.

Type the new name over the old one and press ⏎Enter or click **OK** to rename the directory/subdirectory.

F7—Making a Directory

The Di**r**ectory **M**ake command, or F7, provides an easy way to add directories to your disk. To create a directory off the root, move the selection block to the root and press F7 or click on the command. The screen displays an empty directory block, where you can enter the new directory name (Figure 5.6). Type the new name and press ⏎Enter or click **OK**.

F8—Deleting a Directory

Using NCD utility, you can delete empty directories with the F8 key or the Di**r**ectory **D**elete command. Move the selection block to the directory you wish to delete, and press F8 or choose the command. Unlike with DOS' RD command, you can remove a nonempty directory in NCD. NCD displays a message if you try to delete a directory that contains files.

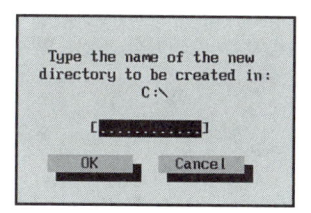

Figure 5.6
Using Directory Make (F7) to create a new directory.

> **TIP:** If you use NCD to create (F7) and remove (F8) your directories, you won't need to rescan the disk with F2. NCD automatically updates the TREEINFO.NCD file when you use F7 or F8 to create or remove directories.

Volume Label Maintenance

DOS allows you to assign a special name, or volume label, to each disk you use. For example, you could assign the volume label MY C DISK to your C: disk or MY FLOPPY to a floppy disk. The DOS LABEL command lets you specify a volume label of up to 11 characters. Norton's NCD utility lets you specify volume labels and provides volume label maintenance help. The active disk's volume label is displayed at the bottom right corner of the NCD screen (Figure 5.7). Press Ctrl + V or choose **D**isk **V**olume **L**abel to display the Volume Label dialog box shown in Figure 5.7.

When the dialog box in Figure 5.7 is displayed, you can do one of two things:

- Change the label by typing over the existing one and pressing ↵Enter.
- Choose the **Delete** button to delete the volume label.

After you make your selection, the dialog box in Figure 5.7 is closed and the new volume label is shown at the bottom of the NCD screen.

Figure 5.7
Pressing Ctrl+V shows the Volume Label dialog box.

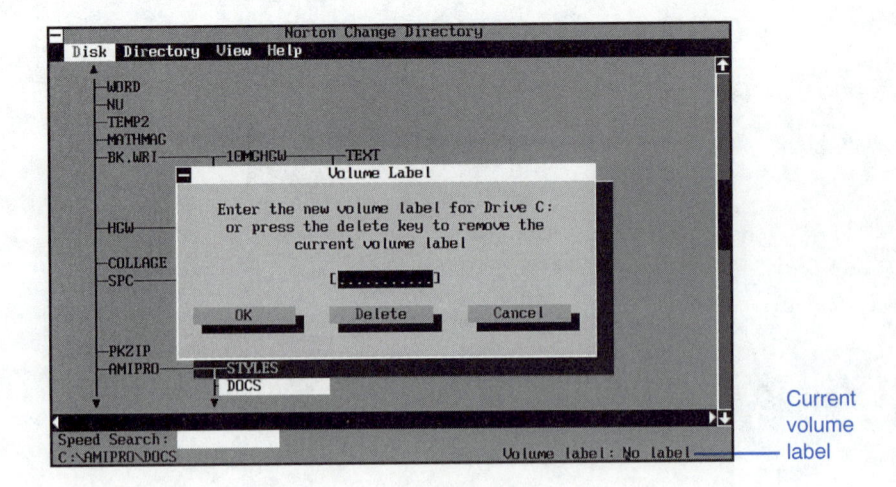

Current volume label

Pruning and Grafting Directories

Moving a directory and its contents, including subdirectories, can be a time-consuming procedure if you use DOS' MD (Make Directory) and COPY commands. Fortunately, NCD offers a Prune & Graft feature that lets you remove (prune) a directory from one location and insert (graft) it at another location on the directory tree.

By default, the Prune & Graft feature is not active. To make it active, press Alt+R or click on Di**r**ectory in the NCD menu bar and select **C**onfigure. The NCD Configuration dialog box, shown in Figure 5.8, appears. Select Enable **P**rune & Graft and press Enter or click OK.

Figure 5.8
Activating Prune & Graft.

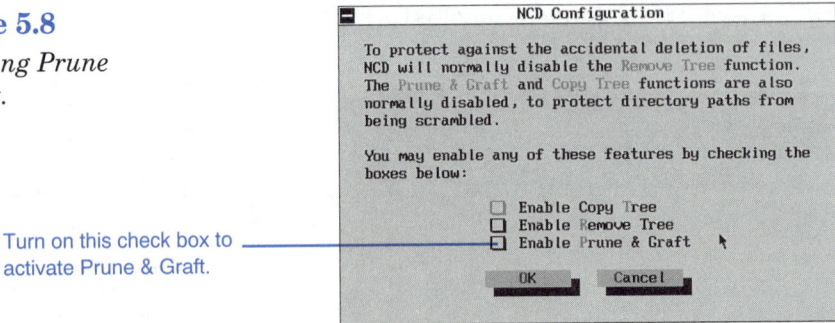

Turn on this check box to activate Prune & Graft.

Managing Your Directories and Disks

Once you've activated Prune & Graft, you can put it to use with the following Quick Steps.

Pruning and Grafting Directories

QUICK STEPS

1. At the main NCD screen, press `Alt`+`G` or choose **Di**rectory **P**rune & Graft.

   The Prune and Graft screen appears.

2. Use the arrow keys or click with the mouse to highlight the name of the directory you want to move.

3. Choose **P**rune.

   The **P**rune command button changes to the **G**raft command button.

4. Use the arrow keys or the mouse to specify the new location for the directory and its contents.

   The highlighted directory name moves to the new location.

5. Choose **G**raft.

   The **G**raft command button once again becomes the **P**rune command button.

6. Use steps 2 through 5 to move other directories, if you wish.

7. To end the Prune & Graft operation, select the **C**lose button.

   The Prune & Graft screen closes. NCD automatically updates the directory tree.

Recovering a Deleted Directory

In Chapter 4, we discussed Norton's UNERASE utility, which allows you to recover accidentally deleted files. As you may already know, DOS has a built-in safeguard that prevents you from accidentally deleting a directory that contains files. However, you could write a batch file that automates the process of first deleting a directory of files and then removing the directory. Regardless of how you lose a directory full of files, to recover those files you must first recover their directory.

Quick Steps

Recovering Deleted Directories with UNERASE

1. Use the NCD utility to move to the parent of the deleted directory. Press Esc.

   For example, if you are trying to recover C:\TEMP, you should use NCD to make the root directory C: active.

2. Type the command UNERASE and press Enter.

   This starts the UNERASE utility and displays the initial UNERASE screen shown in Figure 5.9.

3. Press the up or down arrow key or click with the mouse to highlight the directory you want to recover (for example, ?EMP), then press U or click on the UnErase command button.

   The first character dialog box is displayed.

4. Type the first character of the deleted directory's name (for example, T).

   This recovers the deleted directory and displays the screen in Figure 5.10.

Managing Your Directories and Disks **101**

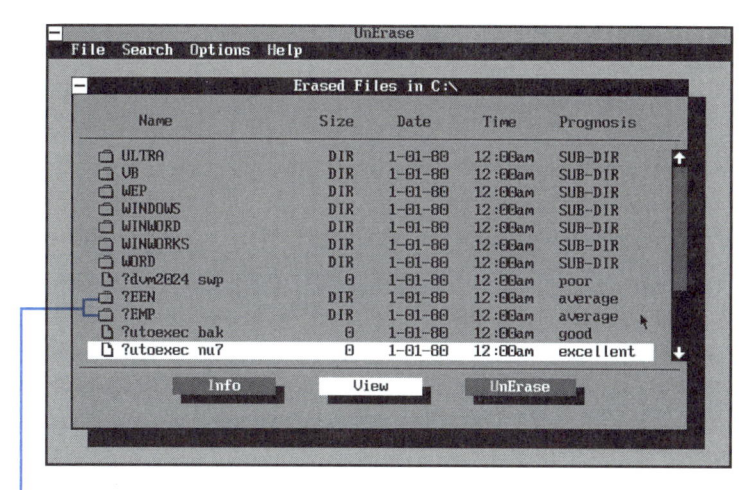

Figure 5.9
The initial UNERASE screen lets you choose the directory to recover.

Directories you can unerase

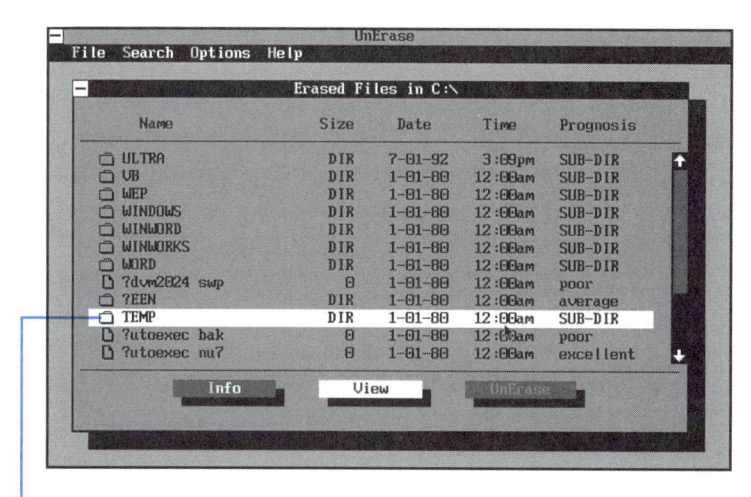

Figure 5.10
When a directory has been successfully unerased, the directory name's first letter appears instead of a question mark.

The first letter in the directory name reappears after it's recovered.

    In Chapter 4's discussion of the UNERASE utility, we saw that a deleted file's name (except for the first character) remains intact in a special table maintained by DOS. The same rule is true for deleted directories; that is why you must supply UNERASE with the first character of the directory you wish to recover.

After Recovering a Directory . . .

After recovering a deleted directory, you might think that you have automatically recovered everything in the directory as well. In reality however, you have only restored the directory name, not its contents. You must then use UNERASE to resurrect the recovered directory's subdirectories/files.

For example, let's assume I have a TEMP directory that contains several files and two subdirectories: WORK and FUN. Let's further assume that the WORK and FUN directories contain several files too. If I accidentally delete the contents of all three directories (TEMP, WORK, and FUN) and the directories themselves, I must use UNERASE twice to recover all the deleted directories.

The first UNERASE that I perform will recover the TEMP directory. Then I must use UNERASE to recover the WORK and FUN subdirectories within TEMP. Once all three directories are recovered I must use UNERASE to recover all the files in TEMP, WORK, and FUN. After I have successfully UNERASEd the directory (Figure 5.10), I can select the recovered directory and press Enter to see what files in that directory can be UNERASEd (Figure 5.11).

Figure 5.11
Using UNERASE displays a list of recoverable files in the UNERASEd directory.

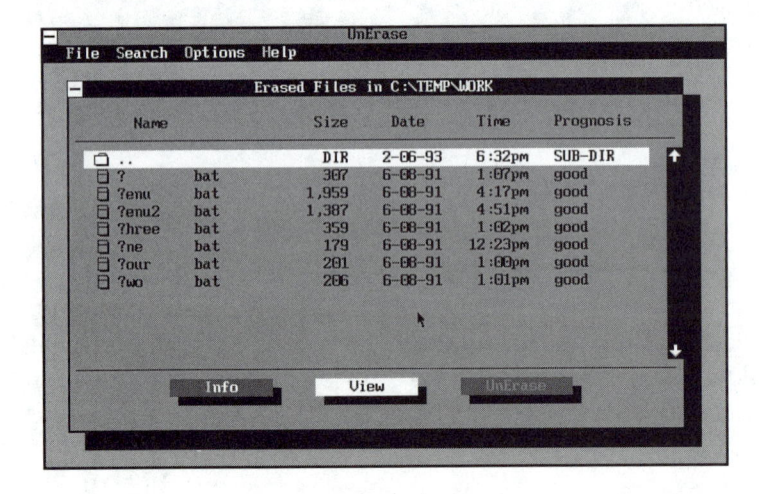

I can then use the steps outlined in Chapter 4 to recover all the deleted files shown in Figure 5.11. Or I can use the Quick Steps outlined earlier in this chapter to recover subdirectories from the recently recovered directory.

Changing the Order of Directories and Files

When you use DOS's DIR command, it scrolls a list of files and directories on-screen. Unfortunately, it does not order the directories and files alphabetically or in any other way to make it easier for you to find the files you're looking for. The Directory Sort utility lets you view files and directories in order according to the sort-keys you select: **N**ame, **E**xtension, **D**ate, **T**ime, and **S**ize. (Note that Directory Sort doesn't actually rearrange the directories on the drive; it only orders their names on-screen for you.)

You can specify more than one sort-key. In that case, Directory Sort orders the files by the primary (first) sort-key first, then uses the second sort-key to break ties, and so on. If the directory you sort (the current directory) contains subdirectories, Directory Sort groups the subdirectories first, then the files. Hidden or system files are not sorted so as not to disturb any protection methods. Table 5.1 lists the default sort orders for the different sort-key types.

Table 5.1
Directory Sort Defaults

Sorting by This Sort-Key…	Orders the Files/Directories…
Name	In alphabetical order
Extension	In alphabetical order
Date	From least recent to most recent
Time	From least recent to most recent
Size	From smallest to largest

Chapter 5

You can display the full Directory Sort dialog box by typing DS at the DOS prompt. (Appendix B explains how to use Directory Sort as a command line utility.) Figure 5.12 shows the Directory Sort screen.

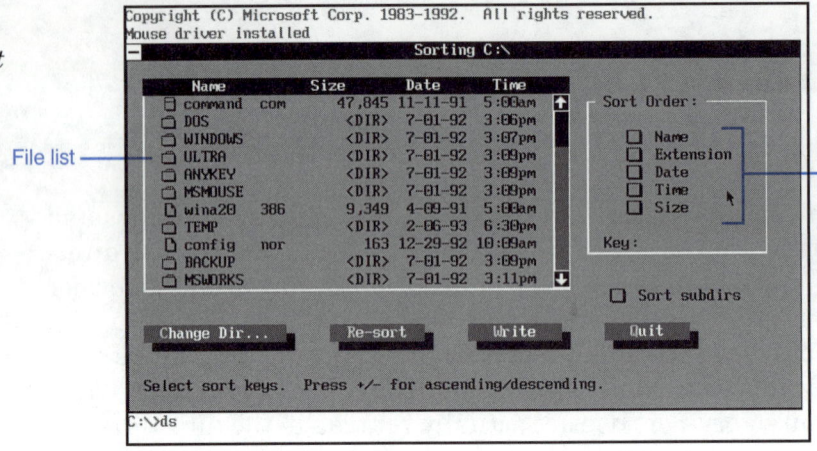

Figure 5.12
The Directory Sort screen.

[Screenshot of the Directory Sort screen, showing the File list on the left and Sort order check boxes on the right]

The following Quick Steps explain how to use the Directory Sort utility.

Using the Full Directory Sort Utility

1. Type **DS** at the DOS prompt or highlight Directory Sort from the Commands list of the main Norton program screen. Press ↵Enter.

   The Directory Sort dialog box appears. The file list box displays the files in the current directory.

2. If necessary, specify another drive and directory by selecting the Change Dir... button.

   Directory Sort displays the Change Directory dialog box.

Managing Your Directories and Disks

3. Type the name of the drive and directory you want to sort, or use the **D**rive and **S**ubdirectories lists to specify the directory. Press ⏎Enter or click **OK**.

   You return to the Directory Sort dialog box, which now displays in the file list box the files and subdirectories in the new drive and directory.

4. Select the sort-keys you want to use in the Sort Order: area by pressing the first letter in the sort-key name or by clicking on it with the mouse. Press – at a sort-key to sort in reverse order.

   A check appears next to each sort-key you choose. The numeral that appears indicates the sort-key's precedence. That is, the first key you choose becomes 1, the primary sortkey, and so on.

5. To sort the files in the subdirectories of the selected directory, press Alt + O or click on the **S**ort subdirs button.

   The Sort subdirs check box is turned on.

6. Press Alt + R, or click **R**e-sort.

   Directory Sort orders the files according to the sort-key(s) you specified and displays the new order in the file list box.

7. If you want to, repeat steps 2 through 6 to sort files in another directory or to re-sort the files in the current directory.

8. Press W or click on **W**rite to write the new file order to disk.

   Directory Sort stores the new file order on disk.

continues

> *continued*
>
> **9.** Press Q, or click on **Q**uit. The Directory Sort dialog box closes, and depending on where you were when you started Directory Sort, the DOS prompt or the main Norton screen appears.

Finding Your Way Through the Disk Forest

After you have created many directories and subdirectories, it is very easy to become lost in the "disk forest." Even if you practice the best disk management techniques, it is possible to forget where you placed a file or two! Fortunately, the FILEFIND utility discussed in Chapter 4 includes two powerful features that let you locate files and text strings. Let's take a look at the file location feature first to see how you can use it to quickly locate a file on your disk.

In This Chapter

Understanding disk structures

Preserving important disk information

Recovering data from an accidentally formatted disk

Copying a disk

Diagnosing and correcting disk problems

Formatting a Floppy Disk with SFORMAT

1. Type the command **SFORMAT** and a disk drive identifier (for example, SFORMAT A:), and press **Enter**.
2. Press **Enter** or click **Format** to accept the default SFORMAT settings.
3. If the warning message is displayed, press **Y** or click **Yes** to continue. Otherwise, wait until a completion message is displayed.
4. Press **Enter** or click **OK**.
5. Choose E**xit**.

Testing a Disk with Norton Disk Doctor (NDD)

1. Type the command **NDD** and press **Enter**.
2. Press **Enter** or click on the **D**iagnose Disk option.
3. Highlight the drive you want to diagnose and press **Enter** or click **D**iagnose.
4. Insert a disk and choose **OK** if needed.
5. Press **Enter** or click **B**egin Test to accept the default settings and begin the surface test.
6. When NDD finds disk errors, it asks if you want to save undo information. Follow the prompts to do so.
7. Press **Enter** or click **R**eport.

Chapter 6

Maintaining Hard and Floppy Disks

This chapter shows you how to avoid accidental data loss and explains the physical layout of DOS disks. First you learn about the fundamental components and structure of DOS disks and how to interpret the disk information reported by Norton's SYSINFO utility. Then we cover disk formatting and copying utilities—and how to recover data from accidentally formatted disks. Chapter 6 concludes with coverage of Norton's Disk Doctor (NDD) utility, which allows you to diagnose and correct disk problems.

Understanding Disk Structures

As the saying goes, "You don't have to know how the engine works before you can drive a car." The same rule holds true for PC users—you don't have to understand the internal workings of a computer to use a PC. A bit of technical insight certainly doesn't hurt, though. In fact, a basic knowledge of PC inner workings is almost mandatory before you can interpret and appreciate the information reported by the more advanced tools in The Norton Utilities.

To work with some of Norton's disk utilities, you must first understand the structure of a DOS disk. You have already been introduced to a few of the terms I will use in this discussion, so let's quickly review those first.

Bits, Bytes, Sectors, and Clusters

You may recall from Chapter 2 that a binary digit, or *bit*, is the smallest piece of data a computer can store. A bit is very simple, and can have a value of only 0 or 1. The discussion in Chapter 2 continued by defining a *byte* as a collection of 8 bits. As many as 256 different values can be indicated by combinations of 1s and 0s in an 8-bit byte.

The computer industry has created a standard for assigning specific 8-bit values for a slew of characters, including all the ones that appear on your PC's keyboard. This standard is called the *ASCII* character set. (ASCII is an acronym for American Standard Code for Information Interchange.)

If a group of bits is called a byte, what do you call a group of bytes? How about a *sector*? A sector consists of 512 bytes. To address an entire disk's data area quickly and easily, DOS works with even larger, more manageable chunks of data called *clusters*.

The number of sectors in a cluster differs among disk types. For example, each cluster on my PC's hard disk is made up of eight sectors, but on a high-density 5 1/4" floppy disk, there is only one sector per cluster. It's not too important to understand why different disk types have different numbers of sectors per cluster. However, you should understand that 8 bits constitute a byte, 512 bytes make up a sector, and a cluster contains one or more sectors (depending on the disk type).

Tracks and Cylinders

Now that you know what sectors and clusters are, let's try to visualize them on a disk. The illustration in Figure 6.1 shows the circular disk platter inside a 5 1/4" disk.

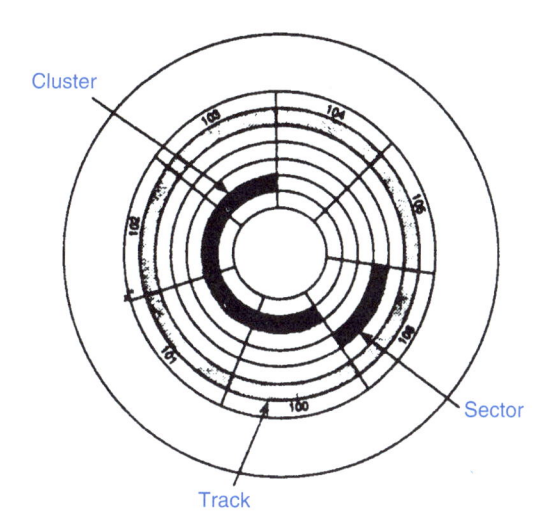

Figure 6.1

Groups of sectors form tracks around the surface of a disk.

As you can see in Figure 6.1, the sectors and clusters are arranged in a circular format; this format resembles the layout of the grooves in a record album. In Figure 6.1, sectors 100 through 106 form a circle on the disk surface. This circle of sectors is called a *track*. These days, virtually all floppy disks are double-sided, which means that there are tracks on both sides of the disk platter.

Now let's expand the discussion to include hard disks. The illustration in Figure 6.2 shows the surface of a hard disk. Hard disks typically contain more than one platter. The hard disk in Figure 6.2 consists of three platters. The platters in a hard disk are stacked fairly close together, and each platter contains tracks, clusters, and sectors just like floppy disks.

On each disk platter, the magnetic material that stores data is aligned in concentric circles called *tracks*. The mechanical heads that read and write data travel along the tracks. Because each platter has two sides, there are tracks on each side of the disk.

Tracks are spaced at even intervals on the surface of each platter so that, for example, the first pair of tracks (top and bottom) on the top platter are precisely above the first pair of tracks on all the other platters. To visualize how the tracks are vertically aligned, look at Figure 6.3, which shows some hard disk platters and an imaginary cylindrical object that appears to cut through the three platters. The collection of vertically stacked tracks intersected by the object in Figure 6.3 is known as a *cylinder*.

Figure 6.2
Hard disks contain several disk platters.

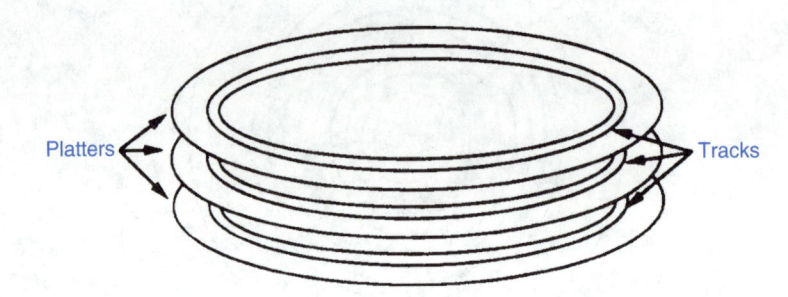

Figure 6.3
Vertically stacked tracks form cylinders.

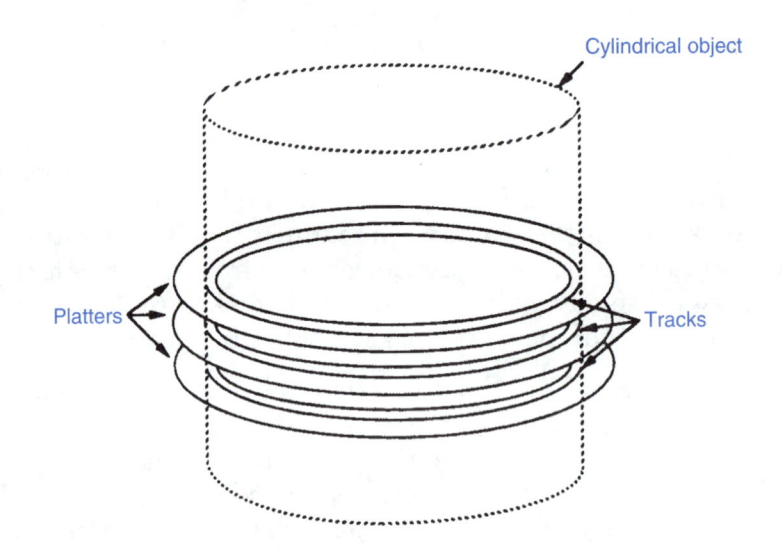

Disk Areas

The terms and concepts discussed so far in this chapter apply to all regions of a DOS disk—that is, the entire disk is made up of bits, bytes, sectors, and so on. There are special regions or areas on a DOS disk where certain pieces of information must reside. These areas are known as the system area and the data area. Three components make up the system area: the boot record, the root directory, and the file allocation table (or, FAT, for short).

Boot Record

The boot record resides in the boot sector, which is the first sector of the first track on the first side of a bootable DOS disk. The boot sector exists on all DOS disks regardless of whether the disk is bootable or not. (When you FORMAT a DOS disk, you can make it bootable by using the /S option, which causes the system files to be copied to the newly formatted disk.) The information contained in the boot record of a bootable disk instructs DOS on how to bring itself up "by the bootstraps" and prepare for your commands.

Root Directory

The root directory area contains information about all the files and directories that reside in the root directory (for example, C:). Each file and directory in the root has an entry in this area that contains information such as name, size, and date/time of creation. One of the most important items in a directory entry is a number that indicates the file or directory's offset in the file allocation table.

File Allocation Table

The *file allocation table* indicates the status of all the clusters on a DOS disk. The information contained in the FAT is so important that DOS actually maintains two copies of the FAT on a disk, just in case something happens to the first copy. Unlike directories, the FAT is organized by clusters rather than by files. There is one entry in the FAT for each cluster on the disk. The illustration in Figure 6.4 shows the relationship between the root directory area and the FAT.

Figure 6.4

Relationship between the root directory area and FAT.

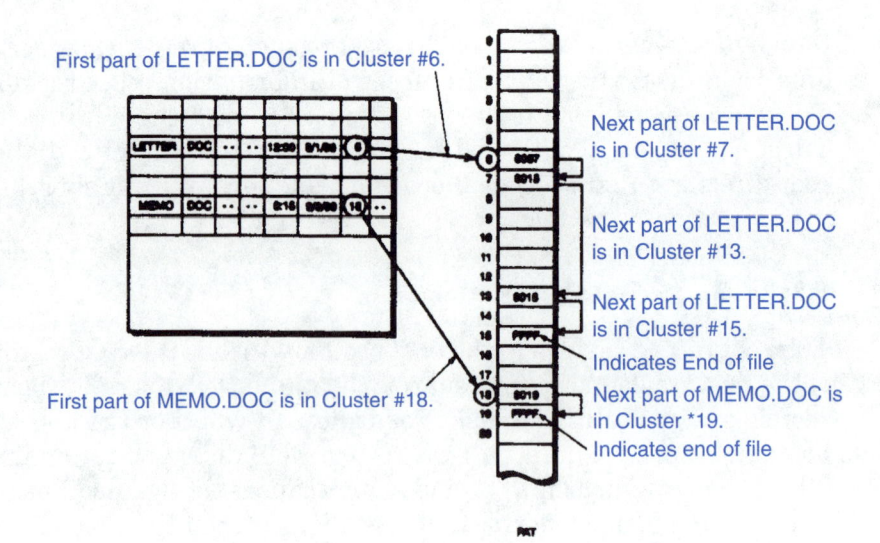

As you can see in Figure 6.4, the contents of the file LETTER.DOC start in cluster #6. Looking at the 6th offset of the FAT in Figure 6.4, we can see that LETTER.DOC continues into cluster #7. The 7th offset of the FAT tells us that cluster #13 is the next cluster in the sequence for LETTER.DOC. Skipping down to the 13th offset of the FAT, we see that the next portion of LETTER.DOC resides in cluster #15. Finally, the 15th offset of the FAT contains the special value 'FFFF', which indicates the end of the file. So LETTER.DOC occupies four clusters on the disk: clusters #6, #7, #13, and #15. Figure 6.4 also shows a directory entry for a file named MEMO.DOC, which occupies two clusters: #18 and #19.

The FAT in Figure 6.4 illustrates an important point about how DOS allocates clusters for a file. Although it is possible for a file to occupy sequential clusters (for example, MEMO.DOC uses clusters #18 and #19), quite often DOS may wind up utilizing nonsequential, or noncontiguous, clusters for a file. (For example, LETTER.DOC, which uses clusters #6, #7, #13, and #15.)

A file that is stored in noncontiguous clusters is called a *fragmented* file. File fragmentation is a leading cause of disk inefficiency because it takes DOS longer to manipulate a file

Maintaining Hard and Floppy Disks 115

whose data is scattered across the disk. In Chapter 7 you'll see how to use Norton's SPEEDISK utility to determine if your disk contains a high percentage of fragmented files. SPEEDISK also lets you defragment your disk by rewriting all the files in contiguous clusters.

Data Area

The last area of a DOS disk is known as the data area. The data area is where all the data for your files and subdirectories is located. All sectors that are not part of the boot record, root directory, or FAT are part of the data area.

Now that you know some of the details behind DOS disk structures, let's revisit the SYSINFO utility and discuss the disk information it reports.

Obtaining Disk Information

Chapter 2's discussion of SYSINFO explained four of the five areas reported by this informative utility. The menu for SYSINFO's fifth area, **D**isks, offers three useful selections: **D**isk Summary, Disk **C**haracteristics, and **P**artition Tables.

Looking at Disk Information with SYSINFO

1. Type the command `SYSINFO` and press `Enter`.   This runs the SYSINFO utility and displays the System Summary screen.

continues

Chapter 6

> *continued*
>
> **2.** Press Alt+D or click on **Disks** in the menu bar. Then choose **Disk Summary**.
>
> This activates the Disks menu, selects the Disk Summary option, and displays the Disk Summary screen (Figure 6.5).
>
> **3.** Press Enter or click on **Next**.
>
> This displays the Disk Characteristics screen (Figure 6.6).
>
> **4.** Press Enter or click on **Next**.
>
> This displays the Partition Tables screen (Figure 6.7).

Figure 6.5

The Disk Summary screen shows information about all disk drives on your PC.

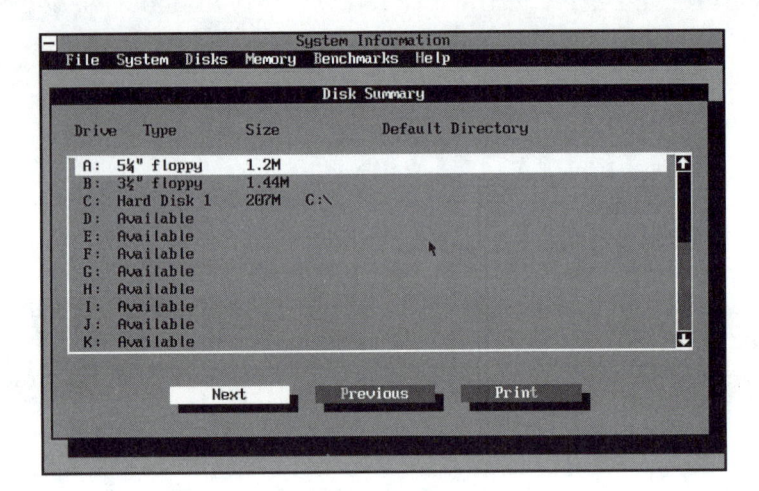

```
┌─────────────────── System Information ───────────────────┐
│  File   System   Disks   Memory   Benchmarks   Help      │
├──────────────────────── Disk Summary ────────────────────┤
│                                                          │
│  Drive    Type           Size      Default Directory     │
│                                                          │
│   A:    5¼" floppy       1.2M                            │
│   B:    3½" floppy       1.44M                           │
│   C:    Hard Disk 1      207M     C:\                    │
│   D:    Available                                        │
│   E:    Available                                        │
│   F:    Available                                        │
│   G:    Available                                        │
│   H:    Available                                        │
│   I:    Available                                        │
│   J:    Available                                        │
│   K:    Available                                        │
│                                                          │
│              Next        Previous        Print           │
└──────────────────────────────────────────────────────────┘
```

Disk Summary

The Disk Summary screen shown in Figure 6.5 shows four pieces of information, or fields, for each drive defined on your PC: Drive, Type, Size, and Default Directory. The first three fields are fairly self-explanatory; they show the drive's one-letter ID (for example,

A:), the drive type (for example, 5 1/4"), and the drive's capacity (for example, 1.2MB). The Default Directory field indicates the drive's default (active) directory. For example, if I change to the WORK directory of my C: drive using CD C:\WORK, WORK becomes the default directory for C:. Even if I move to my D: drive, WORK is still C:'s default directory.

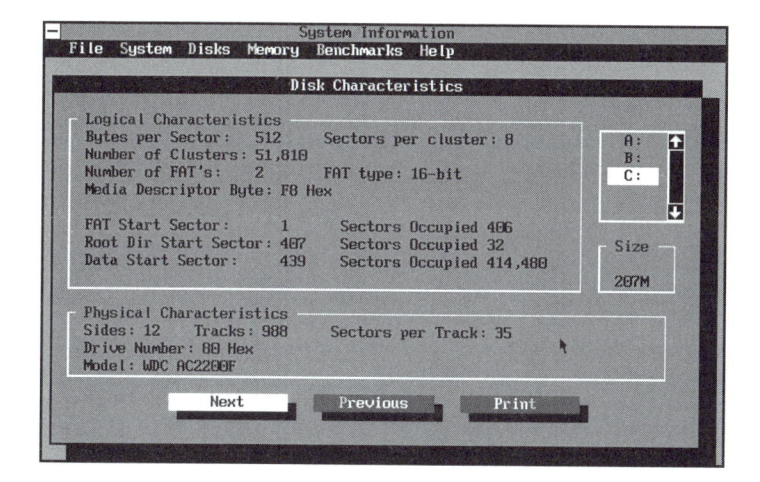

Figure 6.6
The Disk Characteristics screen reports both logical and physical disk information.

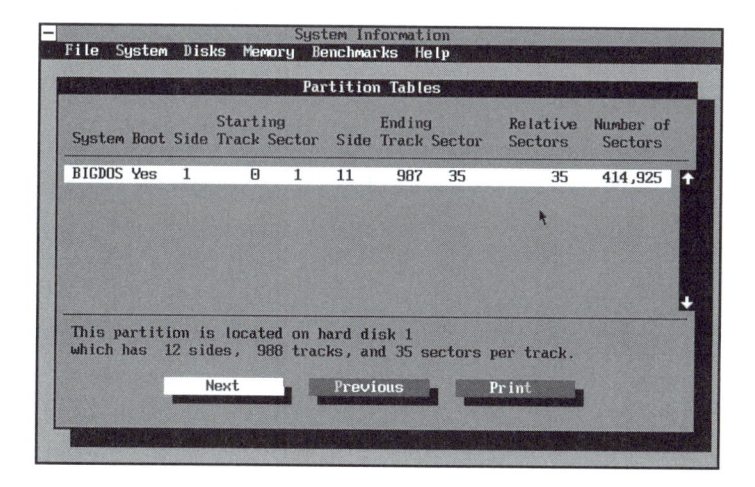

Figure 6.7
Starting and ending partition positions are indicated on the Partition Tables screen.

Disk Characteristics

The Disk Characteristics screen shown in Figure 6.6 has two main areas: Logical Characteristics and Physical Characteristics.

As you can see in the Logical Characteristics portion of Figure 6.6, my C: drive has 512 bytes per cluster and each cluster contains eight sectors. Further, there are 51,810 clusters on the C: drive. Using these figures, we can determine exactly how many bytes can be stored on C:. The formula for total capacity is

Total Capacity =
# of Bytes/Sector x # of Sectors/Cluster x # of Clusters

Now let's insert the values for the C: drive in Figure 6.6 to determine its total capacity:

Total Capacity =
512 Bytes/Cluster x 8 Sectors/Cluster x 51,810 Clusters
Total Capacity = 212,213,760 Bytes

The value shown in the Size area of Figure 6.6, 207M, is an approximation of the exact capacity we calculated.

The rest of the information shown in Figure 6.6 is not very interesting unless you are interested in more low-level details about a disk. The Logical Characteristics portion also contains information about a disk's system and data areas, including the starting sector and number of sectors occupied by the FAT, root directory, and data area. The Physical Characteristics section reports a few other disk-related tidbits including the number of sides, tracks, and sectors per track.

Partition Tables

The Partition Tables screen (Figure 6.7) shows detailed information about each of the partitions defined on your hard disk. Each partition on your hard disk is shown as a line in the Partition Tables screen.

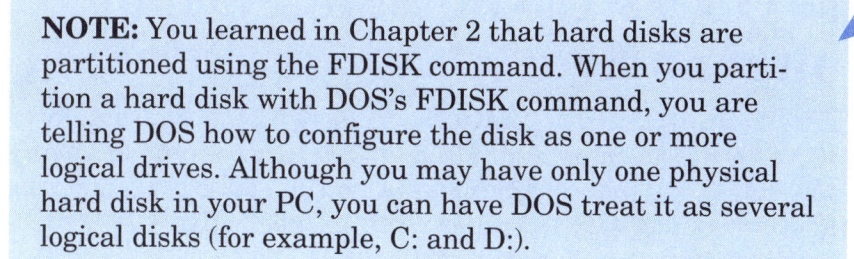

> **NOTE:** You learned in Chapter 2 that hard disks are partitioned using the FDISK command. When you partition a hard disk with DOS's FDISK command, you are telling DOS how to configure the disk as one or more logical drives. Although you may have only one physical hard disk in your PC, you can have DOS treat it as several logical disks (for example, C: and D:).

The Partition Tables screen reports three important pieces of information: whether the partition is bootable (Boot), the partition's starting/ending side/track/sector, and the total number of sectors used by the partition. If you have only one hard disk, and it is not partitioned, you'll only see one disk here.

Formatting Disks

One of the first rules you learn when working with PCs is that all disks, whether hard or floppy, must be formatted (using DOS's FORMAT command) before you can save files on them. DOS's FORMAT command is fairly simple to use. For example, to format the disk in drive A: you use the command FORMAT A:.

As with most DOS commands, FORMAT offers a wide variety of options, and sometimes the meaning of these options is not completely obvious. As mentioned before, the /S option causes FORMAT to place the special system files on the formatted disk to make it bootable. There are other switches too, for formatting disks at different capacities and with different safeguards.

Confusing? Yes it is. Fortunately for us, The Norton Utilities includes a tool that offers a safe and friendly approach to disk formatting.

SFORMAT: The Safe Format Alternative

The SFORMAT utility provides an easy-to-use alternative to DOS's FORMAT command. Although SFORMAT supports many of FORMAT's command line options, you don't need to remember them because SFORMAT allows you to interactively select formatting options on-screen.

Quick Steps: Formatting a Floppy Disk with SFORMAT

1. Type the command **SFORMAT** and a disk drive identifier SFORMAT A:, and press **Enter**.

    This starts the SFORMAT utility and displays the initial Safe Format screen shown in Figure 6.8.

2. Press **Enter** or click on **F**ormat to accept the default SFORMAT settings.

    If files/directories currently exist on the specified disk, a warning message is displayed; otherwise, SFORMAT begins formatting the specified disk.

3. If the warning message is displayed, press **Y** or click **Y**es to continue. Otherwise, wait until a completion message is displayed.

4. Press **Enter** or click **OK**.

    The Safe Format screen reappears.

5. Choose E**x**it.

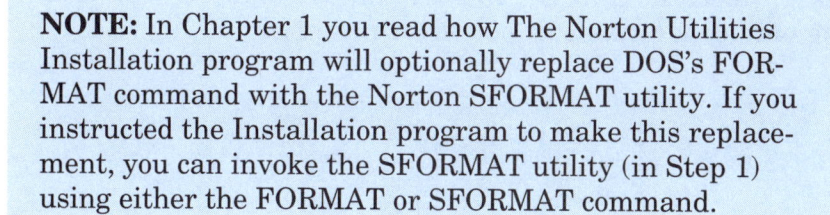

> **NOTE:** In Chapter 1 you read how The Norton Utilities Installation program will optionally replace DOS's FORMAT command with the Norton SFORMAT utility. If you instructed the Installation program to make this replacement, you can invoke the SFORMAT utility (in Step 1) using either the FORMAT or SFORMAT command.

SFORMAT Options

The SFORMAT utility offers several formatting options. The current status of each of these options is shown on the screen in Figure 6.8. Pull down one of the six lists shown in Figure 6.8: **D**rive, **S**ize, Format **T**ype, **Sy**stem Files, **V**olume Label, Save **I**mage Info, and S**a**ve Settings on Exit.

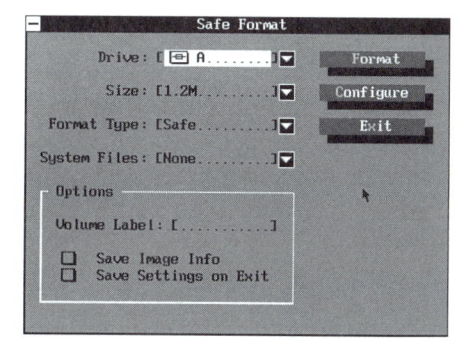

Figure 6.8
SFORMAT offers several disk-formatting options.

The **D**rive list in the Safe Format screen lists all the disk drives SFORMAT can access. The **D**rive list might show only floppy disk drives, since SFORMAT can be configured to prevent formatting of hard disks.

If you wish to allow SFORMAT to format hard disks, select the Configure button, and the screen shown in Figure 6.9 is displayed. Turn on the Allow Hard Disk Formatting check box and press ↵Enter. The initial SFORMAT screen (Figure 6.8) is redisplayed, and the **D**rive list includes all formattable hard disks. Select the Save Settings on Exit option if you want to save the hard disk formatting option for future SFORMAT use.

Figure 6.9
SFORMAT contains a hard disk safety feature that can be bypassed via the Hard Disk Formatting dialog box.

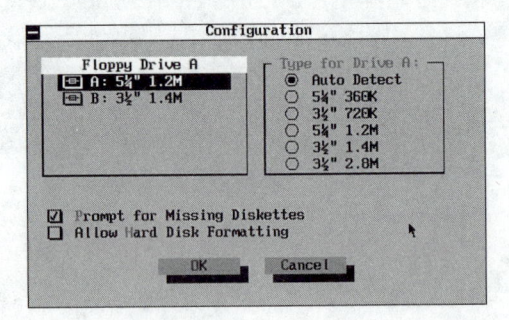

In Chapter 2 you read about the difference between double- and high-density floppy disks. If your PC is equipped with a high-density disk drive, you have the option of formatting either high- or low- (double-) density diskettes. However, keep in mind the warning in Chapter 2: It is not a good idea to format double-density diskettes in a high-density drive.

The SFORMAT utility has the intelligence to know whether the specified drive is a 3 1/2" or 5 1/4" drive. As a result, only valid disk format sizes for the specified drive are displayed in the **S**ize list. (SFORMAT can also support the 2.88MB disk drive if one is attached to your system.)

The Format **T**ype list lets you specify a Safe, Quick, or DOS format. SFORMAT offers three different methods of formatting a disk: Safe mode, Quick mode, and DOS mode. Use the up and down arrow keys and press (Spacebar) or click to select a different Format Mode option.

Safe mode is safe because it does not affect a disk's data areas: It just resets the system area and performs some tests. This allows the Norton UNFORMAT utility (discussed later in this chapter) to easily recover all files from an accidentally formatted disk. Safe mode also happens to be faster than DOS's FORMAT command. Use Safe mode when working with disks that have not previously been formatted.

When you select **Quick mode**, SFORMAT simply clears the disk's file allocation table and root directory; it performs no tests. Use Quick mode whenever you are working with a previously formatted disk. You cannot use Quick mode on disks that have not previously been formatted.

If you select **DOS mode**, SFORMAT emulates DOS's own FORMAT algorithm. This means that any files or subdirectories on the disk will be wiped out and unrecoverable after the format. Use this destructive format option with extreme caution!

The S**y**stem Files list lets you specify whether or not the system files should be copied to the formatted disk. The system files include all the files that make a disk bootable. You have three options for this selection. You can create

- A bootable disk. (Put on disk.)
- A nonbootable disk with room reserved for the system files. (Leave space.)
- A nonbootable disk with no room reserved for the system files. (None.)

> **TIP:** There is an advantage to creating a nonbootable disk with room reserved for the system files: You have the option of easily making the disk bootable in the future (via DOS's SYS command) without having to reformat it.

Use the up and down arrow keys and press (Spacebar) to select a different System Files option.

The **V**olume Label option lets you attach a name (up to 11 characters) to a newly formatted disk. This volume label is displayed every time you use DIR to list the disk's contents. Type in the desired volume label using any of the alphanumeric or symbol keys.

If you select the Save Image Info option, SFORMAT will automatically run another utility, IMAGE. IMAGE saves a copy of the disk's system information in a special hidden file called IMAGE.DAT that another Norton utility (UNFORMAT) can use to recover files if you ever accidentally reformat the disk. (We talk more about IMAGE and UNFORMAT later in this chapter.)

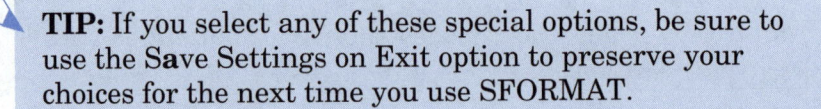

> **TIP:** If you select any of these special options, be sure to use the **S**ave Settings on Exit option to preserve your choices for the next time you use SFORMAT.

Preserving Important Disk Information

In Chapter 4 you learned how to use UNERASE to quickly recover accidentally deleted files. You also learned that you can increase the chances of a successful file recovery by using UNERASE as soon as possible after an accidental deletion. In reality, however, that's not always possible. You may need to recover a file you accidentally deleted yesterday or last week. In addition, recovery of badly fragmented files can be very difficult if not impossible, even with a powerful tool like UNERASE. To keep the odds of file recovery in your favor, I suggest regular use of the Norton IMAGE utility.

Maintaining a Good "Image"

The Norton Utilities tool IMAGE can be used to assist UNERASE and UNFORMAT (discussed later) in data recovery. The IMAGE utility saves a copy of a disk's system area (boot record, FAT, and root directory) in a hidden file called IMAGE.DAT. You may recall that SFORMAT can optionally create an IMAGE.DAT when you

Maintaining Hard and Floppy Disks 125

format a disk. The IMAGE utility gives you the ability to create/update the IMAGE.DAT file to make sure it reflects the most up-to-date system area information.

Quick Steps

Using IMAGE to Guard Against Data Loss

1. Type the command **IMAGE** or highlight it in the Commands list of the main Norton screen. You can include a disk drive identifier (for example, IMAGE C:).

2. Press ⏎Enter.   This starts the IMAGE utility. IMAGE runs by itself and displays the screen shown in Figure 6.10 when it is finished.

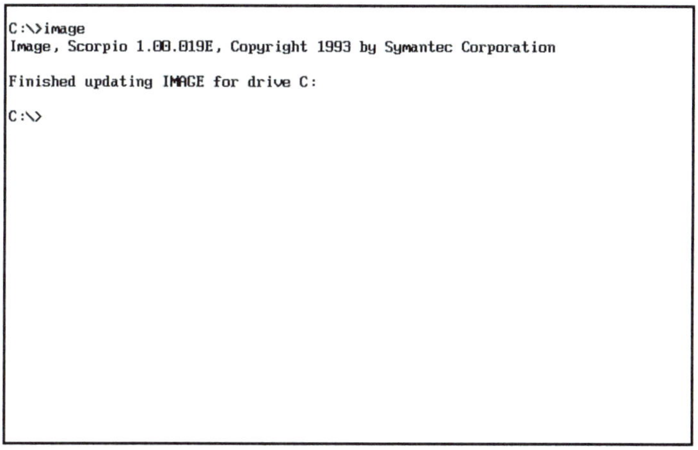

```
C:\>image
Image, Scorpio 1.00.019E, Copyright 1993 by Symantec Corporation

Finished updating IMAGE for drive C:

C:\>
```

Figure 6.10
IMAGE screen.

I highly recommend that you use IMAGE regularly to keep an updated IMAGE.DAT file on each partition of your PC's hard disk. The easiest way to do this is to include the IMAGE command in your AUTOEXEC.BAT file, which executes every time you boot your computer.

You can specify multiple disk drives on IMAGE's command line to update the IMAGE.DAT files for more than one disk partition. For example, the command IMAGE C: D: will update the IMAGE.DAT files on both the C: and D: drives. If IMAGE finds an IMAGE.DAT file on the specified disk, it first renames IMAGE.DAT to IMAGE.BAK and then creates a new IMAGE.DAT file. If you include IMAGE in your AUTOEXEC.BAT file, your hard disks will always contain two generations of system area information that can be used by UNERASE and UNFORMAT.

Recovering Data from an Accidentally Formatted Disk

It's much easier to delete a file accidentally than it is to accidentally format a disk. But since both scenarios are possible, The Norton Utilities include two important tools for data recovery: UNERASE for resurrecting deleted files and UNFORMAT for rescuing data from an accidentally formatted disk. We explored UNERASE in Chapters 4 and 5. Now, let's see how to recover files with the powerful UNFORMAT utility. Note that UNFORMAT is best used in concert with IMAGE, so be sure to turn on the Save Image Info option when you use SFORMAT to format a disk.

TIP: DOS versions 5.0 and above offer their own UNFORMAT command. To make sure you'll be using Norton's version of this command, choose to rename DOS's file to XNFORMAT.COM when you install the Norton Utilities.

Maintaining Hard and Floppy Disks 127

CAUTION

If you want to recover files from an accidentally formatted hard disk and you haven't installed The Norton Utilities yet, do not install the utilities now! The Norton installation program copies all the utilities to your hard disk and may overwrite the files you want to recover. Instead, insert the Norton Emergency Disk 1 into your A: (or B:) drive, substitute A:UNFORMAT (or B:UNFORMAT) for UNFORMAT, and follow the on-screen prompts.

QUICK STEPS

UNFORMATting a Disk

1. Type the command **UNFORMAT** and a disk example, UNFORMAT A:, and press Enter.

    This starts the UNFORMAT utility and displays the IMAGE dialog box shown in Figure 6.11.

2. Press Enter or click **Yes**.

    Unformat asks you to confirm the unformat operation.

3. Press Enter or click **Yes**.

    This initiates the UNFORMAT process. A message appears when IMAGE.DAT is found.

4. Press Enter or click **OK**.

    You are asked to confirm that you want to write the image data to the drive you originally specified.

5. Press Enter or click **Yes**.

    You are asked to specify a **F**ull or **P**artial restore.

continues

continued

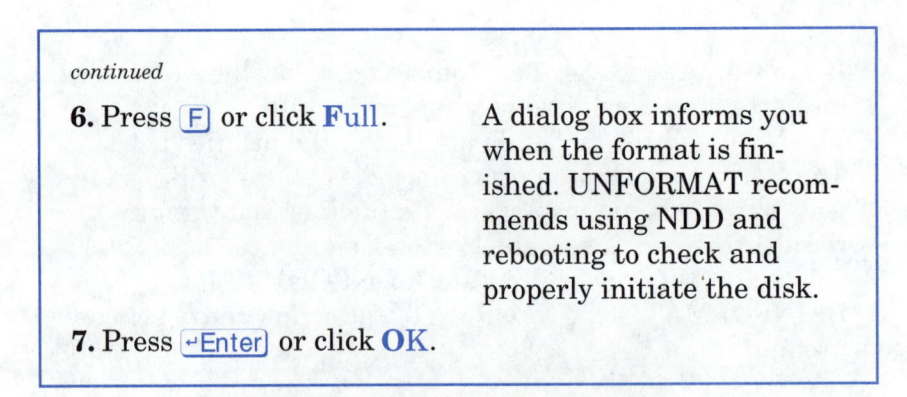

> **6.** Press `F` or click **F**ull. A dialog box informs you when the format is finished. UNFORMAT recommends using NDD and rebooting to check and properly initiate the disk.
>
> **7.** Press `↵Enter` or click **OK**.

Figure 6.11
UNFORMAT will use an IMAGE file if one exists on the formatted disk.

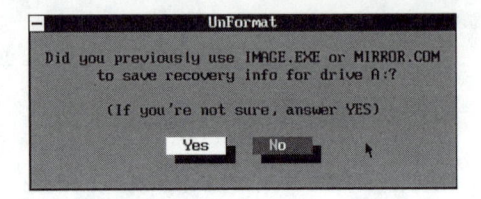

If the disk you want to UNFORMAT contains an up-to-date IMAGE.DAT file, the chances of a complete recovery are excellent. But don't worry if your formatted disk does not contain an IMAGE.DAT file; it is still possible that UNFORMAT will recover everything that was on the disk, if the errant formatting job was done in "Quick" or "Safe" mode.

If the accidental formatting was done with the regular DOS FORMAT command, or with SFORMAT in DOS mode, you're out of luck. These FORMATs overwrite all the data on a disk during the format process, so there's no way to recover the files, even with UNFORMAT.

The Importance of IMAGE

If you have the foresight to always use a nondestructive format, such as the Quick or Safe modes of the Norton SFORMAT utility, you should have no trouble with a full recovery after an accidental format. It is also very important to make certain that all of your disks contain an up-to-date IMAGE.DAT file. (Refer to the SFORMAT and IMAGE utilities for IMAGE.DAT maintenance.)

Perhaps the most important rule to remember for data recovery is to employ the services of a recovery tool like UNERASE or UNFORMAT as soon as possible after the accidental deletion or format occurs. The longer you wait before using UNERASE or UNFORMAT, the greater the chances are of overwriting precious data clusters. If the disk you wish to UNFORMAT was nondestructively formatted and contains an up-to-date IMAGE.DAT file, UNFORMAT should be able to recover all your files with no additional intervention on your part.

> **TIP:** When the UNFORMAT process is complete, you should carefully inspect the contents of the disk and make certain the files and subdirectories are correct. If you determine that some files or subdirectories are missing after an UNFORMAT, you may need to use the UNERASE command to complete the recovery process.

If UNFORMAT is unable to locate an IMAGE.DAT file but is able to recover files and subdirectories, you'll have to do some additional housekeeping when UNFORMAT finishes. Without the IMAGE.DAT file, UNFORMAT does not know the names of a disk's subdirectories. Therefore, UNFORMAT names the subdirectories DIR.0, DIR.1, DIR.2, and so on. You'll need to use the NCD utility to rename these generically named subdirectories.

Without the IMAGE.DAT file, UNFORMAT also has no idea what was contained in the disk's system area (boot record, FAT, and root directory). This means that UNFORMAT cannot recover the files that previously existed in the accidentally formatted disk's root directory. You'll have to manually recover root directory files with the UNERASE utility (refer to the "Manually UNERASEing Files" section of Chapter 9).

TIP: Refer to the DISKTOOL utility discussed in Chapter 9 if the UNFORMATted disk used to be bootable and you want to restore this feature.

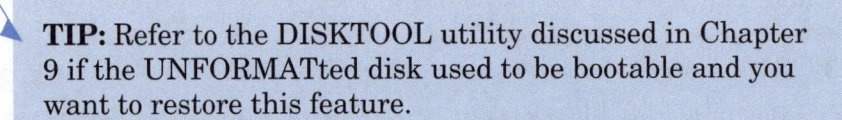

Duplicating a Disk

You can use DOS' DISKCOPY command to copy the files and directories on one disk to another disk of the same size and capacity. However, if you're copying a disk with a capacity of more than 640K, DISKCOPY asks you to swap disks in and out of the drive several times. This is because DISKCOPY stores the data being copied in its conventional RAM, and your system has only 640K (or less) of it available.

Duplicate Disk (DUPDISK), new in version 7.0 of The Norton Utilities, lets you copy (duplicate) a disk of any capacity without repeatedly swapping disks in and out of the drive. Unlike DISKCOPY, DUPDISK is able to use other system resources to hold the data for copying, so it can "remember" more than 640K of data at once.

Use the following Quick Steps to put DUPDISK to work for you. Note that this process overwrites any information that's on the disk to which you're copying.

Quick Steps: Duplicating a Disk

1. Type **DUPDISK** at the DOS prompt or highlight Duplicate Disk in the Commands list of the main Norton screen. Press [↵Enter].

   The dialog box shown in Figure 6.12 appears.

Maintaining Hard and Floppy Disks 131

2. Change the copy **F**rom and copy **T**o drives, if needed.	Note that you can only specify different drives for **T**o and **F**rom if your floppy disk drives are the same size.
3. Press ⏎Enter or click **OK**.	You are prompted to insert the original (source) disk.
4. Place the disk in the drive as requested, and press ⏎Enter or click **OK**.	The Duplicate Diskette box informs you of the copy progress. You are prompted to insert the target disk (disk you're copying to) in the drive.
5. Place the disk in the drive as requested, and press ⏎Enter or click **OK**.	If there are files on the target disk, you are asked whether you want to overwrite them.
6. Press Y or click **Y**es.	DUPDISK asks whether you want to make another copy of the source disk.
7. If you choose **Y**es, repeat steps 5 and 6. If you choose **N**o, press Esc to close the Duplicate Diskette dialog box when it reappears to end the copy process.	

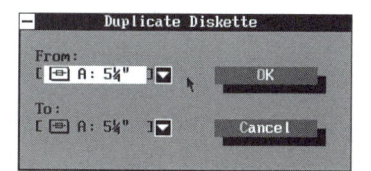

Figure 6.12

The first Duplicate Diskette dialog box.

Diagnosing and Correcting Disk Problems

As an experienced PC user, I've had a few encounters with unreliable hard/floppy disks. Unreliable disks can cause a variety of problems, including corrupt and disappearing files. Although the failure rate for disks is very low, even the slightest disk failure can cause great distress!

Consider this scenario: Let's say you've been working on a report for your boss for several days. The report is quite a few pages long and includes a slew of important tables and figures that have taken hours to create. Just as you are about to print the final copy of the report, your PC informs you that the file is "unreadable," or worse yet, it can't even find the file!

One of the best steps you can take to avoid and correct disk problems like this is to use the Norton Disk Doctor (NDD) utility. Disk Doctor will tell you if a disk is bad before you save or copy data to it—and lose the data. Disk Doctor checks critical disk information, like the file allocation table that tracks where the contents of each file is stored, then tests each and every sector of the disk to see whether it's usuable or bad. Use these Quick Steps to ensure that your disks are in tip top condition.

Quick Steps: Testing a Disk with Norton Disk Doctor (NDD)

1. Type the command **NDD** and press `Enter`.

   This starts the NDD utility and displays the operation screen shown in Figure 6.13.

2. Press `Enter` or click on the **Diagnose Disk** option.

   This displays the Select Drives to Diagnose dialog box.

Maintaining Hard and Floppy Disks **133**

3. Use the arrow keys or the mouse to highlight the drive you want to diagnose, and press `Enter` or click on **D**iagnose. Insert a disk and choose **OK** if needed.

   NDD analyzes several areas of the specified disk; the Surface Test screen shown in Figure 6.14 is displayed when these tests are completed.

4. Press `Enter` or click **B**egin Test to accept the default settings shown in Figure 6.14 and to begin the surface test.

   NDD tests every sector of the specified disk.

5. If NDD finds disk errors, it asks if you want to **C**reate Undo File. Choose this option, insert a disk in the drive, and choose **OK**.

6. Follow prompts to repair any additional errors Disk Doctor finds.

7. NDD displays the screen in Figure 6.15 when the test is complete. Press `Enter` or click **R**eport.

   A report of the NDD session is created that can be viewed on the screen, printed out, or saved to a file.

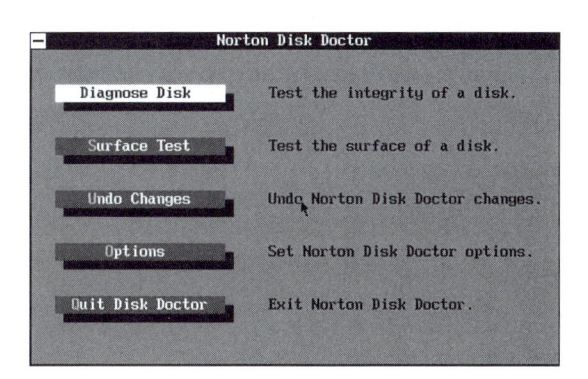

Figure 6.13

Select the desired NDD operation from the Norton Disk Doctor operation screen.

Figure 6.14

The Surface Test screen offers several options for additional NDD disk tests.

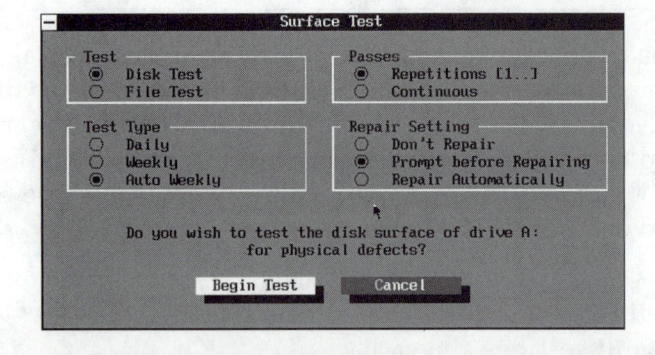

Figure 6.15

The NDD completion screen reports the results of all tests performed.

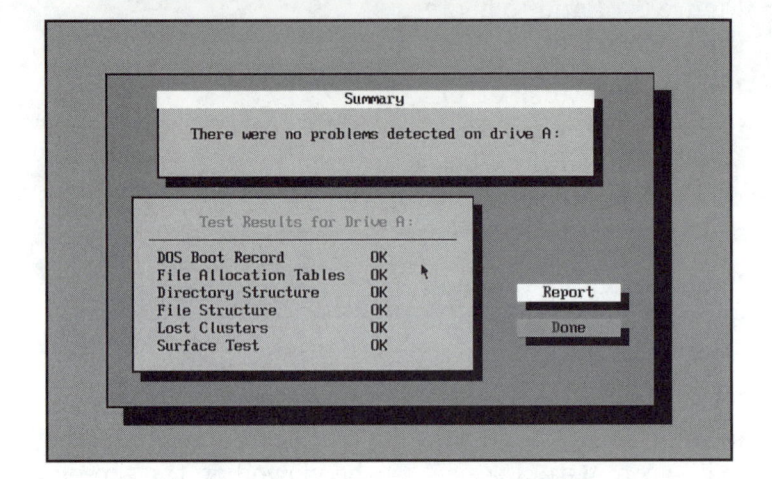

NDD performs a variety of tests in step 3 of the preceding Quick Steps. During these tests, NDD examines the disk's partition table, boot record, file allocation table, directory structure, and file structure. When these tests are complete, NDD examines the disk's FAT in search of lost clusters. A lost cluster is a cluster that does not belong to any file but is shown as being in use in the FAT.

The surface test in step 4 is the last test performed by the Norton Disk Doctor. Depending upon the options selected and the size of the disk being analyzed, the surface test can take anywhere from a few minutes to several hours to complete. When the default options are used, NDD tests each sector of the selected disk once and reports any problems it encounters.

Surface Test Configuration

The screen in Figure 6.14 shows all the options available for the surface test operation. These options can be changed each time you run NDD, or you can modify and save your settings using the **O**ptions button in Figure 6.13.

The Disk Doctor Options screen shown in Figure 6.16 is displayed when you select the **O**ptions button. Press `↵Enter` or click on the **S**urface Test button in Figure 6.16, and the Surface Test Options screen (Figure 6.17) is displayed.

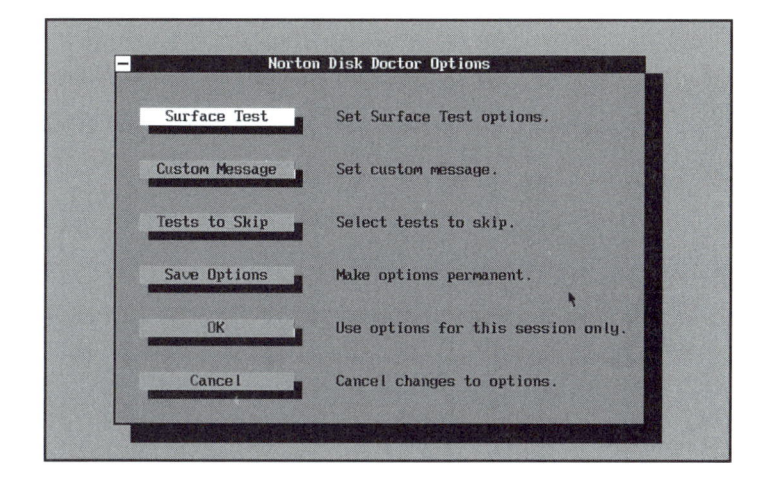

Figure 6.16
You can customize NDD with the Disk Doctor Options screen.

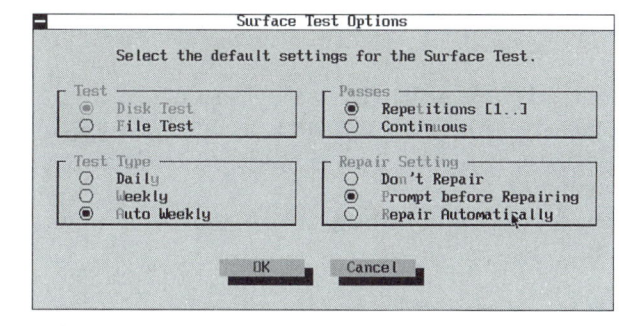

Figure 6.17
The Surface Test Options screen looks very similar to the Surface Test screen (Figure 6.14).

The Surface Test Options screen in Figure 6.17 closely resembles the Surface Test screen in Figure 6.14. Both offer four surface test settings: Test, Passes, Test Type, and Repair Setting. Use the Tab key to jump quickly from one setting area to the next. Then use the up and down arrow keys and the Spacebar to select new surface test settings. Or just click the mouse to make your selection.

The Test option in Figure 6.17 lets you choose between a **D**isk Test and a **F**ile Test. When you select the **D**isk Test option, NDD tests every sector of the selected disk, including those sectors not currently used by any files/directories (such as unused sectors). Select the File Test option if you want NDD to skip unused sectors and test only those sectors currently used by a file/directory.

Use the Passes option to alter the number of times NDD runs the surface test. The default value is 1, but you can specify up to 999 repetitions. When you select the Contin**u**ous option, NDD performs the surface test over and over again until you abort it by pressing `Esc` or by clicking on the left mouse button.

The Test Type option in Figure 6.17 lets you select either a Dail**y**, **W**eekly, or **A**uto Weekly test setting. The Dail**y** test is less sophisticated and time-consuming than the **W**eekly test, but the **W**eekly test can uncover certain disk problems that the Dail**y** test may not detect. The **A**uto Weekly test is a combination of the Dail**y** and **W**eekly tests. When you select **A**uto Weekly, NDD performs a **W**eekly test on Friday and a Dail**y** test every other day of the week.

The last surface test configuration option lets you specify whether NDD should repair any disk problems it encounters. You may choose to

- Prevent NDD from making any repairs.
- Have NDD prompt you before making repairs.
- Let NDD automatically make all repairs without asking for your approval.

NDD repairs disk problems by moving data from questionable clusters to more reliable locations on the disk. Further, NDD marks the questionable clusters as "bad" to prevent DOS from using them in the future.

Once you're satisfied with the surface test settings, press ⏎Enter or click **OK**, then select the Save Options button on the Disk Doctor Options screen (Figure 6.16).

Other Disk Doctor Options

As you can see in the Disk Doctor Options screen (Figure 6.16), NDD offers two other configuration options: C**u**stom Message and **T**ests to Skip. Use the C**u**stom Message option if you want to display a special message when NDD encounters an error in its test process. The Set Custom Message screen shown in Figure 6.18 is displayed when you select the C**u**stom Message button.

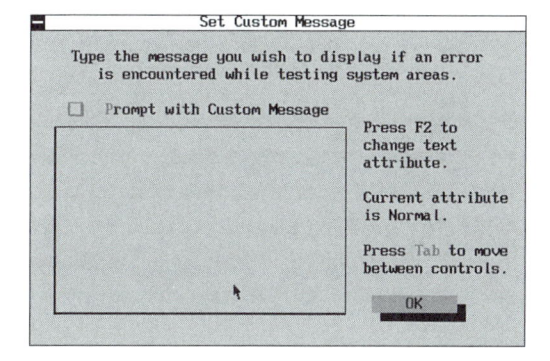

Figure 6.18

Use the Set Custom Message screen to create a special message that will be displayed when NDD encounters an error.

Press Alt + P or click on the **P**rompt with Custom Message option in Figure 6.18, then press Tab⇥ or click in the message box to move the cursor to the message box. Type the desired custom error message in the message box (for example, `NDD has discovered a problem with your disk . . . please call 555-1234 to report this problem!`). Use F2 to select a special attribute for the error message text. Sample text attributes include underline, bold, and reverse video. When you are satisfied with your custom error message, press Tab⇥ or click on the **OK** button, and then press ⏎Enter to return to the Disk Doctor Options screen (Figure 6.16). Finally, select the Save Options button to save your custom error message.

Select the Tests to Skip option shown in Figure 6.16 when you want to prevent NDD from running certain tests on your PC. The Tests to Skip screen shown in Figure 6.19 is displayed when you select this option.

NDD may run into problems during its test process if your computer is not a "true 100% IBM-compatible" PC. Certain compatibility problems may cause NDD to misbehave and lock up your PC. If your PC is having a problem running certain NDD tests, select the Skip option for the those tests and rerun NDD. Be sure to save your Tests to Skip settings by using the Save Options button on the screen in Figure 6.16.

Figure 6.19

You can define which tests NDD should skip using the Tests to Skip screen.

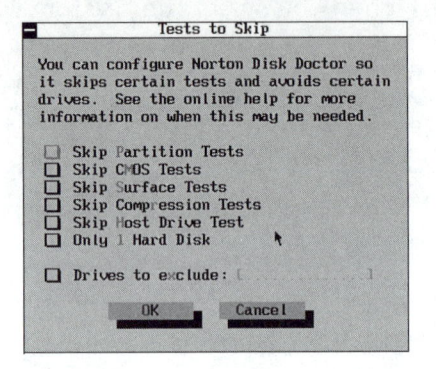

Undoing NDD Repairs

Although NDD does a fine job of repairing most files, it is not infallible; that's why it's a good habit to always check its work. You should always create a report whenever you let NDD make repairs to a disk (refer to step 5 in the NDD Quick Steps). Read through the NDD report to see what files or areas of the disk were repaired. Then check the repaired files to ensure that they truly have been "fixed."

For example, NDD recently repaired a file of mine called MEMO.DOC. I know that MEMO.DOC is a WordPerfect file so I used WordPerfect to load the MEMO.DOC file and check out the repairs. Fortunately, the repairs made by NDD appeared to fix the problems I had been having with MEMO.DOC. But what if my "fixed" file was in worse shape than it was in before NDD made its repairs? It occasionally happens; that's why NDD offers an undo feature.

It takes only a few moments to undo disk repairs made during the last NDD session. This is true because NDD saves disk repair information in a special file called NDDUNDO.DAT. NDD can use this undo data file to restore a disk to the same condition it was in before the disk repairs were made. Select the Undo Changes button on the Norton Disk Doctor operation screen (Figure 6.13), and follow the directions displayed to undo the disk repairs from the last NDD session.

In This Chapter

DOS shells and NDOS

Starting NDOS and getting help

Using NDOS commands

The Norton Utilities program offers the added capability of its own set of DOS-like commands, NDOS, which is compatible with DOS versions 2.1 and later. This chapter introduces you to NDOS and teaches you how to use its flexible features.

- NDOS interprets commands you enter at the prompt to execute system programs, just like DOS.
- NDOS offers enhancements to existing DOS commands, as well as providing over 40 additional commands.
- NDOS offers some flexibility in the ways to enter commands and provides some useful commands that you'll learn about in this chapter.

Chapter

7

Introducing NDOS

Even though DOS has been around for a while in numerous versions, it's not perfect yet (sorry Microsoft). The Norton Utilities includes NDOS, a command processor that works from the command prompt just like DOS does.

A critical advantage to using NDOS is that its versions of familiar DOS features provide new capabilities and command switch options. For example, with NDOS, you can COPY more than one file at a time, as in COPY TEST.DOC MEMO.TXT B:. Also, NDOS includes more than 40 commands DOS doesn't have, such as the ALIAS command, which lets you assign a special name to an often-used command or set of commands.

Loading and Unloading NDOS

To live and breathe and think (so to speak), DOS needs a command processor file that accepts the commands you enter and then tells your system what to do. The default command processor that comes with DOS is called COMMAND.COM, and it loads automatically when you start your system. NDOS's command processor is NDOS.COM. You can run NDOS.COM on top of COMMAND.COM; you don't even have to unload COMMAND.COM first.

> **TIP:** NDOS is automatically installed when you perform a full installation of The Norton Utilities (see Appendix A). To ensure that NDOS is on your system, check your directory containing The Norton Utilities files to see if it contains NDOS's program files: NDOS.COM, NDOSHELP.EXE, and NDOS.INI.

To start NDOS, type **NDOS** at the DOS prompt and press **Enter**. If you didn't add The Norton Utilities to your system's AUTOEXEC.BAT file, first change to the directory where you installed The Norton Utilities by typing **C:\NU** and pressing **Enter**. At the prompt, type **NDOS**, and press **Enter**. NDOS is loaded, and the screen shown in Figure 7.1 appears.

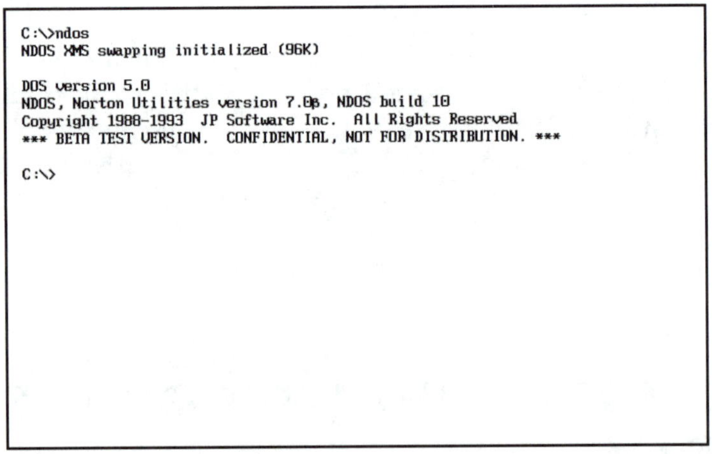

Figure 7.1
NDOS is loaded.

```
C:\>ndos
NDOS XMS swapping initialized (96K)

DOS version 5.0
NDOS, Norton Utilities version 7.0β, NDOS build 10
Copyright 1988-1993  JP Software Inc.  All Rights Reserved
*** BETA TEST VERSION.  CONFIDENTIAL, NOT FOR DISTRIBUTION. ***

C:\>
```

You can return control of your system to COMMAND.COM at any time. Simply type **EXIT** at the prompt and press **Enter**.

Introducing NDOS 143

Getting Help

NDOS comes with a help facility that gives information about each command available. To get help once NDOS is loaded, press F1 at the prompt, or type **NDOSHELP** and press Enter. The NDOS Help screen appears, as shown in Figure 7.2.

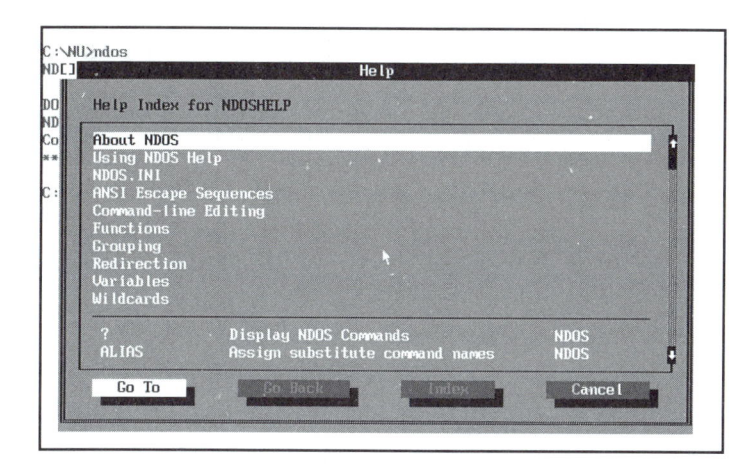

Figure 7.2
The opening NDOS Help screen.

Use the up and down arrow keys or click on a topic with the mouse to move the highlight among the Help screen topics. When the command you want information about is highlighted, press Enter or click on Help to display its Help screen. For example, Figure 7.3 shows the screen that appears when you select DESCRIBE from the main Help screen.

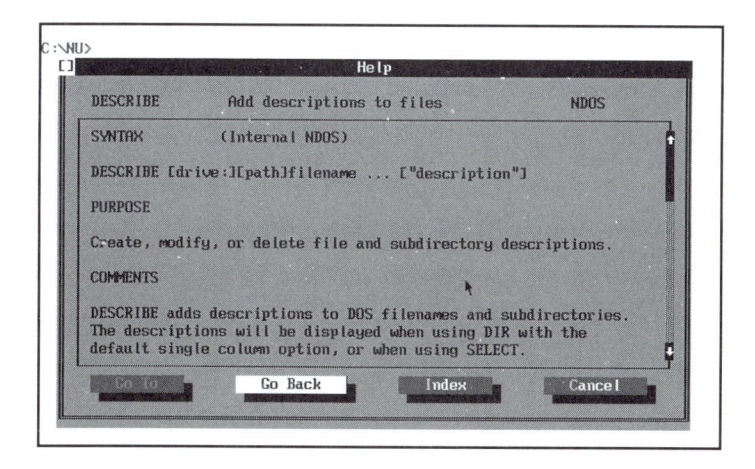

Figure 7.3
The Describe help screen.

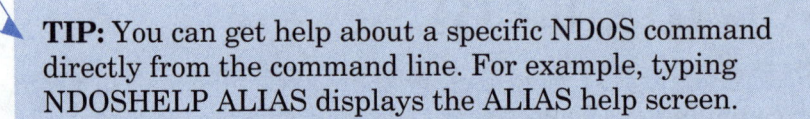

TIP: You can get help about a specific NDOS command directly from the command line. For example, typing NDOSHELP ALIAS displays the ALIAS help screen.

Using NDOS Commands

As you do for DOS commands, enter NDOS commands (with the necessary parameters and switches), and press ⏎Enter to execute them. (You've done this already to start NDOS and get help.) You must enter each command with the appropriate *syntax*. That is, you must follow certain rules in entering the *parameters* (additional information) and *switches* (control options) that go with the command.

For example, when you use the DIR command to list the contents of a directory, it normally displays the file names in a long list that quickly scrolls off your screen. To display the file names in four columns of the screen so you can see more file names, add the NDOS switch /4 to DIR. Type DIR /4 and press Enter, and NDOS lists your files in four neat columns.

The next few sections describe some special options you have for entering NDOS commands and describe a few of the most useful new NDOS commands.

Using NDOS for Single Commands or Batch Files

You can use the /C switch to temporarily load NDOS from DOS, execute an NDOS command or a batch file that includes NDOS commands (see Chapter 8 for more on batch files), then return to DOS. Try the following steps using the NDOS BEEP command, which isn't offered by DOS:

1. If NDOS is loaded, type **EXIT**, and press [↵Enter] to return control of your system to DOS' COMMAND.COM processor.

2. Type **NDOS /C BEEP** and press [↵Enter]. Your computer should beep and return to the prompt (and DOS).

3. Type **BEEP** and press [↵Enter] again. Your system displays the message Bad command or file name, because COMMAND.COM can't execute the BEEP command.

Entering More Than One Command

When COMMAND.COM is running the show, it only lets you enter one command at a time. For example, you have to issue the command COPY *.* A: and press Enter, then type DIR A: and press Enter. In NDOS, you may enter more than one command on the command line before pressing Enter. To do so, simply separate each program command with the caret (^) character. For example, if I typed **DIR C:\MEMOS^BEEP** and pressed [↵Enter], my system would display a list of all the files in the MEMO directory and then would beep.

Repeating Commands

As you execute NDOS commands, NDOS keeps a log of each command you type. (DOS versions 5.0 and 6.0 offer the same feature, but you have to run a separate feature called DOSkey.) You can search through NDOS's list of commands if you would like to reuse one, or if you want to modify and then reuse it. At the prompt, simply press the up arrow key to move back through the commands you executed. Pressing the down arrow will move you back to a more recent command. When the command you want to reissue appears at the prompt, simply press ↵Enter to execute it.

Wild Cards

With DOS commands, you can generally use only two wild card characters per full file name: one in the file name and one in the file name extension. (For example, you could type DIR C:\MEMO\A*.* to display a list of all the files in the MEMO directory that have a file name *starting with* A.) NDOS allows you to use an additional wild card in both the primary file name and the extension. (For example, you could type DIR C:\NU*A*.*X* to find all the files in the NU directory with an A in the file name and an X in the file name extension.)

NDOS recognizes both the * (for multiple characters) and the ? (for single characters) wild cards. In addition, you can use the square brackets, [], to specify a range of characters. For example, DIR [C-D]*.* lists all the files that have names starting with the letters c or d. Using an exclamation mark(!) after the first bracket reverses the result. DIR [!C-D]*.* lists all files *except* those that start with c or d.

Specifying Multiple Files

Just as NDOS can execute multiple program commands by typing one command line, it can execute the specified command(s) on multiple files with dissimilar names. For example, the opening paragraph explained how you can COPY more than one file at a time, as in COPY TEST.DOC MEMO.TXT B:.

Hot NDOS Commands

Although there's not room in this book to review every NDOS command and its syntax, Table 7.1 lists the NDOS commands that beginning users are likely to get the most mileage from. When you become comfortable using the commands in Table 7.1 and are ready to move on to NDOS's more advanced features. If you would like more information about the switches and parameters you can use with the commands in Table 7.1, consult your NDOS Manual that came with The Norton Utilities User's Guide.

Table 7.1
Hot NDOS COMMANDS

Command	Example	Description
?	?	Lists the NDOS commands on-screen
ALIAS/	ALIAS LOOK DIR C:\MEMO	Allows you to specify a new name for a command or
UNALIAS		group of commands you use frequently. (UNALIAS removes the new name assignment.) The example renames the command line DIR C:\MEMO to LOOK.
BEEP	BEEP	Makes your system beep at you.
DESCRIBE	DESCRIBE FUN.TXT "Company picnic details"	Adds a description of up to 40 characters to files and subdirectories.
FREE	FREE C:	Tells you how much disk space, bytes used, and free bytes are on the specified disk. (FREE is much faster than DOS's CHKDSK.)
HISTORY	HISTORY	Lists all the NDOS commands you've used during the current work session.
LIST	LIST CHAP5.DOC	Displays the file contents on-screen, much like DOS's TYPE command. However, with LIST you move forward and backward through the file's pages.

continues

Table 7.1 *Continued.*

Command	Example	Description
MOVE	MOVE FUN.TXT C:\MEMOS\FUN	Moves the specified file from the current directory to the specified destination directory.
SELECT	SELECT COPY (C:\MEMOS*.TXT A:)	Displays a list of the files matching the parameters in the parentheses, so you can choose files on which the specified command will operate. The example displays a list of the files with the .TXT extension in C:\MEMOS; select which of the files in the displayed list to copy to drive A:.

> **CAUTION:** Be careful when you use the ALIAS command not to specify an existing NDOS command name as the alias. This would cause NDOS confusion.

In This Chapter

Using batch files for automation

Batch file syntax

Improving batch files with BE: Batch Enhancer

These are some of the fundamental concepts behind DOS batch files:

- A batch file is an ASCII text file that contains one or more DOS commands.
- Batch files support special command line parameters, looping, and conditional constructs similar to the ones supported by programming languages.
- Besides PAUSE, DOS batch files offer no useful means for accepting user input.
- The Batch Enhancer utility can enhance dull and dreary batch files, letting you add color, sound, and windows.
- You can create script files that quickly execute BE commands. Include script files in batch files.

Chapter 8

Enhancing Your Batch Files

Many PC operations require the same commands to be performed over and over again. For example, I have two subdirectories, WORK\MEMOS and WORK\REPORTS, that contain important work-related files. At the end of each week I have to place the contents of each subdirectory on separate floppy disks for my boss. The DOS commands I execute to perform this operation are shown in Table 8.1.

Table 8.1
DOS Commands for File Backup

DOS Command	Result
CD WORK\MEMOS	Moves to the WORK\MEMOS subdirectory.
COPY *.* A:	Copies the contents of WORK\MEMOS to a floppy disk in the A: drive. (When the COPY is complete, I place a new floppy in the A: drive.)
CD ..\REPORTS	Moves to the WORK\REPORTS subdirectory.
COPY *.* A:	Copies the contents of WORK\REPORTS to the floppy disk in the A: drive.

Using a DOS batch file, I can consolidate all four commands in Table 8.1 into one command.

Creating a Batch File

A batch file is an ASCII text file that contains one or more DOS commands. DOS can get confused if it encounters non-ASCII characters in a batch file. Therefore, you must be careful when determining what text editor to use for writing batch files.

If you are looking for a good text editor, I suggest using either the MS-DOS Editor (EDIT.COM, in DOS versions 5.0 and above) or the Windows Notepad application. DOS' EDLIN text editor (which comes with all versions of DOS) can create ASCII text files, but it's antiquated and hard to use. Even the most modest shareware editors look fully featured when compared to EDLIN!

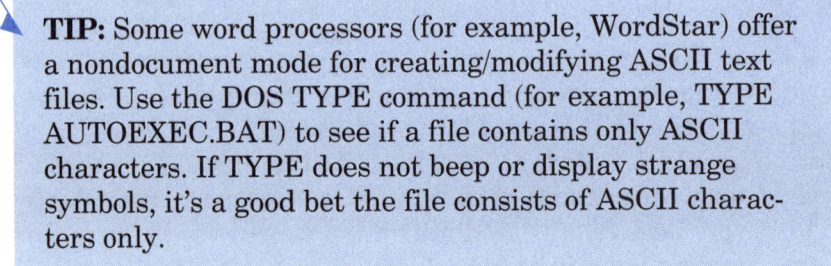

> **TIP:** Some word processors (for example, WordStar) offer a nondocument mode for creating/modifying ASCII text files. Use the DOS TYPE command (for example, TYPE AUTOEXEC.BAT) to see if a file contains only ASCII characters. If TYPE does not beep or display strange symbols, it's a good bet the file consists of ASCII characters only.

See the documentation that came with the text editor of your choice to learn more about using it to create plain text (ASCII files).

A Simple Batch File

When you have selected a text editor, you are ready to start creating batch files. It's not as hard as it sounds; all you have to do is type a list of commands that are to be carried out consecutively. To try it, use your text editor to create a batch file called ONE.BAT using the commands shown in Listing 8.1.

Listing 8.1 ONE.BAT Batch File Listing

```
ECHO OFF
REM This is a simple batch file called ONE.BAT.
REM It performs a DIR of the current directory.
DIR *.*
ECHO ON
REM This is the end of the ONE.BAT batch file.
PAUSE
```

Whew! After you've typed in everying in Listing 8.1, save the file as an ASCII text file named ONE.BAT, and exit to the DOS prompt. Each line of the ONE.BAT batch file in Listing 8.1 is an executable DOS statement. To execute the ONE.BAT batch file, change to the directory where you saved ONE.BAT, type the command **ONE.BAT** or just **ONE** and press Enter (see Figure 8.1).

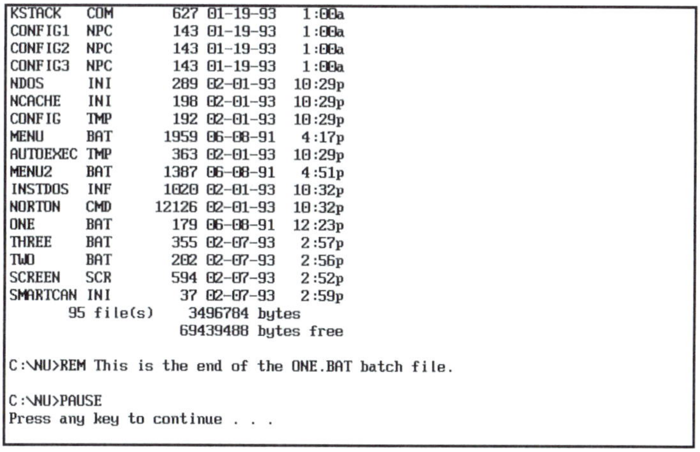

```
KSTACK   COM       627 01-19-93   1:00a
CONFIG1  NPC       143 01-19-93   1:00a
CONFIG2  NPC       143 01-19-93   1:00a
CONFIG3  NPC       143 01-19-93   1:00a
NDOS     INI       289 02-01-93  10:29p
NCACHE   INI       198 02-01-93  10:29p
CONFIG   TMP       192 02-01-93  10:29p
MENU     BAT      1959 06-08-91   4:17p
AUTOEXEC TMP       363 02-01-93  10:29p
MENU2    BAT      1387 06-08-91   4:51p
INSTDOS  INF      1020 02-01-93  10:32p
NORTON   CMD     12126 02-01-93  10:32p
ONE      BAT       179 06-08-91  12:23p
THREE    BAT       355 02-07-93   2:57p
TWO      BAT       202 02-07-93   2:56p
SCREEN   SCR       594 02-07-93   2:52p
SMARTCAN INI        37 02-07-93   2:59p
       95 file(s)    3496784 bytes
                    69439488 bytes free

C:\NU>REM This is the end of the ONE.BAT batch file.

C:\NU>PAUSE
Press any key to continue . . .
```

Figure 8.1
ONE.BAT lists the files in the current directory.

Some of the special batch file statements used in ONE.BAT may not be familiar to you, so let's discuss each command separately.

The ECHO Command

By default, DOS displays, or echoes, each statement on the screen as it executes a batch file. The ECHO OFF command causes DOS to suppress display of subsequent command lines in a batch file. DOS continues to suppress command line displays until it encounters an ECHO ON command.

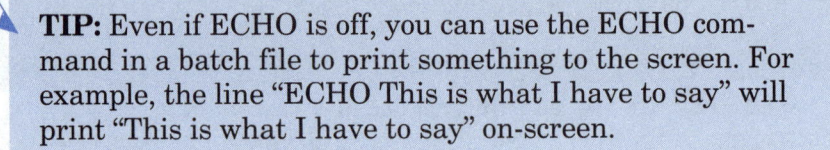

> **TIP:** Even if ECHO is off, you can use the ECHO command in a batch file to print something to the screen. For example, the line "ECHO This is what I have to say" will print "This is what I have to say" on-screen.

The REM Command

You can include comments or notes in a batch file by using the REM command. When DOS encounters a REM command in a batch file, it ignores everything else on that line. The second, third, and sixth lines of ONE.BAT are comment lines. Comment lines can be used to document a batch file's purpose and to explain what is happening at a certain point within the batch file.

The ECHO OFF command at the start of ONE.BAT causes DOS to not display the first two comment lines when the batch file is executed. The comment on line 6 of ONE.BAT is displayed when the batch file is executed because the ECHO feature is turned back on at line 5 (ECHO ON).

The DIR Command

You can run an executable program (for example, files with the .EXE or .COM extensions) or a DOS command in a batch file by specifying the program name/command followed by any required parameters. For example, the DIR command is invoked at the fourth line of ONE.BAT. The next statement in ONE.BAT, ECHO ON, is not performed until DIR finishes execution.

The PAUSE Command

The two lines after the DIR command in Listing 8.1:

```
ECHO ON
REM This is the end of the ONE.BAT batch file.
```

turn the ECHO feature back on and note the end of the ONE.BAT batch file. Actually, the next statement, PAUSE, is the last one in ONE.BAT. The PAUSE command causes DOS to suspend execution of the batch file until you press a key. PAUSE is useful for suspending batch file execution while a user reads a screen, inserts a diskette, and so on.

Batch File Parameters

You have seen examples of some of The Norton Utilities that use command line switches (for example, the /ON in SMARTCAN /ON). Many other DOS applications support command line parameters as well. Because batch files represent a special type of executable file, it should be no surprise that they also support command line parameters. Our next batch file, TWO.BAT (Listing 8.2) shows how to incorporate command line parameters in a simple batch file.

Listing 8.2 TWO.BAT with a Parameter

```
ECHO OFF
REM This is a simple batch file called TWO.BAT.
REM It starts up SMARTCAN with a user-specified
➥parameter.
SMARTCAN %1
ECHO ON
REM This is the end of the TWO.BAT batch file.
PAUSE
```

When you run TWO.BAT, you should include one of the SMARTCAN parameters discussed in Chapter 3 (/ON, /OFF, or /STATUS). For example, if you type

```
TWO.BAT /STATUS
```

and press ⏎Enter, TWO.BAT runs SMARTCAN with a /STATUS parameter, thus showing the status of the SMARTCAN TSR program. The /STATUS parameter on the TWO.BAT command line is passed to SMARTCAN via the %1 operator in the statement SMARTCAN %1.

DOS offers ten unique operators for using command line parameters in batch files: %0 through %9. The leftmost command line parameter is referred to as %0, the next leftmost parameter is %1, and so on.

The next batch file, THREE.BAT (Listing 8.3), illustrates how two parameters can be used in a batch file.

Listing 8.3 THREE.BAT with Two Parameters

```
ECHO OFF
ECHO Hello, %2 !
REM This is a simple batch file called THREE.BAT.
REM We start off by greeting the user.
REM Next, THREE.BAT starts up SMARTCAN with a
REM user-specified parameter.
REM The batch file concludes with another brief
REM message to the user.
SMARTCAN %1
ECHO ON
REM This is the end of the THREE.BAT batch file, %2 !
PAUSE
```

When you run THREE.BAT you must specify two parameters: the parameter for SMARTCAN and your name. For example, I might try

```
THREE.BAT /STATUS LISA
```

The second line in THREE.BAT displays a greeting to the user. Even though the ECHO feature is turned off by the first line of THREE.BAT, we can use ECHO to display a string of characters on the screen. For example, the statement in Listing 8.3 ECHO

Hello, 2%! echoes the message "Hello, Lisa." regardless of whether ECHO is ON or OFF.

The next-to-last line in THREE.BAT also uses %2: REM This is the end of the THREE.BAT batch file, %2 ! This statement displays a batch file termination message with the user's name and illustrates two important points:

- Batch file command-line parameters may be incorporated in remark (REM) statements.

- A parameter can be used in as many different statements within a batch file as is necessary.

Looping Within a Batch File

Creating a batch file is similar to writing a computer program in a language like C, Pascal, or BASIC. Computer programming languages offer a means for user input, output, and comments. We have seen how DOS batch files offer these features as well with PAUSE, ECHO, and REM commands. Another important feature common to programming languages and batch files is the capability to perform the same operation over and over again, or loop. Listing 8.4 illustrates how to use a loop in a batch file.

Listing 8.4 FOUR.BAT with a Looping Construct

```
ECHO OFF
REM This is a simple batch file called FOUR.BAT.
REM FOUR.BAT runs SMARTCAN twice...
REM once for each parameter entry in the FOR loop.
FOR %%a IN (ON STATUS) DO SMARTCAN /%%a
ECHO ON
```

FOUR.BAT uses a FOR loop to run the SMARTCAN utility twice. The syntax of a FOR loop is

```
FOR %%x IN (set) DO statement %%x
```

In short, this syntax means that the specified *statement* will be executed once with each item listed in the set. Each item in the set is a parameter for the statement. Therefore, the FOR loop in Listing 8.4 first executes SMARTCAN /ON, followed by SMARTCAN /STATUS.

You may wonder why the slash (/) appears before the second %%a and not with the ON and STATUS parameters. We must write the parameters without slashes because DOS strips the slash off the parameters in the FOR loop. So if you try to use:

```
FOR %%a IN (/ON/STATUS) DO SMARTCAN %%a
```

DOS will try to run SMARTCAN ON (that is, without the slash preceding ON).

The two %%a's in the FOR loop syntax are referred to as dummy parameters. A dummy parameter acts as a place holder in the FOR statement. The dummy parameter is replaced by each item in the set for every iteration through the loop. In FOUR.BAT, I chose to use the letter "a" (%%a) as the dummy parameter. Actually, you can use any letter in the alphabet after the two percent signs. Perhaps the most important rule to remember is that both dummy parameters in the FOR loop must use the same letter. For example, FOR %%a IN (ON STATUS) DO SMARTCAN /%%z is not a valid FOR loop. In fact, this erroneous FOR loop causes DOS to try to execute SMARTCAN twice with a /%z parameter.

Conditional Execution (IF and GOTO)

One of the minor annoyances with DOS' COPY command is that it lets you overwrite files without warning. The command COPY MYMEMO.DOC YOURMEMO.DOC copies the file MYMEMO.DOC to YOURMEMO.DOC. If a file named YOURMEMO.DOC existed before executing COPY, it is overwritten by MYMEMO.DOC and, probably, is gone forever! You can use a batch file like the one shown in Listing 8.5 to copy individual files and reduce the chance of overwriting important data.

Listing 8.5 C.BAT—An Individual File Copy Utility

```
ECHO OFF
REM This batch file helps you avoid accidentally
REM overwriting important files when using the
REM COPY command.
IF NOT EXIST %2 GOTO end
ECHO WARNING...%2 ALREADY EXISTS!!!
ECHO PRESS CTRL-C TO ABORT THIS COPY...
ECHO PRESS ANY OTHER KEY TO OVERWRITE %2...
PAUSE
:end
ECHO ON
COPY %1 %2
```

I have named the batch file in Listing 8.5 C.BAT as an abbreviation for DOS' COPY command. Rather than using DOS' COPY command to copy MYMEMO.DOC to YOURMEMO.DOC, I can use C.BAT with the following parameters: C MYMEMO.DOC YOURMEMO.DOC. If C.BAT determines that YOURMEMO.DOC already exists, the batch file suspends execution (via PAUSE) and lets you abort the copy by pressing Ctrl + C. You can press any other key to let MYMEMO.DOC overwrite YOURMEMO.DOC. C.BAT uses a couple of special commands to perform this intelligent copy process: IF and GOTO.

The IF command in Listing 8.5 (IF NOT EXIST %2 GOTO end) is read "if the file specified by the second command line parameter (%2) does not exist, go to the 'end' label." In all the previous batch files, we have seen that DOS executes one command after another without skipping any in between. The IF . . . GOTO construction allows us to branch around one or more statements within a batch file. This branching feature illustrates yet another similarity between programming and batch file languages.

Why is it so important to allow branching within a batch file? One of two different situations may arise when running C.BAT: Either the destination file already exists or it does not. C.BAT must act differently depending upon the existence of the destination file.

If the destination file does not exist, we want to copy the source file to the destination file with no further intervention by the user. In this case, the GOTO clause of the IF statement causes control to jump to the next statement after the "end" label. A *label* is an identifier that is preceded by a colon (:) and appears on a line by itself. The ECHO ON statement is the first line executed after this branch (since ECHO ON is the first statement after the ":end" identifier). Then, the file is copied via the COPY %1 %2 statement.

If the destination file does exist, we want to display a message and suspend batch file execution until the user decides whether the file should be overwritten. In this case, the GOTO clause of the IF statement is not executed. Because the condition of the IF statement is not true, the next line in the batch file is executed. More specifically, the three ECHO statements are executed followed by the PAUSE command. At this point, the user can press Ctrl+C to abort the batch file or any other key to overwrite the destination file. If you press a key other than Ctrl+C, the ECHO ON and COPY %1 %2 statements are executed. (Notice that the ":end" identifier line is treated like a REMark and is skipped.)

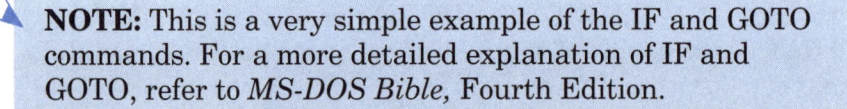

> **NOTE:** This is a very simple example of the IF and GOTO commands. For a more detailed explanation of IF and GOTO, refer to *MS-DOS Bible,* Fourth Edition.

Interactive Batch Files

You have seen how PAUSE can be used to suspend batch file execution until the user presses a key. The previous C.BAT example took PAUSE one step further: It offered a point where the user could press Ctrl+C and gracefully abort batch file execution. PAUSE is the only mechanism DOS provides for user interaction with batch files. What if you want to write a menuing batch file, like the one in Figure 8.2, that lets you select from a list of applications to run?

Enhancing Your Batch Files

It would not be too difficult to write a batch file to display the text shown in Figure 8.2. Further, you could use PAUSE to wait for the user to make a selection. But since there is no way to know what key the user pressed, how would you know which application to start? The answer is simple: Use Norton's Batch Enhancer utility.

Figure 8.2
You can create a menu like this with a simple batch file.

BE: Batch Enhancer

The Batch Enhancer utility is different from the other Norton utilities we have discussed so far. As its name implies, BE can enhance dull and dreary batch files, thus making them more aesthetically pleasing. For my money, however, BE's most important attribute is its ability to handle user entries and permit a batch file to process menu selections. The MENU.BAT listing shown in Listing 8.6 shows how BE can be used in an interactive menuing batch file.

Listing 8.6 The MENU.BAT Batch File

```
ECHO OFF
REM Display application menu
:menu
BE CLS
```

continues

Listing 8.6 Continued

```
BE SA WHITE ON MAGENTA
BE WINDOW 1 1 23 78 BRIGHT WHITE ON BLUE ZOOM
BE WINDOW 6 6 18 74 BRIGHT CYAN ON GREEN SHADOW
BE ROWCOL 6 24 " Please make your menu selection: "
➥ BRIGHT WHITE
BE ROWCOL 8 32 "1 - WordPerfect 5.1" BRIGHT YELLOW
BE ROWCOL 9 32 "2 - NORTON Program" BRIGHT YELLOW
BE ROWCOL 10 32 "3 - DOS Prompt" BRIGHT YELLOW
BE ROWCOL 11 32 "4 - PFS:First Choice" BRIGHT YELLOW
BE ROWCOL 12 32 "5 - Carbon Copy Plus" BRIGHT YELLOW
BE ROWCOL 13 32 "6 - QUIT" BRIGHT YELLOW
BE ROWCOL 15 24
REM Request input from the user
BE ASK "Press 1, 2, 3, 4, 5, or 6..." 123456 BRIGHT
➥WHITE
REM Process the user's entry
IF ERRORLEVEL 6 GOTO quit
IF ERRORLEVEL 5 GOTO ccplus
IF ERRORLEVEL 4 GOTO first
IF ERRORLEVEL 3 GOTO prompt
IF ERRORLEVEL 2 GOTO norton
REM NOTE: No GOTO for WordPerfect is required since it
➥is
REM      started by default with the next executable
REM      statement.
REM WordPerfect 5.1 selection
:wp51
CD C:\wp51
WP
GOTO menu
REM NORTON Program selection
:norton
CD C:\NU
NORTON
GOTO menu
REM DOS Shell selection
:prompt
```

```
REM Inform user how to leave the DOS prompt
BE CLS
BE BOX 5 15 19 65 DOUBLE CYAN
BE ROWCOL 8 25 "YOU HAVE SELECTED TO EXECUTE THE"
➥BRIGHT WHITE
BE ROWCOL 9 25 "DOS PROMPT. THE DOS PROMPT ALLOWS"
➥BRIGHT WHITE
BE ROWCOL 10 25 "YOU TO RUN ANY DOS COMMAND OR" BRIGHT
➥WHITE
BE ROWCOL 11 25 "PROGRAM. WHEN YOU WANT TO RETURN"
➥BRIGHT WHITE
BE ROWCOL 12 25 "TO THE APPLICATION MENU, TYPE" BRIGHT
➥WHITE
BE ROWCOL 13 25 "'EXIT' AND PRESS ENTER." BRIGHT WHITE
BE ROWCOL 16 25 "THIS MESSAGE WILL SELF-DESTRUCT"
➥BRIGHT RED
BE ROWCOL 17 33 "IN 5 SECONDS!!" BRIGHT RED
BE BEEP
REM Delay 5 seconds (90 / 18 = 5 secs.)
BE DELAY 90
BE CLS   C:\COMMAND.COM
GOTO menu
REM PFS:First Choice selection
:first
CD C:\CHOICE
FIRST
GOTO menu
REM Carbon Copy Plus selection
:ccplus
CD C:\CCPLUS
CC
GOTO menu
:quit
BE SA NORMAL
BE CLS
ECHO ON
```

When MENU.BAT is executed, it displays the menu selection screen shown in Figure 8.2. You may have noticed the various BE statements throughout MENU.BAT. For example, the fourth line in MENU.BAT is BE CLS, which illustrates the general syntax for the BE utility. In short, the BE utility name is always followed by a subcommand and, optionally, subcommand parameters. In the BE CLS statement (Listing 8.6), CLS is referred to as the subcommand. Let's look more closely at MENU.BAT and discuss each of the BE subcommands it uses.

The CLS Subcommand

CLS is a BE subcommand that clears the screen and moves the cursor to the *home position* (the top left corner of the screen). I use CLS in MENU.BAT to provide a fresh, blank screen to display my application menu. The DOS CLS command is functionally identical to BE's CLS subcommand.

The SA Subcommand

> **NOTE:** You need to install the DOS device driver ANSI.SYS before you can use the SA subcommand.
>
> 1. Check your DOS directory for ANSI.SYS. (Because my DOS directory is called DOS, this explanation uses the C:\DOS directory. If your ANSI.SYS file resides elsewhere, substitute that location for my C:\DOS specification.)
>
> 2. Look for a file named CONFIG.SYS in the root directory of your C: drive or on your DOS diskette.
>
>   If you cannot find CONFIG.SYS, create in the root directory a CONFIG.SYS file with the device driver DEVICE=C:\DOS\ANSI.SYS in it. Or if your PC does not have a hard disk, use DEVICE=A:\DOS\ANSI.SYS instead.

> If CONFIG.SYS does exist, examine it to see if a DEVICE=ANSI.SYS line exists. If no such line exists, add it.
>
> 3. Reboot to install the ANSI.SYS driver.

The SA subcommand, which is an acronym for Screen Attributes, allows you to set the foreground and background colors on your PC's display. The first example of SA in MENU.BAT sets the foreground color (text) to WHITE and the background color to MAGENTA. The syntax for this usage of SA is

```
BE SA forecolor ON backcolor
```

where *forecolor* and *backcolor* are the foreground and background colors, respectively. There are eight foreground/background colors available with SA:

Black	Magenta
Green	Yellow
White	Cyan
Blue	Red

You may use any combination of these colors for either the foreground or background in SA. Be careful not to set the foreground and background colors to the same value or you will wind up with "invisible" text on your screen.

You may modify the foreground color with either of the two intensity values BRIGHT or BLINKING. For example, the statement BE SA BRIGHT WHITE ON BLUE changes the foreground color to BRIGHT WHITE and the background color to BLUE.

As you can see, the SA subcommand lets you customize your screen using your favorite foreground/background colors. You can use the other form of the SA subcommand when you want to return the screen to the default colors. The syntax for this other SA form is

```
BE SA main-setting
```

where *main-setting* is either NORMAL, REVERSE, or UNDERLINE.

The second-to-last statement in MENU.BAT BE SA NORMAL resets the foreground and background colors to their default values (for example, on some EGA monitors, the default values are WHITE on BLACK). Also, NORMAL turns off the REVERSE and UNDERLINE main-setting switches if they are on. You should experiment with different foreground/background colors and main-setting values to see what combination you prefer.

The WINDOW Subcommand

The next two lines in MENU.BAT

```
BE WINDOW 1 1 23 78 BRIGHT WHITE ON BLUE ZOOM

BE WINDOW 6 6 18 74 BRIGHT CYAN ON GREEN SHADOW
```

use the WINDOW subcommand to place two windows on the screen. The syntax for the WINDOW subcommand is

```
BE WINDOW top left bottom right attributes
```

where *top*, *left*, *bottom*, and *right* are the window coordinates and *attributes* specifies characteristics about the window. Valid attributes include any of the colors in Listing 8.6 and the special window options SHADOW and ZOOM.

Window coordinates are specified by row and column where the top left corner of the screen is row 0 column 0. Column values increase from left to right across the screen and row values increase from top to bottom.

Window colors are specified with the format

```
BE WINDOW border-color ON fill-color
```

where *border-color* is the color BE will use to draw the window border and *fill-color* is the color BE will use to fill the window.

When BE draws a window with the SHADOW option, it places a see-through shadow along the bottom and right sides of the window to create the illusion of a three-dimensional object. Windows drawn with the other special option, ZOOM, appear to explode onto the screen.

With this knowledge, we can now analyze the statement

```
BE WINDOW 1 1 23 78 BRIGHT WHITE ON BLUE ZOOM
```

which draws a window from row 1 column 1 to row 23 column 78. This BLUE window is drawn with a BRIGHT WHITE border. Finally, the ZOOM option is used to create the exploding visual effect.

The ROWCOL Subcommand

The next several statements in MENU.BAT use the ROWCOL subcommand to place colored text on the screen. The syntax for ROWCOL is

```
BE ROWCOL row column text color
```

where *row* and *column* specify where the *text* should be located, and *color* is any one of the colors in Listing 8.6. These colors may also be modified by the intensity values BRIGHT or BLINKING. So the statement

```
BE ROWCOL 6 24 " Please make your menu selection: "
↪BRIGHT WHITE
```

places the statement Please make your menu selection: in BRIGHT WHITE text on the 6th row starting in the 24th column. Several ROWCOL statements are used together to create the application menu shown in Figure 8.2. The last ROWCOL command used for the menu is BE ROWCOL 15 24, which places the cursor on row 15 column 24 but does not display any text. This cursor placement is important for the next statement in MENU.BAT which uses the ASK subcommand.

The ASK Subcommand

The ASK subcommand is the key to interactive batch files with the BE utility. The syntax for ASK is

```
BE ASK text keys color
```

where *text* is the prompt to display in *color*, and *keys* are the valid keys that the user may press. For example, the statement

```
BE ASK "Press 1, 2, 3, 4, 5, or 6..." 123456 BRIGHT
➥WHITE
```

displays the BRIGHT WHITE prompt Press 1, 2, 3, 4, 5, or 6... and waits for the user to press one of the numeric keys 1 through 6 (123456). BE sounds an error tone if you try to press a key not listed in the "keys" list. When you press a valid key, BE places a value in a special location called ERRORLEVEL.

The ERRORLEVEL Variable

ERRORLEVEL is a variable whose value may be set by either DOS or an executable program, such as Norton's BE utility. Once a program like BE sets ERRORLEVEL, a batch file may perform conditional operations based upon ERRORLEVEL's value. BE sets ERRORLEVEL to

- 1   if the first key in the "keys" list was pressed
- 2   if the second key in the "keys" list was pressed, and so on.

The five IF statements

```
IF ERRORLEVEL 6 GOTO quit
IF ERRORLEVEL 5 GOTO ccplus
IF ERRORLEVEL 4 GOTO first
IF ERRORLEVEL 3 GOTO prompt
IF ERRORLEVEL 2 GOTO norton
```

branch to different parts of MENU.BAT depending upon the value of ERRORLEVEL. Because of a quirk with the ERRORLEVEL feature, you must always list the "IF ERRORLEVEL . . . GOTO . . ." statements in descending order of ERRORLEVEL value. Also note that there is no IF statement to check for an ERRORLEVEL value of 1.

Since the batch file commands for menu selection #1 (WordPerfect 5.1) appear immediately after the last IF statement, there is no need to perform a GOTO. DOS automatically executes the next sequential batch file statement if ERRORLEVEL is not 2 when the `IF ERRORLEVEL 2 GOTO norton` statement is executed.

Each block of application statements in MENU.BAT is fairly straightforward. In general, a CD is performed to switch to the application's directory, the application is executed, and the menu is redisplayed. The only exception to this general flow is the DOS Shell menu selection, which uses a few more BE subcommands.

The BOX Subcommand

When option #3 (DOS Prompt) is selected in MENU.BAT, the screen is cleared and a box is displayed with the BOX subcommand whose syntax is

```
BE BOX top left bottom right attributes
```

where *top*, *left*, *bottom*, and *right* are the box coordinates, and *attributes* specifies characteristics about the box. Valid attributes include any of the colors in Listing 8.6 and the special box border options SINGLE and DOUBLE. By default, boxes are drawn with a SINGLE line border.

For example, the statement

```
BE BOX 5 15 19 65 DOUBLE CYAN
```

draws a DOUBLE-line border CYAN box from row 5 column 15 to row 19 column 65. Several ROWCOL statements are then used to display information about the DOS Prompt option.

The BEEP Subcommand

The BEEP subcommand is also used within the batch file logic for the DOS Shell selection. The statement BE BEEP plays a tone through your PC's internal speaker. If you are musically inclined, you can use BEEP to play a simple song or just a few random notes. The syntax for BEEP is

    BE BEEP /D# /F# /R# /W#

and each option is defined as shown in Table 8.2.

Table 8.2
BEEP Subcommand Options

Option	Meaning
/D#	Duration or length of tone to play in 18ths of a second (for example, /D9 equals 9/18 or 1/2 second).
/F#	Frequency of the tone in cycles per second (for example, /F262 represents a frequency of 262 cycles per second [Hz] or a musical note "C").
/R#	Number of times to repeat the tone (for example, /R4 repeats the tone four times).
/W#	How long to pause, in 18ths of a second, after playing the specified tone (for example, /W18 equals a pause of 1 second).

The DELAY Subcommand

The DELAY command offers an easy-to-use method of freezing a screen for a period of time without waiting for the user to press a key to continue. The syntax for DELAY is

    BE DELAY time

where *time* is expressed in 18ths of a second. So the statement BE DELAY 90 in Listing 8.6 causes the MENU.BAT batch file to suspend execution for 90/18 or 5 seconds.

Enhancing Your Batch Files

> You can customize MENU.BAT to work with the applications on your system. Just edit all the lines corresponding to the entry you want to replace. For example, to replace the PFS:First Choice entry, you would edit lines 12, 21, and 55 through 58. You can copy the MENU.BAT file to other systems so that you can, for instance, provide a consistent menu for all the computers in your company. Make sure, however, that all the computers have the programs listed in MENU.BAT, or that you've edited MENU.BAT to reflect what's really on each system.

Batch Enhancer Script Files

When you run the MENU.BAT batch file, the menu lines appear on-screen one at a time, with a slight pause before each line appears. This is because it takes DOS time to find and execute the BE commands included in MENU.BAT. You can, however, make it easier to execute a series of BE commands by including them in a script file. When you include the BE commands in a script file, the Batch Enhancer can execute them much more quickly. Let's revisit the MENU.BAT example to explore the power of script files.

Look at Listing 8.6. The lines of MENU.BAT included in Listing 8.7 build the menu's lines on-screen and request the user's input.

Listing 8.7 The SCREEN.SCR Script File

```
BE SA WHITE ON MAGENTA
BE WINDOW 1 1 23 78 BRIGHT WHITE ON BLUE ZOOM
BE WINDOW 6 6 18 74 BRIGHT CYAN ON GREEN SHADOW
BE ROWCOL 6 24 " Please make your menu selection: "
➥BRIGHT WHITE
BE ROWCOL 8 32 "1 - WordPerfect 5.1" BRIGHT YELLOW
BE ROWCOL 9 32 "2 - NORTON Program" BRIGHT YELLOW
BE ROWCOL 10 32 "3 - DOS Prompt" BRIGHT YELLOW
```

continues

Listing 8.7 Continued

```
BE ROWCOL 11 32 "4 - PFS:First Choice" BRIGHT YELLOW
BE ROWCOL 12 32 "5 - Carbon Copy Plus" BRIGHT YELLOW
BE ROWCOL 13 32 "6 - QUIT" BRIGHT YELLOW
BE ROWCOL 15 24
REM Request input from the user
BE ASK "Press 1, 2, 3, 4, 5, or 6..." 123456 BRIGHT
➥WHITE
```

If you remove these lines from MENU.BAT and save them as a separate script file, you can include a command for MENU.BAT to run that script file, which will build the menu screen much more quickly. To do so:

1. Use your text editor to remove the lines in Listing 8.7 from MENU.BAT and save them as a file called SCREEN.SCR. Or you can simply use the text editor to create and name that file.

2. Open the MENU.BAT file and delete the lines shown in Listing 8.7, if you haven't done so.

3. In place of the lines you've deleted (immediately following the command BE CLS), type the command BE C:\NU\SCREEN.SCR. (Substitute the drive and directory where you've saved SCREEN.SCR for C:\NU.)

4. Save the updated MENU.BAT. Listing 8.8 shows the new MENU.BAT file.

Listing 8.8 The Revised MENU.BAT File

```
ECHO OFF
REM Display application menu
:menu
BE CLS
BE C:\NU\SCREEN.SCR
REM Process the user's entry
IF ERRORLEVEL 6 GOTO quit
IF ERRORLEVEL 5 GOTO ccplus
IF ERRORLEVEL 4 GOTO first
```

Enhancing Your Batch Files

```
IF ERRORLEVEL 3 GOTO prompt
IF ERRORLEVEL 2 GOTO norton
REM NOTE: No GOTO for WordPerfect is required since it
REM       started by default with the next executable
REM       statement.
REM WordPerfect 5.1 selection
:wp51
CD C:\wp51
WP
GOTO menu
REM NORTON Program selection
:norton
CD C:\NU
NORTON
GOTO menu
REM DOS selection
:prompt
REM Inform user how to leave the DOS prompt
BE CLS
BE BOX 5 15 19 65 DOUBLE CYAN
BE ROWCOL 8 25 "YOU HAVE SELECTED TO EXECUTE THE"
➥BRIGHT WHITE
BE ROWCOL 9 25 "DOS PROMPT. THE DOS PROMPT ALLOWS"
➥BRIGHT WHITE
BE ROWCOL 10 25 "YOU TO RUN ANY DOS COMMAND OR" BRIGHT
➥WHITE
BE ROWCOL 11 25 "PROGRAM. WHEN YOU WANT TO RETURN"
➥BRIGHT WHITE
BE ROWCOL 12 25 "TO THE APPLICATION MENU, TYPE" BRIGHT
➥WHITE
BE ROWCOL 13 25 "'EXIT' AND PRESS ENTER." BRIGHT WHITE
BE ROWCOL 16 25 "THIS MESSAGE WILL SELF-DESTRUCT"
➥BRIGHT RED
BE ROWCOL 17 33 "IN 5 SECONDS!!" BRIGHT RED
BE BEEP
REM Delay 5 seconds (90 /18 = 5 secs.)
BE DELAY 90
BE CLS
C:\COMMAND.COM
```

continues

Listing 8.8 Continued

```
GOTO menu
REM PFS:First Choice selection
:first
CD C:\CHOICE
FIRST
GOTO menu
REM Carbon Copy Plus selection
:ccplus
CD C:\CCPLUS
CC
GOTO menu
:quit
BE SA NORMAL
BE CLS
ECHO ON
```

Now, when you run MENU.BAT, the initial menu screen appears much more quickly. In addition to creating script files to include in batch files, you can create ones for use from the DOS prompt.

> **CAUTION:** Batch Enhancer script files can contain only BE commands. DOS commands are not recognized.

Other Batch Enhancer Commands

In addition to those BE commands we've already described, there are several others you'll find particularly helpful when creating batch and script files. Table 8.3 lists these commands and gives a brief description of each. A complete discussion of these commands is beyond the scope of this book but can be found in The Norton Utilities User's Guide.

Table 8.3
Other BE Commands

Command	Use to
EXIT	End execution of a BE script file.
GOTO	Control the starting point for executing a script file (works only with BE script files).
JUMP	Specify branching in BE script files.
MONTHDAY	Return the system day and month as a code for use by the batch file.
PRINTCHAR	Display the specified characters on-screen in the specified colors.
REBOOT	Have a batch file execute a warm boot of your computer.
SHIFTSTATE	Report to the file whether the Shift, Alt, or Ctrl key is depressed.
TRIGGER	Pause a batch file and restart it at the specified time.
WEEKDAY	Return the system day of the week as a code for use by the batch file.

In This Chapter

Miscellaneous disk tools, including how to create a rescue disk

Using the disk editor

Manually UNERASEing files

Making a Disk Bootable

1. Type **DISKTOOL** at the DOS prompt or highlight Disk Tools in the Commands list of the main Norton screen. Press [↵Enter].
2. Highlight the Make a Disk Bootable selection in the Procedures box, and press [↵Enter] or click Proceed.
3. In the disk selection box, highlight the drive letter of the disk you wish to make bootable (for example, A:), and press [↵Enter] or click **OK**. If you select a floppy disk drive in this step, DISKTOOL will ask you to insert a disk in the drive and press Enter or click **OK**. DISKTOOL then begins the process of making the selected disk bootable.
4. When the procedure is done, press [↵Enter] or click **OK**.

Creating a Rescue Diskette

1. Type **RESCUE** at the DOS prompt or highlight Rescue Disk in the Commands list of the main Norton screen. Press [↵Enter].
2. Choose Create. The Create Rescue Disk screen appears.
3. If necessary, change the designation of the drive to **S**ave Rescue Information To and change the Rescue **D**iskette Type.
4. Click on the Create button or press [Alt]+[C].
5. To bypass the warning, press [↵Enter] or click **OK**. The Rescue utility saves your PC's system information on the rescue diskette.
6. Press [↵Enter] or click **OK** when the procedure is done.

Chapter

9

Recovery Techniques

This chapter explains the mysteries behind some of the more advanced disk-related tools in The Norton Utilities. The tools covered in this chapter on the utilities offer a wide range of disk recovery power.

First, you'll learn how to make a disk bootable, how to undo a RECOVER operation, and how to revive a defective diskette. Next, you can try your hand at editing file defects. Finally, you can learn how to rebuild an erased file cluster by cluster.

Miscellaneous Disk Tools

In earlier versions of The Norton Utilities (before release 5.0), the Norton Disk Doctor included a feature called Common Solutions. The Common Solutions available through NDD let you perform three useful disk operations: make a disk bootable, recover from DOS's RECOVER command, and revive a defective diskette.

In version 7.0 of The Norton Utilities, the three operations that used to be part of NDD's Common Solutions are now available in a separate utility called DISKTOOL. The DISKTOOL utility also offers a couple of other valuable disk tools that let you mark bad clusters and save/restore important hard disk configuration information.

Using DISKTOOL to Make a Disk Bootable

In order for a disk to be considered bootable, it must contain a couple of special hidden system files and DOS's command interpreter, COMMAND.COM. The Quick Steps outlined here place COMMAND.COM and the hidden system files on the specified disk.

> **NOTE:** DOS's SYS command is capable of copying the system files to a formatted disk, if none of the needed areas on the disk are being used. However, the SYS command for some older versions of DOS copies only the hidden files and does not copy COMMAND.COM. You have to manually copy COMMAND.COM after running SYS to make a disk bootable.

The DISKTOOL utility can make a formatted disk bootable regardless of whether space was allocated for system files when the disk was originally formatted. (Refer to the SFORMAT Options section of Chapter 6 for a discussion of placing system files on a disk during the format process.)

Making a Disk Bootable

1. Type **DISKTOOL** at the DOS prompt or highlight Disk Tools in the Commands list of the main Norton screen. Press ⏎Enter.

   This runs the DISKTOOL utility and displays the Disk Tools screen (see Figure 9.1).

Recovery Techniques 179

2. Highlight the Make a Disk Bootable selection in the Procedures box, and press ⏎Enter or click **Proceed**.

   This displays a disk drive selection dialog box.

3. Highlight the drive letter of the disk you wish to make bootable (for example, A:), and press ⏎Enter or click **OK**.

   If you select a floppy disk drive in this step, DISKTOOL will ask you to insert a disk in the drive and press Enter or click **OK**. DISKTOOL then begins the process of making the selected disk bootable.

4. When the procedure is done, press ⏎Enter or click **OK**.

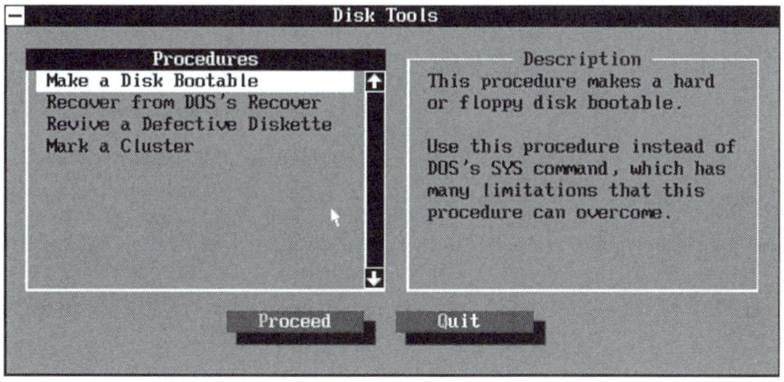

Figure 9.1

The DISKTOOL utility offers several selections for disk operations.

Backtracking after a Disk RECOVERy

If you've ever used the DOS RECOVER command to rescue files from a defective disk, you're probably familiar with the mess it can create. When you ask RECOVER to recover a disk (for example, **RECOVER A:**) it gathers all the files and directories on the disk, places them in the root directory, and gives them meaningless names like file0001.rec, file0002.rec, and so on. When RECOVER is finished, it's up to you to inspect each of the filexxxx.rec files and determine its real name and whether it represents a file or a directory! Use the DISKTOOL utility instead of RECOVER, or use it to undo the mess created by RECOVER and return a disk to a more acceptable condition.

Quick Steps: Undoing a Disk RECOVERy

1. Type the command **DISKTOOL** or highlight Disk Tools in the Commands list of the main Norton screen. Press Enter.

   This runs the DISKTOOL utility and displays the Disk Tools screen.

2. Highlight the Recover from DOS's Recover selection in the Procedures box, and press Enter or click Proceed.

   This displays a RECOVERy information screen.

3. Read the information presented in the RECOVERy information screen and press Enter or click OK.

   This displays a disk drive selection dialog box.

4. Highlight the drive letter of the disk you wish to unRECOVER (for example, A:), and press Enter or click OK.

   If you select a floppy disk drive in this step, DISKTOOL will ask you to insert a disk in the drive and select OK. DISKTOOL then displays a couple of warnings before actually performing unRECOVER.

5. Select the Yes button for each message to continue the unRECOVER operation.

DISKTOOL does the best it can to return a disk to its preRECOVER condition, but it cannot recreate the names of the files and directories in the root directory; RECOVER zaps them permanently. Therefore, DISKTOOL is forced to use generic names for root directory entries when it undoes the RECOVER operation. When you inspect the contents of a disk after undoing a RECOVER, you'll notice that DISKTOOL uses generic names for root directory entries. For example, the files in the root directory are named file0001, file0002, and so on, and the directories are named DIR0000, DIR0001, and so on. You must rename these root directory entries to reflect their original names. The non-root directory entries (subdirectories and files in directories/subdirectories) on an unRECOVERed disk should appear as they did before the RECOVER operation.

Reviving a Defective Diskette

The third item in the Procedures box of the Disk Tools selection screen (Figure 9.1), Revive a Defective Diskette, lets you reformat a questionable disk without destroying the disk's contents. You should use this selection if you cannot read files from a disk and you want to preserve the data it contains. To revive data from a defective diskette, select the Revive a Defective Diskette option and follow the simple directions provided by the DISKTOOL utility.

Marking Clusters

In Chapter 6, you learned that the Norton Disk Doctor (NDD) can diagnose and correct many common disk problems. When NDD finds a questionable cluster, it can move that cluster's data to a new location and mark the bad cluster so DOS doesn't try to use it in the future. The DISKTOOL utility also lets you mark bad clusters so DOS doesn't try to use them for data storage. As with NDD, to mark a bad cluster, select the Mark a Cluster option from the Procedures box of the Disk Tools screen (Figure 9.1), and follow the directions that are displayed.

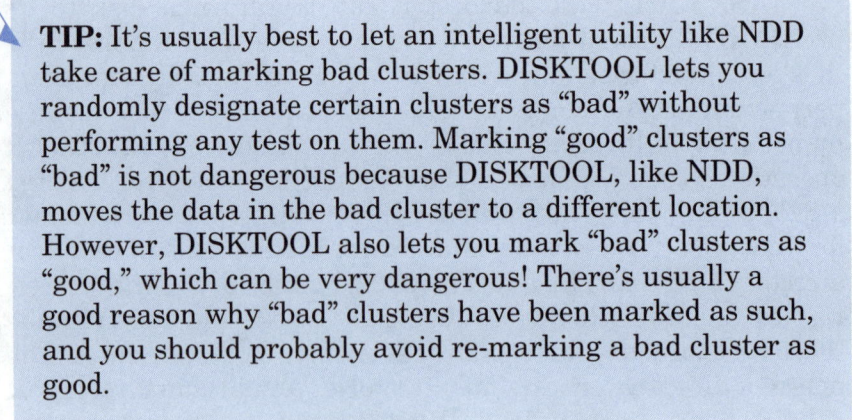

TIP: It's usually best to let an intelligent utility like NDD take care of marking bad clusters. DISKTOOL lets you randomly designate certain clusters as "bad" without performing any test on them. Marking "good" clusters as "bad" is not dangerous because DISKTOOL, like NDD, moves the data in the bad cluster to a different location. However, DISKTOOL also lets you mark "bad" clusters as "good," which can be very dangerous! There's usually a good reason why "bad" clusters have been marked as such, and you should probably avoid re-marking a bad cluster as good.

Creating a Rescue Diskette

You should have created a Rescue Diskette when you installed the utilities; however, if you didn't, you can use the RESCUE utility to create one at any time. The RESCUE utility lets you create a rescue diskette containing the following system parameters: partition tables, boot records, and CMOS values. If your PC ever loses track of any of this system information, you can use the RESCUE utility to restore the values from the rescue diskette.

Creating a Rescue Diskette

1. Type RESCUE at the DOS prompt or highlight Rescue Disk in the Commands list of the main Norton screen. Press Enter.

    This displays the Rescue Disk screen.

2. Choose Create.

    The Create Rescue Disk screen appears (see Figure 9.2).

Recovery Techniques **183**

3. If necessary, change the designation of the drive to **S**ave Rescue Information To and change the Rescue **D**iskette Type.

4. Click on the **Create** button or press `Alt`+`C`.

   A warning appears informing you that the procedure will overwrite whatever is on the disk.

5. Press `Enter` or click **OK**.

   The Rescue utility saves your PC's system information on the rescue diskette.

6. Press `Enter` or click **OK** when the procedure is done.

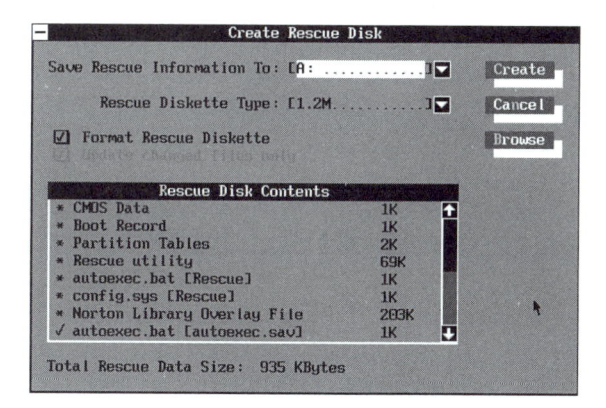

Figure 9.2
Use this screen to create a rescue diskette.

Use the other RESCUE selection, **R**estore, as a last resort when you cannot access partitions on your hard disk and the Norton Disk Doctor utility cannot revive the disk.

Using the Disk Editor

You can use many tools to view the contents of files on your disks. The DOS TYPE command offers one of the easiest ways to view, or dump, a file. To display the contents of a file called LETTER.DOC, use the command TYPE LETTER.DOC. TYPE does a pretty good job as long as the file you specify consists solely of displayable ASCII characters (like AUTOEXEC.BAT and CONFIG.SYS). If you try to use TYPE to view the contents of an executable file (for example, TYPE NORTON.EXE), however, you'll wind up with a bunch of gobbledygook on your screen, and your PC may even beep a few times!

As you can see, we need something more powerful than TYPE if our goal is to view the contents of any file on a disk. To complicate matters further, what if you want to browse through other nonfile areas of a disk, such as the boot record, FAT, or unused clusters? Better yet, what if you're interested not only in viewing but also in modifying or editing the contents of any area of a disk? The Norton Utilities include a disk editor (DISKEDIT), which lets you perform a wide variety of tasks including viewing and editing virtually any byte on a disk.

Quick Steps: Browsing Through Files with DISKEDIT

1. Type the command **DISKEDIT** or highlight Disk Editor in the Commands list of the main Norton screen. Press ↵Enter.

   A message tells you that Disk Edit is in read-only mode.

2. Press ↵Enter or click **OK**.

   DISKEDIT scans your drive and displays the DISKEDIT screen shown in Figure 9.3.

Recovery Techniques 185

> 3. Use the **O**bject menu to change the active drive/directory if necessary.
>
> 4. Double-click on the desired file or highlight it and press ⏎Enter. — Displays a hexadecimal/ASCII view of the selected file (Figure 9.4).

Active drive and directory

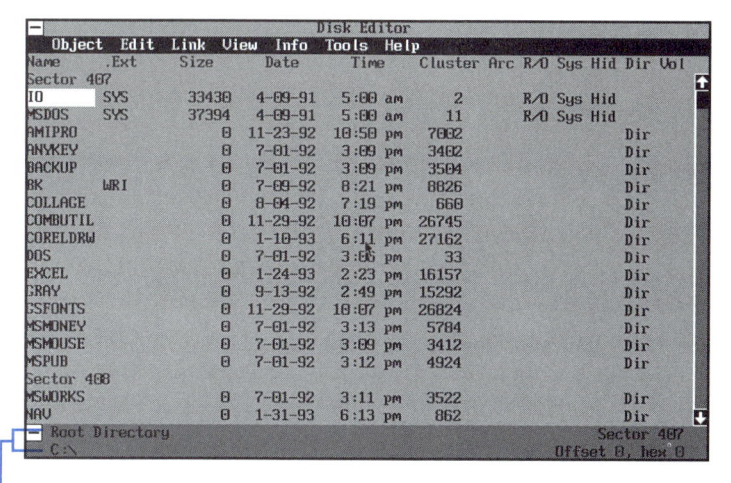

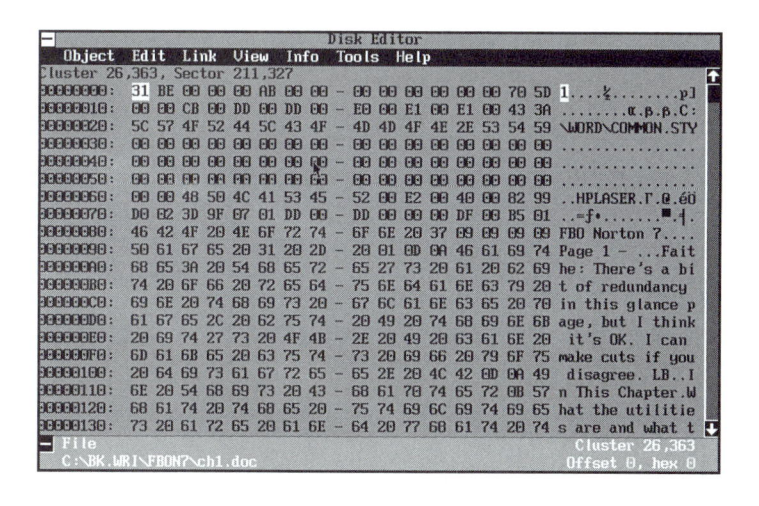

Figure 9.3
This DISKEDIT listing screen shows a listing of the active directory.

Figure 9.4
Here, DISKEDIT shows a hexadecimal/ASCII view of a file.

Double-click anywhere on the displayed file to return to the directory list.

> **TIP:** Choose **T**ools Co**n**figuration, then press Alt+R to turn off the **R**ead Only check box, which lets you edit your file. You should probably leave DISKEDIT in read-only mode until you become more familiar with how the utility works.

A Note on Hexadecimal Notation

Most of the information shown in Figure 9.4 may not be meaningful to you if you're unfamiliar with *hexadecimal notation*. The hexadecimal (hex) numbering system is very similar to the decimal number system we use every day. In the decimal number system, values are written using some combination of the ten digits 0 through 9 (for example 1, 490, and 27,662). These same ten digits are used by the hex number system along with six additional values, A through F.

Valid hex numbers include 4A, 11, and 3FC. It is customary to prefix a hex number with a dollar sign ($) to avoid ambiguity with decimal numbers. So our list of valid hex numbers may also be written as $4A, $11, and $3FC.

You don't have to understand hex to use DISKEDIT! In fact, you don't even have to know how to convert between hex and decimal. All you have to do is move over to the column of ASCII text at the right. In fact, you can only edit your data files in **H**ex view. You can't edit a file when you view it as **T**ext.

Working with the Hexadecimal/ASCII View

Each row of information in Figure 9.4 shows the hexadecimal and ASCII values of 16 bytes in the selected file. The column of numbers along the left side of Figure 9.4 shows the *offset* (in hex) of the first byte in each row. The offset is a position indicator that is relative to the beginning of the selected file. For example, the first byte in the file is at offset 0, the second byte is at offset 1, the third byte is at offset 2, and so on.

The row of hex values starting at offset 00000060 is

```
00 00 48 50 4C 41 53 45 - 52 00 E2 00 40 00 82 99
```

> **NOTE:** The dash between 45 and 52 shows the midpoint of the line of 16 bytes and is not part of the data itself.

You can use any of the arrow keys to move the cursor from one row or byte to another. When you're viewing a file with DISKEDIT, two highlight blocks are used in conjunction with the blinking cursor. The highlight blocks work together to easily show the selected byte's location in both the hex and ASCII portions of the line. You can move the blinking cursor from the hex highlight box to the ASCII highlight box, or vice versa, by pressing Tab.

You can modify any of the values in the selected file if DISKEDIT is not restricted to read-only mode. DISKEDIT accepts byte modifications in either hex or ASCII depending on the location of the blinking cursor; simply type the new hex/ASCII value(s) over the existing value(s). Press Enter when you are finished entering changes, and DISKEDIT will display a dialog box indicating which cluster was modified. You then have the opportunity to write or discard your changes and return to the DISKEDIT Directory Listing screen.

Selecting Other Views and Objects

The hex/ASCII view shown in Figure 9.4 is useful when you're looking for a detailed view of the selected file. DISKEDIT offers several other views depending on the type of data you're working with. The file we viewed earlier is a text file that is somewhat difficult to read using the hex/ASCII view. The file is shown in a more readable format if you select the as Text option from the View menu (Figure 9.5).

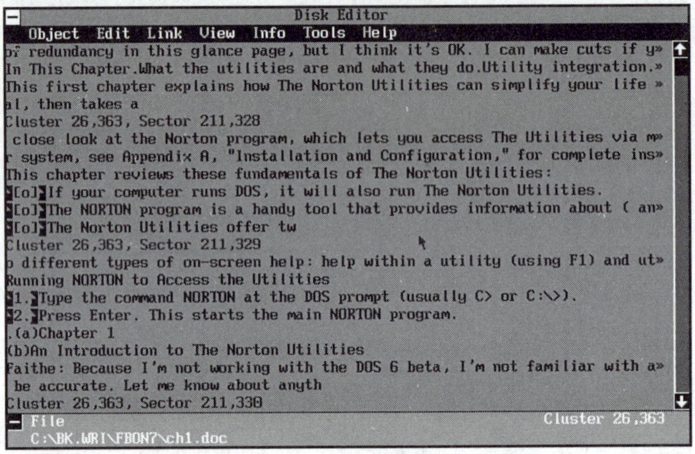

Figure 9.5

The View as Text option shows your file in a much more readable format. Note that you can't edit the file in this view.

DISKEDIT has enough intelligence to select the appropriate view depending on the type of object being displayed. For example, the As Directory option is used to display the directory listing in Figure 9.3.

DISKEDIT's Object menu lets you change the active drive/directory. The Object menu also provides several other selections, including an option to display either the primary or secondary copy of the active drive's FAT. The screen in Figure 9.6 is displayed when you select the 1st FAT option from the Object menu.

Recovery Techniques   189

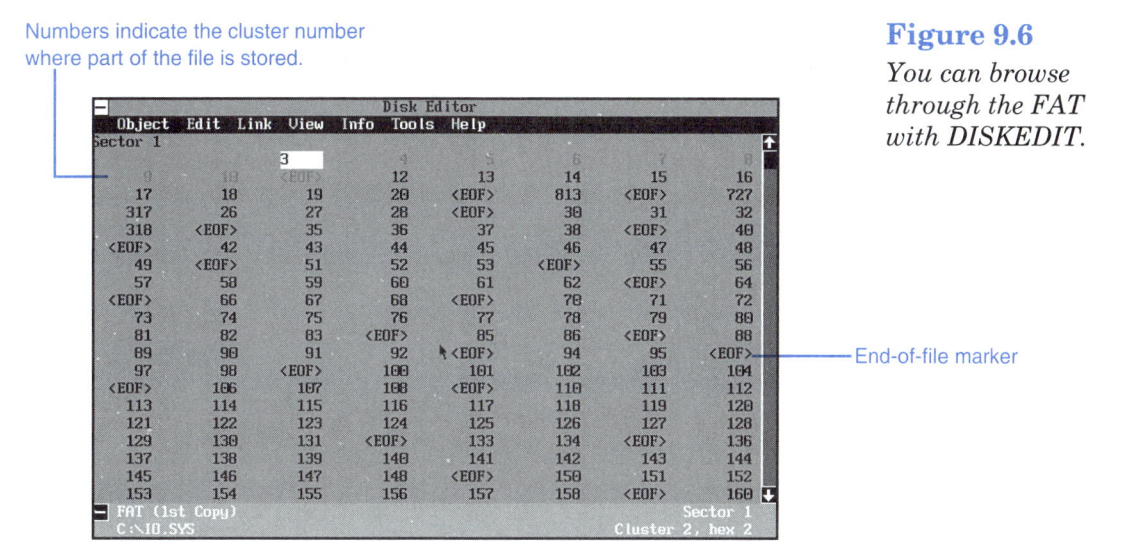

Numbers indicate the cluster number where part of the file is stored.

[Figure: DISKEDIT screen showing FAT (1st Copy) for C:\IO.SYS, Sector 1, Cluster 2, hex 2, with cluster numbers and <EOF> markers]

End-of-file marker

Figure 9.6
You can browse through the FAT with DISKEDIT.

When DISKEDIT displays a FAT, it shows the information in a FAT-view format. You can use the arrow keys to highlight different clusters in the FAT-view. Each value shown in the FAT-view screen indicates the status of a particular cluster.

It's very easy to trace through the chain of clusters used in a file, especially since DISKEDIT highlights the chain in a special color (or places double greater-than signs [>>] next to each cluster in the chain on a monochrome monitor). If you're curious to find out what file the highlighted chain of clusters represents, press ↵Enter, and the directory screen is displayed. The file represented by the chain of clusters on the FAT screen is automatically highlighted on the directory screen. As you saw earlier, you can press ↵Enter again to view the contents of that file.

Select **M**emory Dump from the **O**bject menu (or press Alt + M) to display a dump of your system's memory on-screen. When you select this command, the Memory Dump dialog box appears, asking you to specify starting and ending addresses of the memory to dump. Do so, then press ↵Enter or click **OK**. The screen shown in Figure 9.7 appears, displaying the hex and ASCII contents of your system's memory.

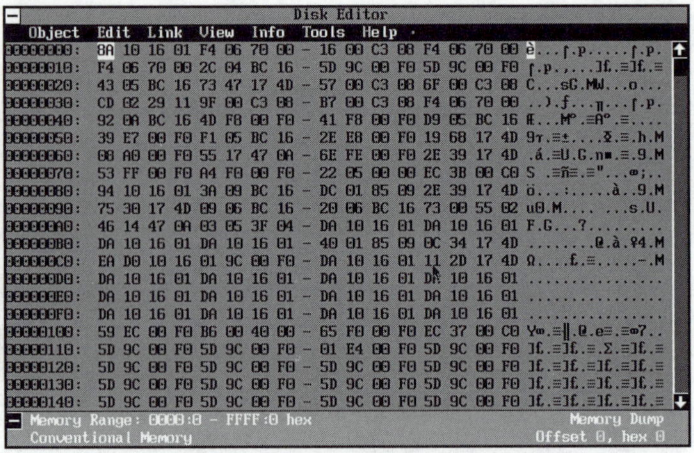

Figure 9.7
An example memory dump.

> **CAUTION**
>
> DISKEDIT is perhaps the most powerful and flexible Norton utility. It's so powerful, in fact, that in the hands of a novice user it can be quite lethal! Accidental modification of the wrong byte in a file, FAT, directory, and so on may cause major headaches for you and anyone else who uses your PC. So be careful when using DISKEDIT. As a precaution, you may want to consider leaving the DISKEDIT utility in read-only mode (use the Configuration... selection in the Tools menu).

Printing Your Selection

When you view an object on-screen, you have the option to print the object's contents. To do so, select **Print Object As** from the **T**ools menu or press Ctrl+P. The Print As dialog box appears, as shown in Figure 9.8. As you can see, you can either print the object to your printer or to disk. And, just as you can select several different on-screen views for objects, you can print several views. After you've made your dialog box selections, choose OK to print.

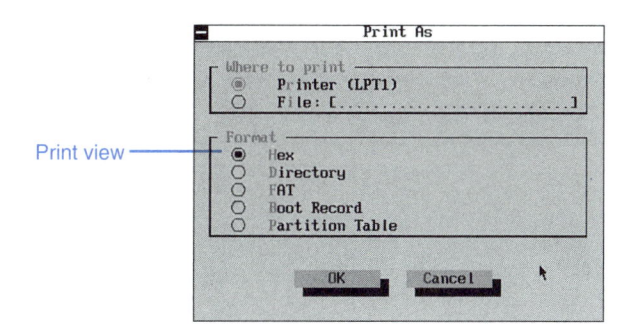

Figure 9.8
DISKEDIT's Print As dialog box.

DISKEDIT provides one way to repair a defective file. But, you can't use DISKEDIT unless you have recovered the defective file so that your system can read it. If you've accidentally deleted a file but couldn't automatically recover it with UNERASE, read on to see how to use the advanced features of UNERASE to manually recover accidentally deleted files.

Manually UNERASEing Files

In Chapter 4 you learned how to use Norton's UNERASE utility to resurrect accidentally deleted files. The unerase process can be very quick and simple if there has been little disk activity since the accidental deletion. Every time you copy a file, save a file from a word processor, or perform a similar operation, you run the risk of overwriting the unprotected data of a deleted file. Therefore, the chances of recovering an accidentally deleted file are best if you run UNERASE immediately after the deletion.

The UNERASE utility reports a recovery prognosis for each deleted file it finds on your disk (see Figure 9.9).

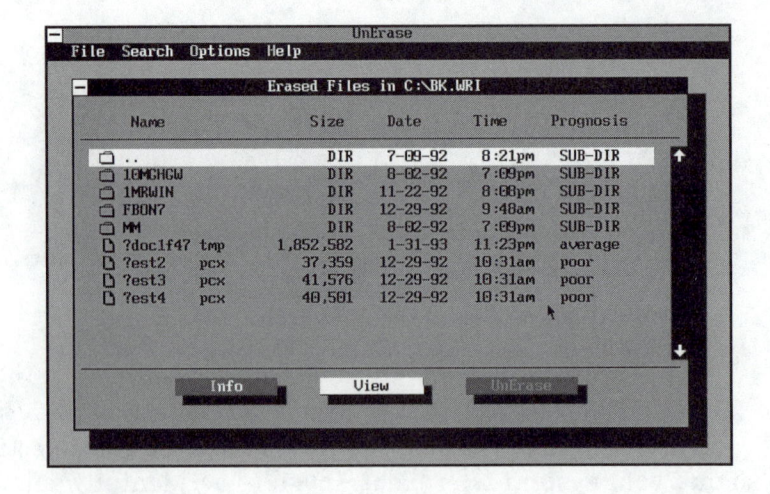

Figure 9.9
The UNERASE screen reports a poor recovery prognosis for the ?est2.pcx file.

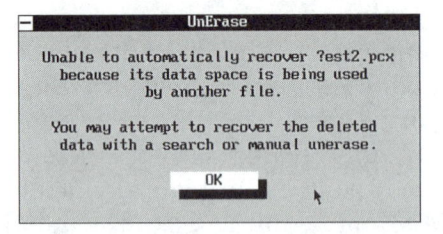

Figure 9.10
UNERASE displays a failure message if automatic recovery is unsuccessful.

UNERASE usually has no problem automatically recovering deleted files with an "excellent" or "good" prognosis. If you're trying to recover a file with an "average" or "poor" prognosis, however, you'll probably need to help UNERASE with the recovery process. Regardless of the prognosis listed, you should first try the automatic method to recover the deleted file by choosing UnErase. If UNERASE displays a message similar to the one shown in Figure 9.10, you'll have to try to manually recover any of the file's data that may still reside on the disk.

Choose OK, then select the Manual UnErase option from the File menu to begin the manual recovery process. UNERASE then asks you to supply the first character of the name of the file to be recovered. After you type the file name's first character, the Manual UnErase screen in Figure 9.11 is displayed.

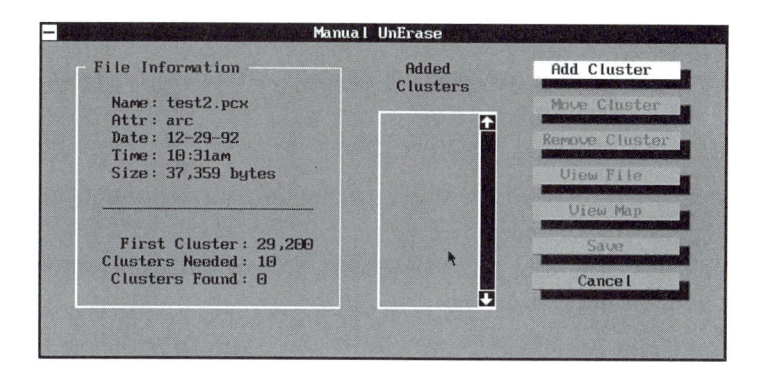

Figure 9.11
Use the Manual UnErase feature to recover files that cannot be unerased automatically.

The panel on the left side of the Manual UnErase screen shows the file information UNERASE was able to locate including the file's name, attributes, time/date stamps, and size. The File Information panel also reports cluster information as you manually rebuild the deleted file.

The right side of the Manual UnErase screen contains several buttons you can select during the manual recovery process. Select the Add Cluster button to start rebuilding the file, and the screen in Figure 9.12 will be displayed.

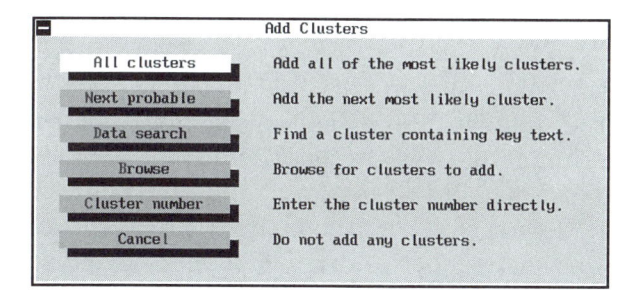

Figure 9.12
UNERASE offers several ways to add clusters to a file as you recover it.

Even though UNERASE may not be able to recover a deleted file automatically, it can still offer some useful information about which clusters the file occupied. The first time you try to manually unerase a file, you should select the All clusters button in Figure 9.12. When you select this button, UNERASE uses all available information to try to piece together the clusters from the deleted file. The Manual UnErase screen (Figure 9.11) is redisplayed after UNERASE gathers all the likely clusters for the file. Select the View File button in Figure 9.11 to have a look at the clusters that UNERASE has gathered.

Depending on what the View File selection displays, you may want to either save the file with the recommended clusters or try another manual recovery approach. If you want to save the recovered file, press [Esc] to return to the Manual UnErase screen, and select the Save button.

If the data contained in the recommended clusters doesn't even resemble the previous contents of the deleted file, you can try another, less automated mode of manual recovery. Press [Esc] a couple of times to return to the initial UnErase screen (Figure 9.9), then follow the directions provided earlier to reach the Add Clusters screen (Figure 9.12).

Rather than letting UNERASE guess at the entire chain of clusters for the deleted file, you can select the Next probable or Data search buttons to build the cluster chain manually. The Data search feature is particularly useful when trying to recover text files because you can search the entire disk for a specific string of characters. As you manually add each cluster to the chain, be sure to use the View File button to monitor the contents of the rebuilt file.

UNERASE is a powerful tool, but it's not without limitations. If some of the clusters from a deleted file have been overwritten, you cannot completely recover the file with UNERASE; however, you can still use UNERASE to recover manually as many clusters as possible. Now let's take a look at three important utilities that can improve the efficiency and speed of your hard disk.

In This Chapter

Viruses and disk protection

Protecting sensitive files

Wiping files from a disk

Preventing Unauthorized Disk Write Activity

1. Type **DISKMON** at the DOS prompt or highlight Disk Monitor on the main Norton screen. Press `Enter`.
2. Press `Enter` or click on **D**isk Protect.
3. Select the **E**ntire Disk option then the **O**n button.
4. Press `Esc` or click on **Q**uit. DISKMON is activated as a TSR utility.

Encrypting a File with DISKREET

1. Type **DISKREET** at the DOS prompt or highlight Diskreet on the main Norton screen. Press `Enter`.
2. Select the **F**ile menu.
3. Select the **E**ncrypt option.
4. Change to the drive and directory that holds the file you want to encrypt. Highlight the file you want to encrypt on the Fi**l**es list.
5. To accept the default encrypted file name, leave it in the **T**o box.
6. Choose Enter **P**assword. Enter a secret password for the encrypted file (minimum of six characters) and press `Enter`.
7. Choose **R**e-Enter Password. Type the secret password again for verification and press `Enter`.
8. Press `Enter` or click **OK**. A message appears asking if you want to wipe the original file.
9. Choose **D**elete or **C**ancel.

Chapter 10

Security Techniques

As computer users increasingly share information through networks, on-line services and bulletin boards, and disk swapping, security is becoming an increasingly important issue. Sharing files in any way can transmit computer viruses. And when other users have access to your system, there is a chance of them seeing confidential data. This chapter discusses utilities which help you keep your system free from viruses and which enable you to keep your data private—even when you delete the data!

You'll first examine the DISKMON utility, which lets you monitor all disk activity on your system—a valuable tool for preventing computer viruses from wreaking havoc. Then you'll learn about utilities that let you encrypt a file (put it into an ureadable code) and wipe a file from a disk (so another user can't unerase it and view it).

Viruses and Disk Protection

A *computer virus* is a program that can cause irreversible damage to the data on your hard disk. Viruses are the computer equivalent of bacterial warfare; they are usually created by mischievous computer-whiz types.

Viruses can find their way to your PC in a variety of ways. As a result, it's usually very difficult to determine exactly how and when a computer got "infected." To complicate matters, most viruses operate "behind the scenes" and can completely obliterate your hard disk before you know what's happened! To discover how to find and remove viruses that may have invaded your system, read Chapter 13, "Protecting Your System with Norton AntiVirus."

Monitoring Disk Activity

Norton's DISKMON utility is a TSR utility that lets you monitor all disk activity on your system and that can prevent computer viruses from destroying the contents of your hard disk. DISKMON also offers a disk park feature that protects your hard disk from damage when you move your PC from one location to another.

QUICK STEPS

Preventing Unauthorized Disk Write Activity

1. Type DISKMON at the DOS prompt or highlight Disk Monitor in the Commands list of the main Norton program screen. Press ⏎Enter.

    This runs the DISKMON utility and displays the Disk Monitor screen shown in Figure 10.1

2. Press ⏎Enter or click on Disk Protect.

    This selects the Disk Protect button and displays the Disk Protect screen shown in Figure 10.2.

3. Select the Entire Disk option, then choose the On button.

    This redisplays the Disk Monitor screen and shows the updated status of the Disk Protect feature.

Security Techniques

> **4.** Press [Esc] or click on **Q**uit. This DOS prompt returns, and DISKMON is activated as a TSR utility.

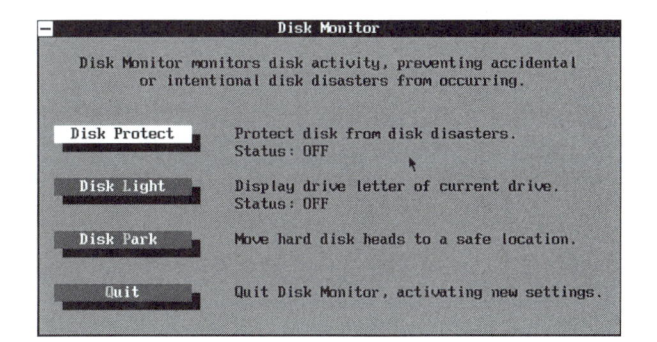

Figure 10.1
The Disk Monitor screen offers access to three useful disk utilities.

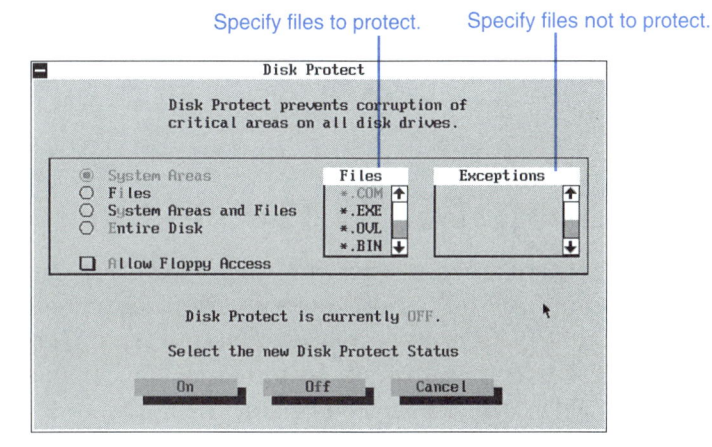

Figure 10.2
Use the Disk Protect feature to prevent unauthorized disk access.

When DISKMON is installed with the Entire Disk option, you will be notified before data is written to any disk on your PC (including both hard and floppy drives). The Disk Monitor dialog box shown in Figure 10.3 is displayed before each disk write operation.

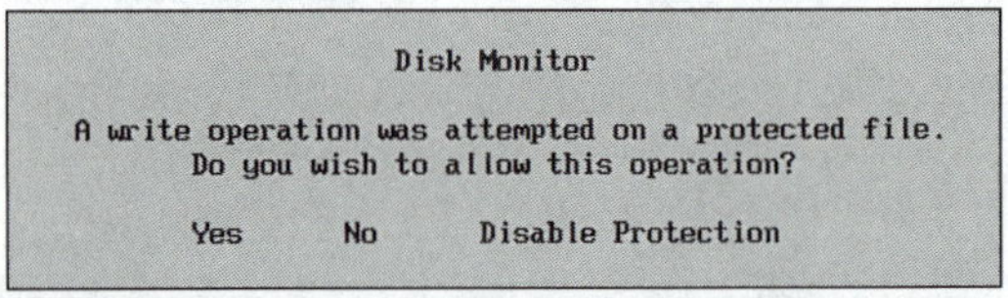

Figure 10.3
The Disk Monitor dialog box pops up whenever an application tries to write to a protected disk.

```
                    Disk Monitor
    A write operation was attempted on a protected file.
           Do you wish to allow this operation?

           Yes      No      Disable Protection
```

Press Y to permit or N to prohibit the write operation when the dialog box in Figure 10.3 is displayed. The Disk Monitor dialog box may pop up several times during one file copy or save operation. Press D to temporarily disable the disk monitor feature when the Disk Monitor dialog box is displayed.

> **TIP:** You can also disable the disk monitor directly from the DOS prompt by executing the command DISKMON /PROTECT-. To reactivate the disk monitor, execute the command DISKMON /PROTECT+ at the DOS prompt.

Disk Monitor Options

The Disk Protect screen shown in Figure 10.2 offers several disk monitor options. If you're not concerned with entire disk protection, you can elect to protect just the **S**ystem Areas (boot record, FAT, and root directory) or files. In addition, you can use the **Fi**les option and Files and Exceptions lists in Figure 10.2 to specify exactly which files you do and do not want protected. For example, let's say you want to monitor all Microsoft Excel spreadsheet data files except for those whose file names start with TEMP. You could specify *.XLS in the Files column and TEMP*.XLS in the Exceptions column of the Disk Protect screen. Finally, the **S**ystem Areas and Files option lets you protect both your system data and the files you specify.

Depending on the Disk Protect level selected, certain disk operations may cause the Disk Monitor dialog box (Figure 10.3) to pop up several times for write acknowledgment. The disk format process is a good example of an operation that can cause an enormous number of acknowledgment requests. The **A**llow Floppy Access option listed in the Disk Protect screen lets you work with floppy disks without being bothered by the Disk Monitor dialog box. You should consider activating this option if you need to format floppy disks fairly often.

Disk Light

In addition to the Disk Protect feature already discussed, the DISKMON utility lets you monitor all disk activity (disk reads and writes) more simply. When DISKMON's Disk Light feature is activated, the TSR program displays the ID of the drive where disk read/write activity is occurring. The active disk drive ID (for example, C:) is displayed in the top right corner of the screen. Use the /LIGHT+ and /LIGHT– options to turn the Disk Light feature on and off from the DOS command line (for example, DISKMON /LIGHT– disables the Disk Light feature).

> **NOTE:** The Disk Protect and Disk Light features will display messages only while your monitor is in text mode. If you are running a graphics mode application (like Microsoft Windows), DISKMON cannot display Disk Protect/Light messages.

Parking Your Hard Disk

Before you move your PC from one position or location to another, it is very important to prepare your hard disk for the relocation process. Hard disk drives are very sensitive devices and can easily be damaged while in transit. Use DISKMON's Disk Park feature to ensure your hard disk's safety before moving your PC. When you select the Disk **P**ark button on the Disk Monitor screen (Figure 10.1), the Disk Park dialog box shown in Figure 10.4 is displayed.

Note that some hard disk drives park automatically each time you shut down your computer. It won't hurt your system to park such a disk drive with DISKMON. If you're not sure whether your drive parks automatically, you should use DISKMON, especially when moving your computer.

Figure 10.4
Park your hard drive to prevent damage during transportation of your PC.

As the dialog box in Figure 10.4 notes, DISKMON has parked your hard disk, and you should immediately power down your PC. I suggest using DISKMON to park your hard disk every day before you turn off your PC; you never know when you may need to move your system. You can also use DISKMON's /PARK option to park your disk directly from the DOS prompt (for example, DISKMON /PARK).

Protecting Sensitive Files

The DOS ATTRIB command and Norton's FILEFIND utility can both be used to turn on the hidden file attribute for any personal/sensitive files you want to protect on your PC. (So can the File Attributes command line utility, which is described in Appendix B.) This is a good way to keep confidential files private since hidden files do not appear in directory listings. However, if someone is clever enough, they can use ATTRIB or The Norton Utilities to unhide your hidden files and expose your secrets.

Encrypting Files

To more effectively protect your private files, you should use Norton's DISKREET utility, which encrypts, or encodes, files so

Security Techniques

nobody else can interpret them. DISKREET is superior to encryption features offered in application programs such as word processors. When you use a word processor's or other application's encryption feature, you can still view the file contents at the DOS prompt by using the TYPE command. Or, you can view such a file with the DISKEDIT utility. Only DISKREET's encryption method prevents you from using either of the methods I just mentioned to view the contents of your encrypted file.

QUICK STEPS

Encrypting a File with DISKREET

1. Type **DISKREET** at the DOS prompt or highlight Diskreet in the Commands list of the main Norton screen. Press ↵Enter.

   This runs the DISKREET utility and displays the Diskreet screen shown in Figure 10.5.

2. Open the **F**ile menu.

   The **F**ile menu is displayed.

3. Select the **E**ncrypt option.

   This displays the encryption file selection screen shown in Figure 10.6.

4. Use the **D**rive and **D**irectories lists to move to the directory that holds the file you want to encrypt.

5. Choose the **F**iles list, then use the arrow keys to highlight the file you want to encrypt and press ↵Enter.

   This displays the Encrypt a File screen.

6. To accept the default encrypted file name, leave it in the **T**o box.

   continues

Chapter 10

continued

7. Choose **Enter Password**. Enter a secret password for the encrypted file (minimum of six characters) and press ⏎Enter.

8. Choose **Re-Enter Password**. Type the secret password again for verification and press ⏎Enter.

   DISKREET encrypts the selected file and displays a message when the process is complete.

9. Press ⏎Enter or click **OK**.

   A message appears asking if you want to wipe the original file.

10. Choose **Delete** or **Cancel**.

Figure 10.5
Use DISKREET to protect personal files.

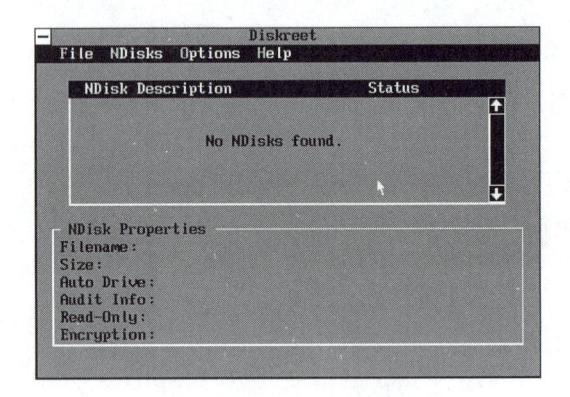

Figure 10.6
Use the encryption file selection screen to specify which file(s) you wish to encrypt.

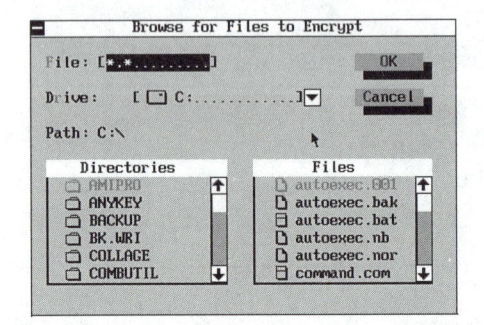

Be careful when selecting an encryption password for step 6. You'll need to specify this password later when you try to decode, or decrypt, the file. Don't use simple passwords like your name, address, or phone number, because they are obvious choices for others who may try to decrypt your files. On the other hand, don't use passwords that you might easily forget, because there's no way to reveal an encrypted file's password. If you forget the password, you may never be able to decrypt the file.

Encryption Options

Select the Options menu, then choose File to display the File Encryption Options screen shown in Figure 10.7.

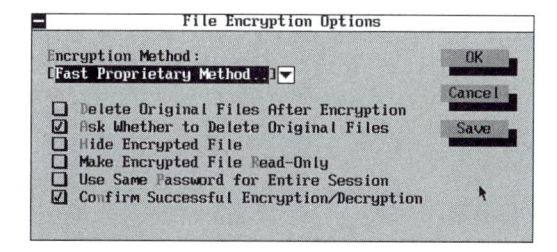

Figure 10.7
DISKREET offers several encryption options.

The DISKREET utility offers two methods of file encryption. The default DISKREET encryption method uses a proprietary encoding technique, and the other method uses the Data Encryption Standard (DES) technique, which has been approved by the U.S. Government as a highly secure encryption standard. Use the pull-down list to select the desired encryption method.

The other options shown in Figure 10.7 let you specify whether:

- The original file should be deleted after encryption.
- A message should appear to let you confirm the deletion of the original file.
- The encrypted file's read-only and hidden attributes should be set.

- The same password should be used for encryption throughout the DISKREET session.
- A message should appear to confirm successful encryption.

The password retention option is a handy feature if you want to encrypt several files with the same password. When this option is turned on, you have to enter the encryption password only once during the DISKREET session. Use the up and down arrow keys and the **Spacebar** or click with the mouse to select the desired DISKREET options, then select the **S**ave button to preserve the settings.

Decrypting Files

The DISKREET file decryption process is very similar to the encryption process. Pull down the **File** menu and select the **D**ecrypt option to display the Browse for a File to Decrypt screen shown in Figure 10.8.

Figure 10.8

Use the Browse for File to Decrypt screen to specify which files you wish to decrypt.

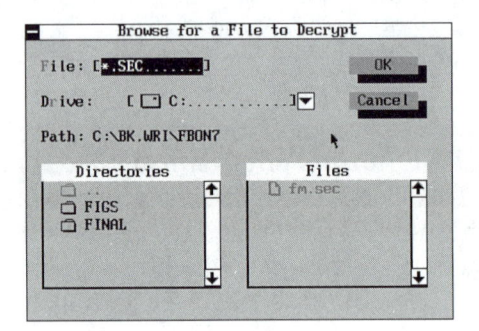

Select the directory/drive and highlight the file you want to decrypt. Then press **Enter** or click **OK**. The password request screen will be displayed. Enter the password you used to encrypt the file, and press **Enter**. If you enter the correct password, DISKREET will decrypt the specified file and display a message when the process is complete. (If you left the original file on disk, Diskreet will ask whether you want to overwrite the original file with the decrypted one before it finishes the decryption.)

Removing a File Permanently with WIPEINFO

In Chapter 4, I explained how the UNERASE utility can recover deleted files. Although it is convenient to have a recovery feature available, sometimes you really want to delete a file so no one else can see what it contained (for example, personnel records or top secret memos).

If you copy enough files to a disk, you may eventually overwrite the unprotected clusters of all deleted files. But this could take a long time (especially if you have a large hard disk partition), and there is no way to guarantee that it would overwrite all the deleted files. If you are really determined to obliterate a file, you may even consider FORMATting the disk. This approach is a bit drastic and may not work anyway since files can often be recovered from recently formatted disks (thanks to Norton's UNFORMAT utility!).

If you truly need to eradicate a file from a disk you should use Norton's WIPEINFO utility. Norton's WIPEINFO utility overwrites a file's clusters, thereby removing the file's data from a disk.

> **CAUTION**
> Use WIPEINFO with extreme caution because it overwrites a file's data clusters and makes recovery via UNERASE impossible.

Chapter 10

QUICK STEPS

Wiping a File from a Disk

1. Type `WIPEINFO` at the DOS prompt or highlight Wipe-Info in the Commands list of the main Norton screen. Press [↵Enter].

    This starts the WIPEINFO utility and displays the screen shown in Figure 10.9.

2. Press [↵Enter] or click on Files.

    This selects the default Files selection in Figure 10.9 and displays the Wipe Files screen.

3. Type the drive, directory, and name of the file to be wiped (for example, C:\WORK\JUNK.DOC) and press [↵Enter] or click on Wipe.

    A warning message is displayed.

4. Press [W] or click on Wipe to acknowledge the warning message.

    The Wiping Files screen is displayed.

5. Select the file, then press [W] or click on Wipe to wipe the selected file.

    WIPEINFO wipes the file and displays a completion message.

Figure 10.9
The WipeInfo screen lets you decide whether to wipe files or an entire disk.

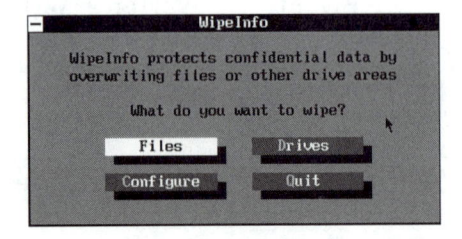

WIPEINFO Configuration

WIPEINFO overwrites each byte in every cluster of the specified file with the default value, 0. Therefore, if you look at the clusters previously occupied by JUNK.DOC, all you will see is a bunch of zeroes. If you want, you can change this value to any other number. You can also select the number of times you want the file wiped, for extra security. Select the Configure button on the WIPEINFO screen shown in Figure 10.9 to access the Wipe Configuration screen (Figure 10.10).

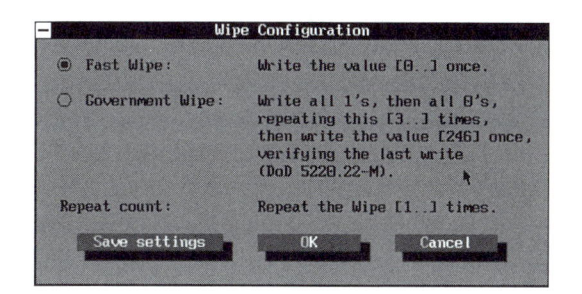

Figure 10.10
Select the desired WIPEINFO settings with the Wipe Configuration screen.

There are two Wipe options available in WIPEINFO: **F**ast Wipe and **G**overnment Wipe. WIPEINFO was configured with the **F**ast Wipe option when we eradicated the JUNK.DOC file in the previous Quick Steps. WIPEINFO overwrites each byte in a file one time with the specified value (0). You can change the 0 to another value by pressing Tab or clicking to move the cursor to the **F**ast Wipe default value field, and then typing a new value. After you change the overwrite value, choose **S**ave settings to save the new WIPEINFO configuration setting.

If you use WIPEINFO with the **G**overnment Wipe option shown in Figure 10.10, each wiped file is overwritten seven times with the following overwrite values:

Overwrite #	Overwrite Value
1	1
2	0
3	1
4	0
5	1
6	0
7	246

The Wipe Configuration screen in Figure 10.10 lets you change the number of times the 1/0 overwrite combination will be performed (the default is three times). You can also specify a different overwrite value for the final overwrite (the default value is 246). Press [Alt]+[G] or click on the Government Wipe option.

If you are the kind of person who worries whether the refrigerator light goes off when the door closes, you will appreciate the Repeat count option shown in Figure 10.10. The default repeat count is 1, but you can tell WIPEINFO to repeat the wipe as many as 999 times! So if you use the **G**overnment Wipe option and change the Repeat count to 4, each file will be overwritten 28 times (4 X 7 = 28)! Note, however, that increasing the repeat count increase the time it takes to wipe the specified information.

Wiping a Disk

WIPEINFO also lets you wipe an entire disk. Why would you want to wipe an entire disk? During the course of regular PC use, you are creating, copying, and deleting files that may contain sensitive data. As a result, some of this sensitive information may remain in unused clusters (because the DEL command doesn't remove a file's data from the disk). When the disk wipe feature is selected, WIPEINFO overwrites every part of the specified disk, including the unused clusters.

> **CAUTION** Use the WIPEINFO utility with extreme caution because it overwrites a file's data clusters and makes recovery with UNERASE impossible.

Security Techniques 211

Quick Steps

Wiping a Disk with WIPEINFO

1. Type the command **WIPEINFO** or highlight WipeInfo in the Commands list of the main Norton program screen. Press `Enter`.

   This starts the WIPEINFO utility and displays the WIPEINFO screen shown in Figure 10.9.

2. Choose the **Drives** command button.

   This displays the Select Drives to Wipe screen shown in Figure 10.11.

3. Use the arrow keys and press `Spacebar` or double-click with the mouse to select the drive(s) to wipe.

4. Press `Enter` or click **OK**.

   A warning screen is displayed reminding you that you are about to destroy the contents of the disk in the specified drive.

5. Press **W** or click **Wipe** to continue the disk wipe process.

   WIPEINFO begins wiping the specified disk. A completion message is displayed when the wipe process is finished.

6. Press `Enter` or click **OK** to acknowledge the wipe completion message.

   The WIPEINFO screen is redisplayed.

Figure 10.11
The Select Drives to Wipe screen lets you select which drive(s) you want to wipe.

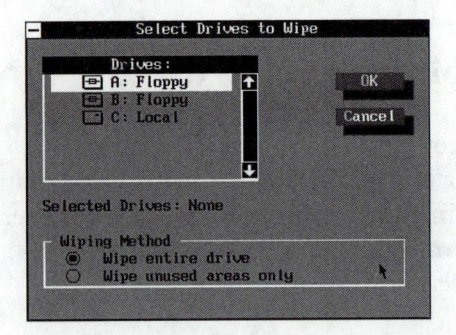

Depending upon whether you reconfigured WIPEINFO, WIPEINFO overwrites each byte in every cluster of the disk one or more times. You can also specify what value WIPEINFO should use when overwriting data on a disk. Refer to the WIPEINFO Configuration section for a full discussion of wiping options.

In This Chapter

Defragmenting your hard drive with SPEEDISK

Setting up Norton Cache to make RAM more effective

Calibrating your hard drive

Defragmenting Your Disk

1. Type **SPEEDISK** at the DOS prompt or highlight Speed Disk on the main Norton screen. Press Enter.
2. Highlight the drive you want to optimize. Press Enter or click OK.
3. Press Enter or click Optimize to accept the recommended method and begin disk optimization.

Calibrating Your Hard Disk

1. Type **CALIBRAT** at the DOS prompt or highlight Calibrate on the main Norton screen. Press Enter.
2. Press Enter or click Continue to acknowledge the Calibrate information dialog box. If it's the first time you've run CALIBRAT, you see a screen advising you to back up your hard disk.
3. Press Enter or click Continue.
4. Press Enter or click Continue.
5. Follow the on-screen prompts until you see a report screen or a chart with different interleaves set.
6. If you choose Done from the report screen, Calibrate performs a pattern text and low-level format of the disk. If you see the interleaves screen, choose an interleave rate, then choose the Continue button. Calibrate performs a nondestructive format and changes the disk interleave factor to the recommended optimal value. Follow the on-screen instructions to create a Calibrate report and/or exit the utility.

Chapter **11**

Making Your System More Efficient

You can use several tricks to make your PC operate at its peak performance level. I use the Norton Control Center utility (discussed in Chapter 2) to set my keyboard rate at the fastest setting. This step alone can create the illusion of a much faster PC! The Norton Utilities include three other tools that you can use to optimize your hard disk's performance. When used properly, these disk optimization tools can significantly increase the performance of even the slowest hard disk.

Using SPEEDISK

A badly fragmented disk is one of the most common causes of sluggish PC performance. The fragmentation that results from the everyday process of copying and deleting files can cause even the fastest hard disk to appear to be as slow as molasses! Use the Norton SPEEDISK utility regularly to keep your hard disk defragmented and efficient.

Chapter 11

> ## Quick Steps: Defragmenting Your Disk
>
> 1. Type **SPEEDISK** or highlight Speed Disk in the Commands list of the main Norton screen. Press ⏎Enter.
>
>   This runs the SPEEDISK utility and displays a drive selection dialog box.
>
> 2. Use the up and down arrow keys or the mouse to highlight the drive you want to optimize. Press ⏎Enter or click **OK**.
>
>   SPEEDISK analyzes the selected disk and displays the recommended optimization method (Figure 11.1).
>
> 3. Press ⏎Enter or click **Optimize** to accept the recommended method and begin disk optimization.
>
>   SPEEDISK optimizes the specified disk and displays a message when the process is complete.

Figure 11.1
SPEEDISK recommends a Full Optimization.

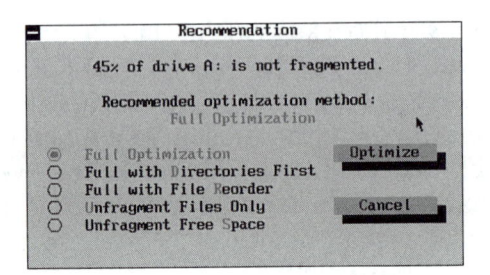

```
┌─ Recommendation ──────────────────────┐
│                                       │
│    45% of drive A: is not fragmented. │
│                                       │
│    Recommended optimization method:   │
│           Full Optimization           │
│                                       │
│   ⦿ Full Optimization       ┌────────┐│
│   ○ Full with Directories   │Optimize││
│     First                   └────────┘│
│   ○ Full with File Reorder  ┌────────┐│
│   ○ Unfragment Files Only   │ Cancel ││
│   ○ Unfragment Free Space   └────────┘│
└───────────────────────────────────────┘
```

SPEEDISK offers five different methods of optimization, ranging from a full optimization to a file sort, which simply rearranges the order of files on the disk. After you specify which disk to optimize, SPEEDISK analyzes the disk and determines which optimization method should be used. You can accept SPEEDISK's recommended optimization method, or you can select a different method. Select the **Optimization Method** option from the **Optimize** menu to see the list of optimization methods offered (Figure 11.2).

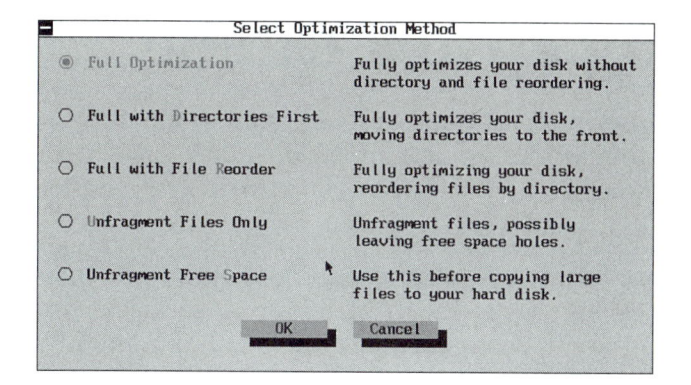

Figure 11.2
You can choose from several optimization methods.

Of the five optimization methods offered, the **F**ull Optimization and **U**nfragment Files Only methods are perhaps the most valuable. When the **F**ull Optimization method is used, SPEEDISK defragments files and moves all unused clusters to one contiguous area on the disk. **F**ull Optimization is the most time-consuming method offered by SPEEDISK, but it also organizes the disk in the most efficient manner possible. Full with **D**irectories First and Full with File **R**eorder not only optimize the disk, but also order the directories and files.

In contrast, the **U**nfragment Files Only method is less time-consuming than **F**ull Optimization, but it doesn't create the most efficient disk possible. As its name implies, the **U**nfragment Files Only method concentrates on unfragmenting files on the specified disk. However, there's no guarantee that every single file will be unfragmented when the optimization process is complete. Further, a disk optimized with the **U**nfragment Files Only method will probably still contain "holes" of noncontiguous unused clusters.

Use the **F**ull Optimization method monthly and the **U**nfragment Files Only method weekly to maintain a highly efficient and organized disk.

Using a Disk Cache

Disk read/write operations are very slow compared to the time required to manipulate data in RAM. A disk cache utility maintains frequently accessed disk data in a RAM buffer to help expedite disk read/write operations.

Before a time-consuming disk read operation is performed, the disk cache checks its RAM buffer to see if it contains the requested data. If the requested data is found in the RAM buffer, the cache can provide it to DOS without having to perform a timely disk read operation. Similarly, the cache utility may buffer several disk write operations and perform them together in a more efficient manner.

NOTE: The Norton Utilities Installation program includes an option to automatically install the cache utility. You can use the NUCONFIG program (described next) to install the cache utility if you skipped that step in the installation process.

To utilize the NCACHE caching programs, you must use NUCONFIG to install it. Type **NUCONFIG** at the DOS prompt. Select the Startup Programs option. In the dialog box that appears, highlight Start Norton Cache and press (Spacebar). Select either Load from CONFIG.SYS or Load from AUTOEXEC.BAT from the Loading section of the screen. Choose OK, then choose Save. You can then exit NUCONFIG.

After you add the NCACHE statement to your CONFIG.SYS file, you must reboot to activate the cache utility.

NCACHE and Microsoft Windows

NCACHE is compatible with the memory usage of Windows 3.x. When you run Windows 3.x in enhanced mode, it can (and does) use some of the memory held by NCACHE. To specify a minimum amount of expanded or extended memory for NCACHE when you're running Windows 3.x in enhanced mode on your system, you can use NUCONFIG to load NCACHE from your CONFIG.SYS file. Then you can edit the DEVICE line for NCACHE to add the EXT and EXP commands with parameters. (Or you can start NCACHE from the DOS prompt with the desired parameters and memory specifications.) For more on the EXT and EXP command parameters, see The Norton Utilities User's Guide.

Using CALIBRAT

The Calibrate utility is perhaps the most powerful disk optimization tool included in The Norton Utilities. CALIBRAT (short for Calibrate) performs rigorous pattern testing to check how well your system can read and write data to every sector on a disk. If you encounter problems storing data to a disk, run Calibrate. Otherwise, Symantec recommends you run Calibrate every three months to maintain your hard drive.

Calibrate also may test your hard disk's *interleave factor*. The interleave factor indicates how sectors are laid out within each track on a disk. The disk in Figure 11.3 has a 1:1 (pronounced "one to one") interleave factor, which means that each sector is adjacent to the next consecutive sector.

> **NOTE:** CALIBRAT cannot adjust the interleave on IDE or SCSI drives, and 90% of the drives in today's computers are one or the other. These drives are generally optimized by the manufacturer.

Figure 11.3
CALIBRAT shows that this disk has a 1:1 interleave factor.

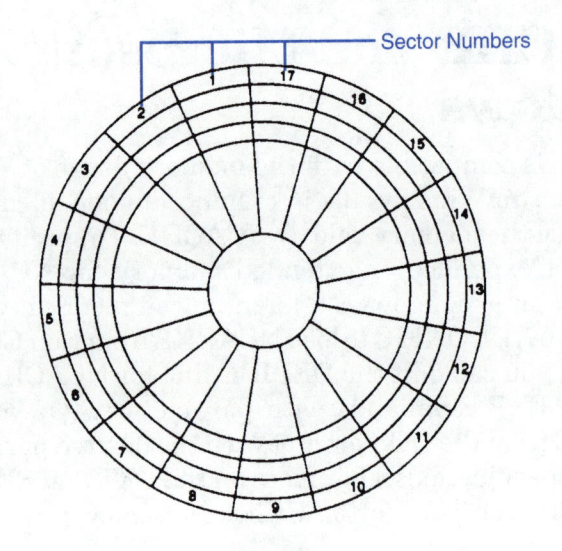

The disk in Figure 11.4 has a 2:1 interleave factor, which means that you must skip a sector to get to the next consecutive one.

Figure 11.4
This disk has a 2:1 interleave factor.

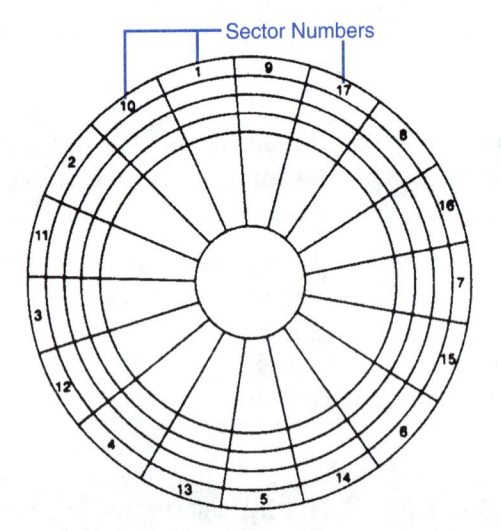

Similarly, a 3:1 interleave factor means that you must skip two sectors to get to the next consecutive one.

Making Your System More Efficient

Your hard disk's interleave factor was probably set by the disk's manufacturer or your PC dealer when the disk was installed. Regardless of how your disk's interleave factor was set, a different interleave factor may produce a faster, more efficient hard disk. Use the CALIBRAT utility to determine and/or modify your hard disk's interleave factor.

> **CAUTION**
>
> Always back up your hard disk before modifying the interleave factor with CALIBRAT. (See the Norton Backup program discussed in Chapter 12.) In addition, you need to plan ahead before using the following procedure. Calibrate's pattern testing can take several hours. Consider starting the test after you're finished working on your system for the day, so it will be ready to go the following morning.

QUICK STEPS

Calibrating Your Hard Disk

1. Type the command CALIBRAT or highlight Calibrate in the Commands list of the main Norton screen. Press `Enter`.

    This runs the CALIBRAT utility and displays a Calibrate information dialog box.

2. Press `Enter` or click Continue to acknowledge the Calibrate information dialog box.

    If it's the first time you've run CALIBRAT, you see a screen advising you to back up your hard disk.

3. Press `Enter` or click on Continue.

    This displays an information dialog box that explains each of the tests that will be run on the specified disk.

continues

continued

4. Press ⏎Enter or click on Continue.	CALIBRAT performs a series of integrity and performance tests on your hard disk.
5. Follow the on-screen prompts until you see a chart with different interleaves set.	
6. If you choose **Done** from the screen shown in 11.5, Calibrate performs a pattern text and low-level format of the disk. If you see the interleaves screen, choose an interleave rate and choose the Continue button.	CALIBRAT performs a nondestructive format, and changes the disk interleave factor to the recommended optimal value. Follow the on-screen instructions to create a CALIBRAT report and/or exit the utility.

As indicated in step 6 of the preceding Quick Steps, CALIBRAT performs a nondestructive format of the specified hard disk when it alters the interleave factor. In other words, none of your disk's data should be lost during this format process. However, you should *always* back up your disk before changing the interleave factor with CALIBRAT.

In This Chapter

Setting up the Norton Backup

How to back up your hard disk

How to restore data from backup diskettes

How to create macros to simplify your backups

Installing the Norton Backup

1. Insert the Norton Backup Disk #1 in drive A: or B:. Change to that drive by typing **A:** or **B:** and pressing `Enter`.
2. Type **Install** and press `Enter`.
3. Select **Black & White** or **Color** for your display.
4. Respond to the dialog boxes that ask you to indicate a directory to install to, personalize your copy of The Norton Backup, and configure the program to run with your system. Swap disks in and out of the drive when prompted.
5. When the installation is finished, choose **Go to Program**. The Norton Backup screen appears.

Running the Basic Backup

1. Select **Backup** from the main menu.
2. Specify the drives to Ba**c**kup From and **B**ackup To.
3. Choose a Backup T**y**pe.
4. Select **Options** to check or change the Basic options.
5. If you want to check or change which files are set to be backed up, choose **Select Files**. Select (or deselect) the directories and files to be backed up. When all files are selected, click on **OK**.
6. Select **Start Backup**.
7. Insert and replace diskettes as prompted. When the backup is complete, you are returned automatically to the DOS prompt (if the **Q**uit after Backup option is set to On), or a Backup is complete message appears.
8. Select **OK** at the prompt to complete the backup.

Chapter **12**

Using the Norton Backup

The Norton Backup, which is a separate program by Symantec, provides a simple means of protecting your information and the time it took you to create it. The program "backs up" (copies) files from your hard disk onto floppy diskettes in a special compressed format. If your hard disk files become lost or damaged, you can "decompress" and restore them from your backup diskettes onto your hard disk.

This chapter covers the most important information you need to know about Backup—how to install it, back up and restore files, and create macros to make your backups easier.

Be Safe—Back It Up!

How can you lose files from a hard disk? Let me count the ways. Your hard disk can "crash" due to power spikes, system failure, or physical damage. You can inadvertently erase files or directories. You can accidentally reformat your hard disk. You can even lose your hard disk contents to a computer virus.

Regular backup of your hard disk files prevents their total loss in the event of disaster. The frequency with which you back up your hard disk depends on how often you use it and how sensitive or difficult it is to recreate your files. With the Norton Backup, you can easily back up all files on a daily basis. Many users, however, find that a complete monthly backup, with weekly or daily backups of new or changed files only, is adequate for their needs.

Norton Backup Options

The Norton Backup provides options that let you set your backup frequency, select the files that you want to back up, specify the degree of compression (which determines whether a backup requires more diskettes or more time), choose whether you want the accuracy of copied data verified (which also affects speed), and more.

The options available to you depend on which of the three Norton Backup levels you use:

Basic   You can select which files to back up, modify your setup, specify simple options, schedule automatic backups, and create macros.

Advanced   You can do everything from Basic, plus choose from more backup options and create scripts that automate file selection.

Preset   You can preview backups and save your backup routine so that you can rerun it automatically.

In this chapter, we'll be working mostly with the Basic level. Most beginners will find everything they need there.

Installing and Configuring Backup

Before you can perform your first backup, you must install and configure the Norton Backup. Both procedures are easy and quick, with on-screen prompts guiding you each step of the way. In the following sections, you will learn how to install, configure, start, and exit from the Norton Backup, as well as how to use the On-Line Help system.

As you run the installation, dialog boxes both provide information and ask for input. You provide some of the input by selecting items on the screen. To select an item using the keyboard:

- Highlight it by pressing [Tab] or the arrow keys, then press [Spacebar].

- To turn a checkbox on or off, highlight it and then press [Spacebar].

- Use [Backspace] and [Del] to erase characters that you type. (If a choice has a highlighted selection letter, you can choose it by pressing the selection letter or pressing [Alt] plus the selection letter.)

To select an item using the mouse, position the cursor over the item, and click the left button.

Note that you use these same methods to make selections when you're running the Norton Backup program.

Installing the Norton Backup

Installation is a three-step process, as shown on the initial Norton Backup Install screen in Figure 12.1. The final step begins program configuration, which is explained in the next section.

Figure 12.1
The main Norton Backup Install screen shows the steps Install leads you through.

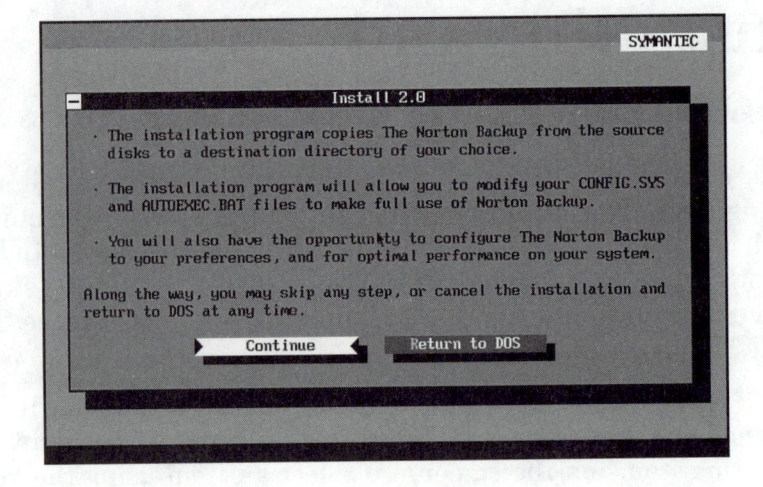

During installation, you will be asked to make some decisions, such as:

- Where the Norton Backup will be installed. Unless you specify otherwise, the program is installed on your hard drive (C:) in a directory called NBACKUP.

- Whether or not you want the Norton Backup to revise the PATH command in your AUTOEXEC.BAT file so that you can run the Norton Backup from any directory. This is a good idea, because it saves you the trouble of changing to the NBACKUP directory before running the program.

- Whether or not you want the program to change your CONFIG.SYS file to set the BUFFERS parameter at 30. This allows you to run the Norton Backup more efficiently.

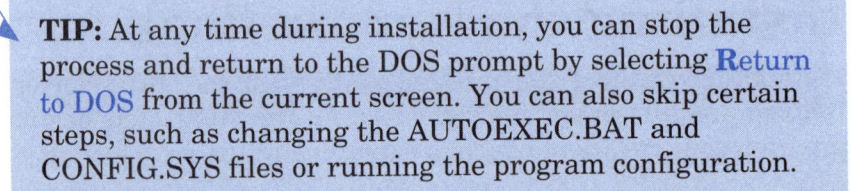

TIP: At any time during installation, you can stop the process and return to the DOS prompt by selecting Return to DOS from the current screen. You can also skip certain steps, such as changing the AUTOEXEC.BAT and CONFIG.SYS files or running the program configuration.

Using the Norton Backup

The Norton Backup Installation **Q**UICK STEPS

1. Insert the Norton Backup Disk #1 in drive A: or B:. Change to that drive by typing **A:** or **B:** and pressing `Enter`.

    The A> or B> prompt appears.

2. Type **INSTALL** and press `Enter`.

    Install asks you to specify your monitor's display colors.

3. Select **B**lack & White or **C**olor.

    The Install screen appears (Figure 12.1).

4. Select **C**ontinue.

    The program searches for existing Norton Backup files, then asks for the drive and directory on which the program will be installed. C:\NBACKUP is the default.

5. Type in a new drive and/or directory name if you do not want the default. (For example, C:\BU.)

    The new name replaces the default.

6. Select **C**ontinue.

    Install begins copying the backup files to your hard drive.

7. When install prompts you to place another disk in the drive, insert the disk in the specified drive and press `Enter`.

    After the last disk, Install asks if you want to add Norton Backup Help to your DOS help file.

8. Choose **A**dd Help or **D**on't Add Help.

    Install asks you to personalize your copy of The Norton Backup.

continues

Chapter 12

continued

9. Type your name. Press `Tab`. Type your company name. Press `Enter` twice.

    Install asks what Program Level you want to use with Backup (Figure 12.2).

10. Select a program level and click **OK** or press `Enter`.

    Install continues to prompt you to test and configure your system. The configuration is described in detail in the next section.

11. Continue responding to the configuration prompts. When finished, choose **S**ave.

    Install tells you it's creating the DEFAULT.SET file.

12. Choose **C**reate.

    Install asks if you want to go to DOS or return to the Norton Backup program.

13. Choose **G**o to Program.

    The Norton Backup screen appears.

Figure 12.2

The Norton Backup Configuration screen shows setup options. The Program Level dialog box appears automatically.

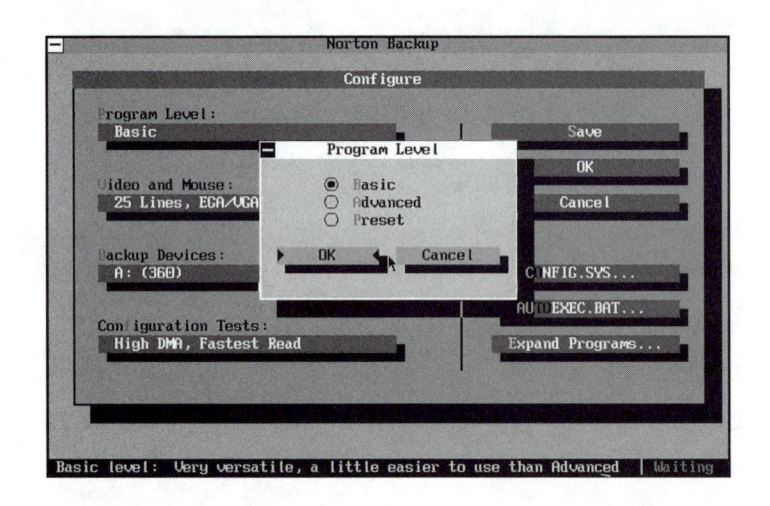

Configuring the Norton Backup for Your System

The install process lets you automatically configure The Norton Backup for your system. You also can reconfigure Backup at any time by selecting Configure from the Norton Backup main menu, displayed when you start the program.

The Norton Backup Configuration screen (see Figure 12.3) shows several setup parameters for which you will choose options. These are described next.

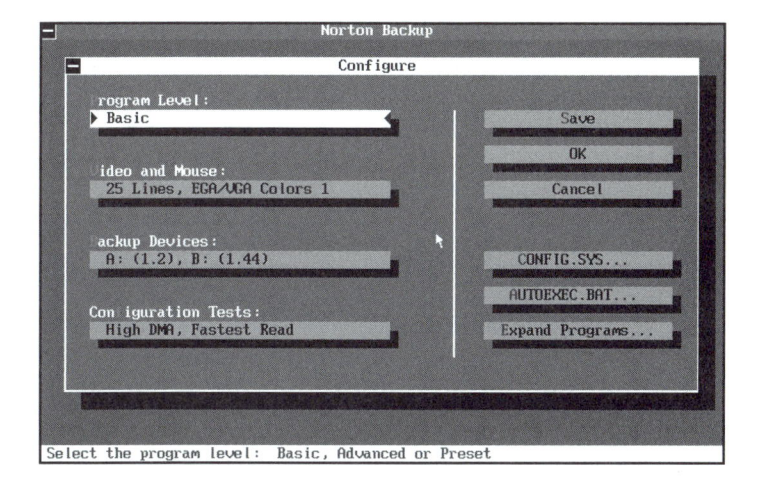

Figure 12.3
Use this screen to configure The Norton Backup.

Program Level

You selected a program level during installation (see Figure 12.2). The default program level is **B**asic. Leave the setting as **B**asic until you become more experienced with the Norton Backup. It is easy to change the setting later if you desire.

Video and Mouse Settings

The **V**ideo and Mouse settings let you configure your screen display and mouse. The Screen Options configuration settings are set automatically to match your monitor; accept the default settings unless you are sure that they are incorrect.

Chapter 12

Turn on the Reduce Display Speed option if you have an older CGA monitor that is subject to "snow." Turn off the Expanding Dialog option if you want dialog boxes to pop on the screen rather than appear more gradually. Choose the Custom Colors option to display a dialog box that lets you customize screen colors.

Use the Mouse Options to customize the mouse for ease-of-use. The Double-Click setting determines how rapidly one click must follow another to be recognized as a double-click. Slow allows a longer interval; the default is Medium.

The Sensitivity setting determines the distance that the cursor moves across the screen when you move the mouse. It can be set to Default, Low, Medium, or High. The Acceleration setting determines the acceleration of mouse movement. Turn on the Left-Handed Mouse check box to reverse the operation of mouse buttons.

> **CAUTION** Don't choose the Hard Mouse Reset option unless you're having trouble getting your mouse to work with The Norton Backup.

Backup Devices

The Backup Devices configuration option lets you tell Backup what kind of floppy drives you'll be using for backups. Choose Auto Config to have Norton Backup confirm what method it can use to detect when you've changed disks (or a tape) during a backup procedure.

Configuration Tests

The Configuration Tests are conducted automatically. You only have to do two things:

- Approve their continuation at various points by selecting OK from a dialog box.
- Insert floppy diskettes when prompted by the Insert Diskette message within flashing brackets.

The diskettes do not need to be formatted, but they do need to match the floppy disk drive configuration (size and density) set up earlier.

The **D**MA Test checks whether Norton Backup can access your hard and floppy drives simultaneously, and sets the appropriate Direct Memory Access option. The **C**ompatibility Test runs a mini backup and checks the results, then sets the Disk Log Strategy option.

> **CAUTION**
>
> The first Configuration Test, the Direct Memory Access (DMA) test, checks your computer's DMA chip to make sure the Norton Backup uses the chip's optimum speed. Some DMA chips may fail the test and cause the computer to "freeze." If this occurs, simply turn your computer off and on again, then restart the program by typing nbackup at the DOS prompt.

Working with the Norton Backup

If you did not choose **G**o to Program after installation (or when you want to use the program in the future), you can start the Norton Backup from any directory on your hard disk (that is, if you let Install alter your AUTOEXEC.BAT file). For example, you can start the program from any of the following prompts:

```
C:\>
C:\WORDS>
C:\NBACKUP>
```

To start the program, simply type

nbackup

Chapter 12

and press <kbd>Enter</kbd>. This takes you to the Norton Backup main menu, shown in Figure 12.4. From this menu you can choose from several options: **B**ackup, **C**ompare, **R**estore, Backup **S**cheduler, Co**n**figure, or **Q**uit.

Figure 12.4

Use the Norton Backup main menu to start the backup or restore process, compare backup files, schedule backups, change configuration options, or exit the Norton Backup.

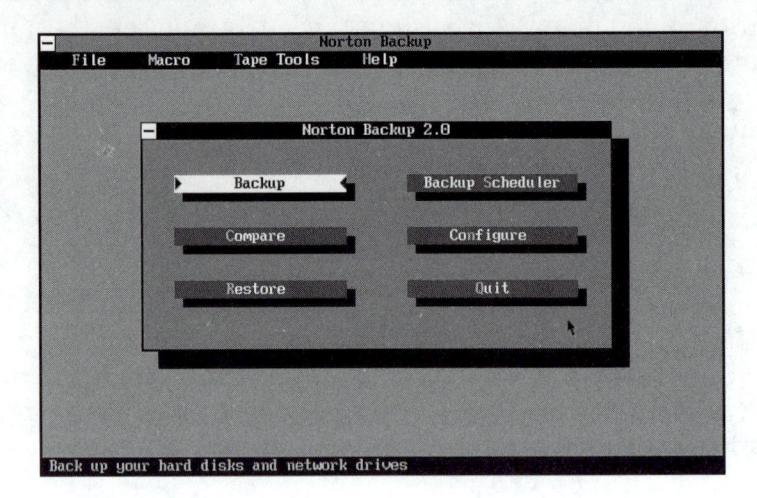

Getting Help When You Need It

Although the Norton Backup is easy to use, you may occasionally need help with a particular operation or may desire more information on available options. This help is available at any time from within the program through the On-Line Help system. To enter this system, press <kbd>F1</kbd> or choose the **Help** command from the menu bar, then choose **Index**. A screen similar to the one shown in Figure 12.5 appears.

The help screen shows information related to the operation that you were performing when you entered the Help system. You can scroll the screen to read additional information using the arrow keys or the mouse scroll bar.

Some words or phrases on the screen may be highlighted or displayed in a different color. These phrases are linked to additional information on specific topics, which you can also select. Use <kbd>Tab</kbd> to highlight a linked phrase, then press <kbd>Enter</kbd> to display the information—or click on the phrase with the mouse.

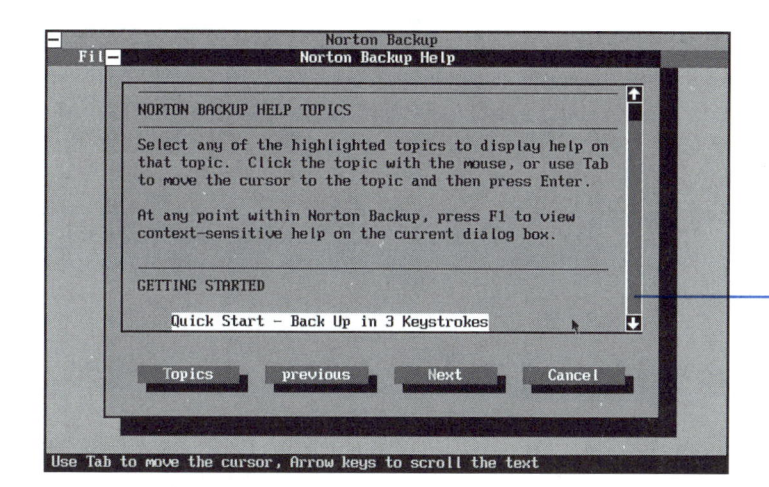

Using the Norton Backup

Figure 12.5
The Norton Backup Help screen displays information on the last operation you were performing.

Scroll bar

At the bottom of the screen is a menu of additional Help options:

*T*opics displays an index of all Help topics. Select a topic from the list to see more detailed information on it.

*P*revious shows the last help screen viewed. If you are at the initial help screen, this option is not available.

*N*ext shows the next available help screen on the topic selected.

Cancel or *Esc* takes you out of the on-line Help system and returns you to the screen from which you left.

If an option is not available, the highlight will skip over it when you attempt to select it.

Exiting the Program

When you are finished using the Norton Backup, exit the program by selecting **Q**uit from the main menu (Figure 12.4) or by choosing E**x**it from the **F**ile pull-down menu. This returns you to the DOS prompt from which you started the program.

Chapter 12

> **NOTE:** If you select the Quit After Backup (or Quit After Restore) from the Options screen of either operation, the program quits automatically when the operation is complete and returns you to the DOS prompt. These options are explained later in the chapter.

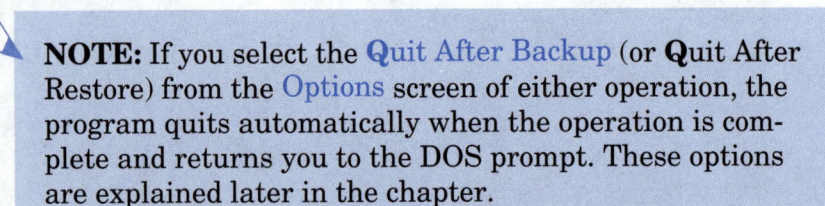

The Basic Backup

The Basic backup gives you considerable power and a number of options for protecting your hard disk files. Even though it is not as fully featured as the Advanced backup, it gives you as much control as you are likely to need in the beginning.

The following Quick Steps for the Basic backup take you through the process quickly—more information on each step is provided in the sections that follow.

Quick Steps: Running the Basic Backup

1. Select Backup from the main menu.

   The Norton Basic Backup screen appears, as shown in Figure 12.6.

2. If you want to back up a different drive than the one currently displayed, select the new drive(s) in the Backup From box.

   `All files` appears next to the selected drive.

3. If you want to change the floppy disk drive that the backup files will be copied to, select the Backup To box. Choose the drive you want in the window that appears, then select OK.

   The Norton Basic Backup screen reappears with the new floppy disk drive shown.

Using the Norton Backup

4. If you want to specify a different type of backup than the one shown, select the Backup Type box. Choose the desired type in the window that appears, then select OK.

   The Norton Basic Backup screen reappears with the new backup type shown.

5. Select Options to check or change the Basic options.

   The Backup Options window appears.

6. Select the desired options by turning on the check boxes. Select OK.

   This sets your options, and the Norton Basic Backup screen reappears.

7. If you want to check or change which files are set to be backed up, choose Select Files. Otherwise, skip to step 9.

   The Backup Files screen appears. If you are running Backup for the first time, all files in all directories in the selected drive are marked for backup. Otherwise, the files last selected for backup are marked.

8. Select (or deselect) the directories and files to be backed up. Select Display to check and change any file display options. When all files are selected, click on OK.

   The Norton Basic Backup screen reappears.

9. Select Start Backup.

   The Norton Backup screen appears, and the backup begins.

   continues

Chapter 12

> *continued*
>
> **10.** Insert diskettes as prompted.
>
> The backup begins and the lower left corner of the screen displays its progress. When the backup is complete, you are returned automatically to the DOS prompt (if the **Q**uit after Backup option is set to On), or a `Backup is complete` message appears.
>
> **11.** Select OK at the prompt to complete the backup.
>
> You are returned to the main menu.

Figure 12.6
The Norton Basic Backup screen prompts you for backup information and options.

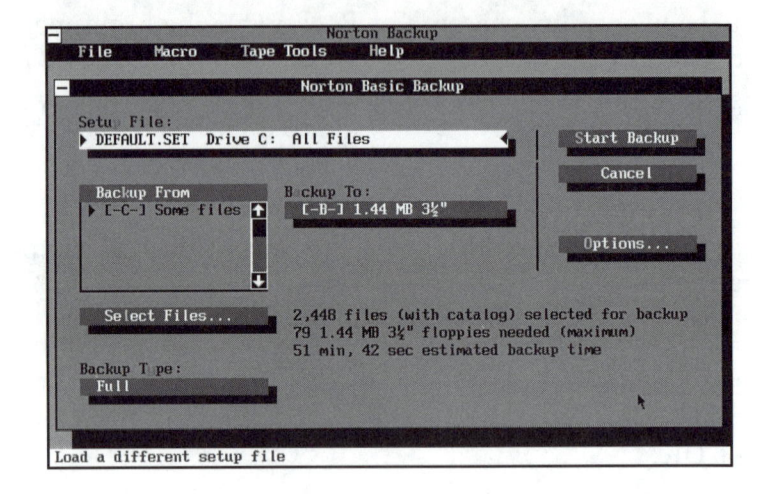

Selecting the Backup Drives

You may back up files from one or more hard drives. The Ba**c**kup From option in the Norton Basic Backup screen shows all drives available on your system. The current drive (whether selected or not) is marked with an arrow. When you choose Se**l**ect Files, the contents of the current drive are displayed.

Using the Norton Backup

The **B**ackup To drive is the drive onto which you will save the backup files. The default floppy disk drive selected by the program appears in this box. If you want to change this drive, select Backup To, then select a different drive from the list displayed.

> **CAUTION**
>
> Although you can specify a hard disk drive to back up to, your resulting backup files will do you little good in the event of a total hard disk disaster. It is better to back up your files onto floppy diskettes.

Selecting the Backup Type

There are five types of backups from which you can choose:

- **F**ull
- **I**ncremental
- **D**ifferential
- Full **C**opy
- Incremental Cop**y**

To understand the differences among these types, you must know how files are marked, or *flagged*. When a file is created or changed (worked with in any way), it is marked with one type of flag. When a file is backed up, it is marked with another type of flag. In this way, the program is always able to tell which files have been backed up and which files have been changed since they were backed up.

Full Backup

A full backup backs up all files that you select and flags them as backed up. When you first back up your hard disk, you should perform a full backup. After that, you may need to do a full backup only once a week or once a month, depending on how often you use your computer.

Incremental Backup

An incremental backup backs up only the files whose flags indicate that they were created or changed since your last full backup. After these files are backed up, they will be flagged as backed up. In subsequent backups, if these files have not been changed, they are not backed up again. However, the next time you work with the files, they are again marked as changed and included in your next backup.

Use this type of backup if you work with many different files. Keep your set of disks from the full backup separate, and use different diskettes for each incremental backup.

Differential Backup

A differential backup is similar to an incremental backup. It backs up all selected files that you have worked with since your last backup. Unlike an incremental backup, however, it does not flag the files as backed up. As a result, the files are backed up again on your next backup, even if they haven't been changed. Use this type of backup if you work with the same few files every day and want a continuously updated set of backup files.

Full Copy

This type of backup backs up all selected files, regardless of whether they have been changed or not. It does not flag the backed up files, so it does not affect full or incremental backups that you have regularly scheduled. Use this type of backup when you want to transfer files from one location to another.

> **CAUTION** Do not confuse a Full Copy backup with the DOS COPY command. With COPY, files on the floppy are ready to use; with Norton Backup, Full Copy, you must restore the files before you can use them.

Incremental Copy

An incremental copy is similar to a full copy, but it backs up only selected files that have changed since the last backup of any type and does not change the backed up flag on any files copied.

Selecting Backup Options

The **O**ptions that you select in a Basic level backup determine the speed of your backup operation, the number of backup diskettes required, the accuracy of the backup, and other factors, all of which are explained in the following sections. These options, shown in Figure 12.7, can be set to On or Off only. After all options are set to your satisfaction, select OK to return to the Basic Backup screen.

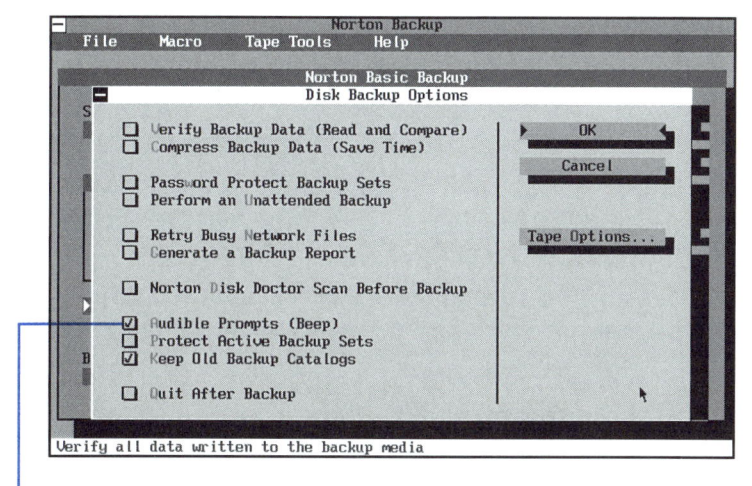

Figure 12.7
A check mark indicates that an option is on. If you're not running Norton Backup in graphics mode, an X between two brackets indicates that an option is selected.

NOTE: Although some of the options you set affect the backup time and the number of backup diskettes, their effect may not be reflected in the estimated backup time and in the number of diskettes shown on the Basic Backup screen.

Verify Backup Data (Read and Compare)

This option instructs the program to check the backed up data to make sure there are no errors in it and that it matches the original data. In a Basic backup, only the highest level of verification—Read and Compare—is available. This ensures an accurate data transfer; it also slows down the backup by as much as 50% when turned on.

Compress Backup Data (Save Time)

This option saves the data in a compressed format that requires fewer backup diskettes. There are higher levels of compression available in an Advanced backup, which save even more diskette space. However, they slow down the backup process more.

Password Protect Backup Sets

Improve the security of your system by assigning a password to backup files. When you use this option, only someone who knows the password can compare and restore the backup files.

Perform an Unattended Backup

Turn this feature on so that The Norton Backup supplies automatic answers to prompts and proceeds with the backup.

Retry Busy Network Files

Leave this option off so that The Norton Backup will skip locked files on a network. If Backup repeatedly tries to access files, backup time is substantially increased.

Generate a Backup Report

Choose to create a report of the details of the backup, including backup date and time, the setup and catalog file names, options settings, files processed, and more. Use the **File Print** command to output a hard copy of your report.

Norton Disk Doctor Scan Before Backup

If you've installed The Norton Utilities in a C:\NU or C:\NORTON directory, you can turn on this option so that your hard drive is scanned and errors are corrected before the backup begins.

Audible Prompts (Beep)

This option adds a beep to prompts during the backup. This is a useful option if you don't want to sit and watch the screen during your entire backup.

Protect Active Backup Sets

Check this option so that Backup warns you if you try to backup over a disk that contains a file from your current backup set of disks.

Keep Old Backup Catalogs on Hard Disk

A backup catalog provides an index of your backed up files and is necessary for the restore operation. Normally, when you perform a full backup, all interim catalogs since the prior full backup are deleted. With this option on, catalogs from previous backups are saved, so you can restore files from earlier backups. However, these catalogs do occupy space on your hard disk.

Quit After Backup

With this option on, the program automatically returns you to the DOS prompt rather than the program main menu when the backup operation is finished.

Selecting Files to Back Up

You can back up all files in all directories on your hard disk, or you can back up only selected files in selected directories. The Select

Backup Files screen, shown in Figure 12.8, is where you make your selections.

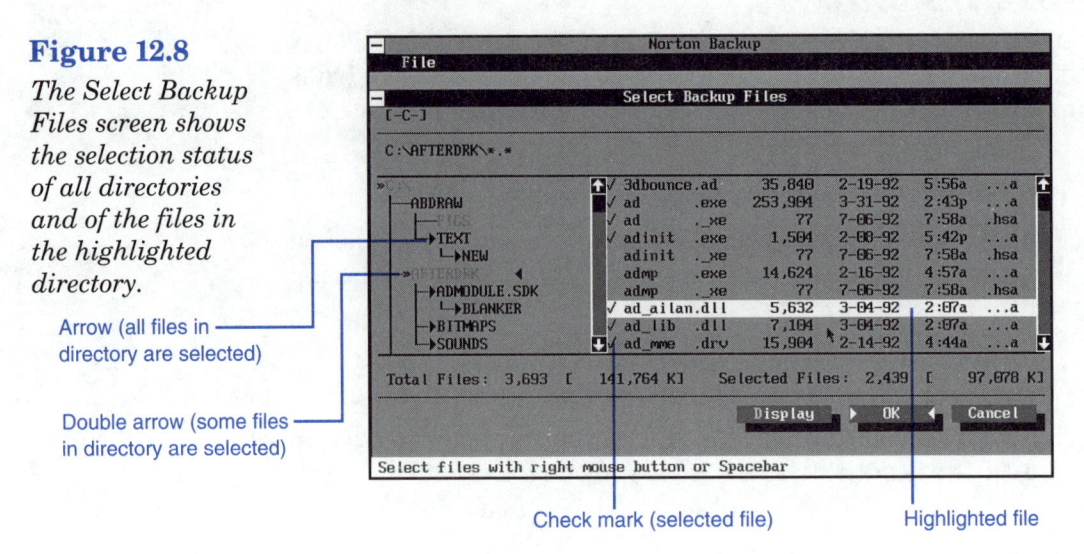

Figure 12.8

The Select Backup Files screen shows the selection status of all directories and of the files in the highlighted directory.

Arrow (all files in directory are selected)

Double arrow (some files in directory are selected)

Check mark (selected file)   Highlighted file

The directories are listed on the left side of the screen; the files in the highlighted directory are listed on the right side of the screen. Files and directories are marked as follows:

- An arrow to the left of a directory means that all files in it are selected for backup.
- A smaller double arrow means that some files in the directory are selected for backup.
- A checkmark next to a file name means that the file is selected for backup.

To select a file, use the mouse or arrow keys to highlight it, then press Spacebar.

> **TIP:** Use the **F**ile menu to **C**opy selected files to a diskette, to **D**elete the file that's highlighted (not selected with a checkmark beside it) in the file list, or to **V**iew the contents of the highlighted file if it's in one of the many formats that Backup lets you view.

When you have selected all the files to include in the backup, select OK. If you change your mind about your file selections, select Cancel to return to the Norton Basic Backup screen without changing your original file selections.

The Display Option

This option lets you choose the way in which files are sorted and displayed on the Select Backup Files screen. It also lets you display information about the size and number of selected files. Choosing this option brings up the Display Options dialog box, shown in Figure 12.9.

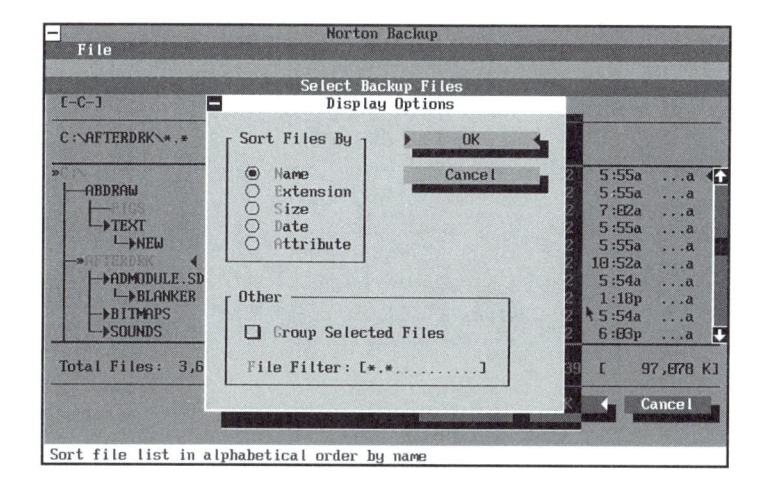

Figure 12.9

The Display Options dialog box lets you arrange selected files for easier viewing.

The first display option, Sort Files By, lets you arrange the displayed files by file **N**ame, **E**xtension, **S**ize, **D**ate, or **A**ttribute (hidden, archived, and so on). For example, if you arrange files by name, they are sorted alphabetically. If you arrange them by size, they are sorted with the largest files first. Arranging by date sorts files with the most recently created files first.

The **F**ile Filter option lets you limit the range of files that are shown in the file list. The default shown in Figure 12.9 is *.*, which means that all files in the directory are displayed. If you changed this default to *.COM, then only files with the COM extension would be displayed. If you changed it to ANSI.*, then only files with the file name ANSI and any extension would be displayed.

> **NOTE:** Any files selected before you set a file filter remain selected, even though they are not displayed on the file list.

Turning on the **G**roup Selected Files option causes all selected files in a directory to be grouped together at the start of the file list, followed by unselected files.

> **NOTE:** All of the backup selections you make are stored automatically in a *setup file*. In a Basic backup, this file is named DEFAULT.SET. This file loads automatically and sets the default settings for all backups and restores until you change the settings again. In an Advanced backup, you can save setup files under other names.

Starting the Basic Backup

When you are ready to begin the backup operation, select Start Backup from the Norton Basic Backup screen (Figure 12.6). The backup progress screen shown in Figure 12.10 appears.

Once the backup begins, you simply insert floppy diskettes when prompted. An estimate of the number of diskettes you will need is shown in the lower right window of the screen. This estimate is based on the last backup you performed. If you have changed the compression option since your last backup, you may need more or fewer diskettes than the estimate shows.

Using the Norton Backup

Figure 12.10
The backup progress screen shows the status of your backup operation.

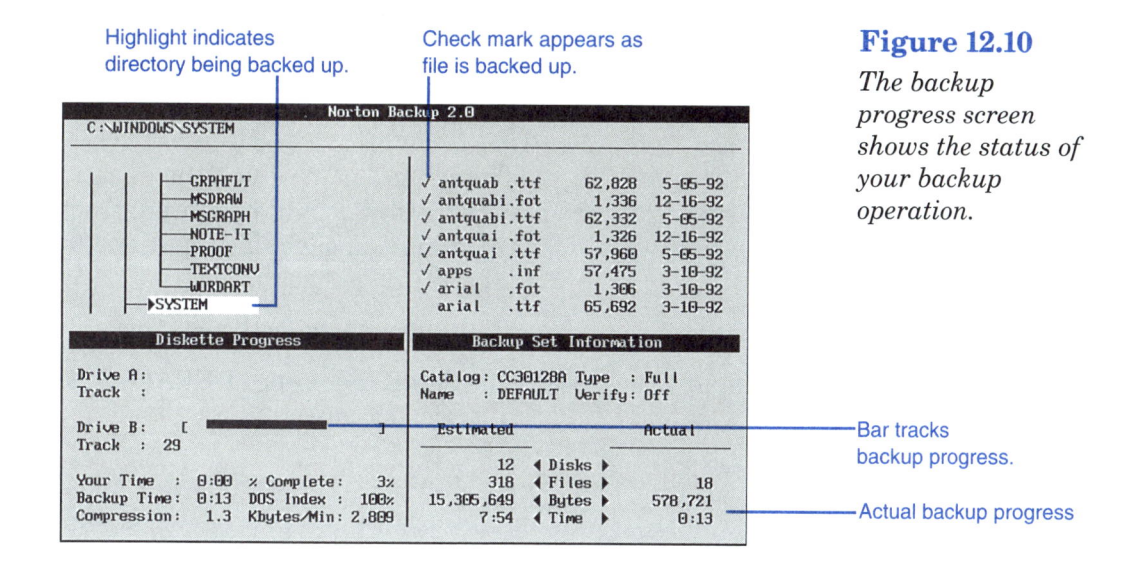

After you insert each diskette, a bar moves across the bracketed area next to the drive letter in the Diskette Progress area, tracking the actual transfer of data until the diskette is full.

> **NOTE:** During backup, the disk drive light on your computer always remains on, even while you are removing and inserting diskettes. This is normal and not a cause for alarm.

Other information shown on the screen during backup includes:

Your Time	The time it takes you to swap diskettes.
Backup Time	The computer's time backing up files.
Compression	The amount that files are being compressed as they're stored on the backup diskettes.
% Complete	How much of the backup is complete (useful for estimating how many more diskettes you may need).

DOS Index	An indicator of the program's efficiency.
Kbytes/Minute	The amount of data being backed up per minute.
Catalog	The name under which the backup catalog (index) will be stored. (Include this name on each backup diskette label.)
Type	The backup type you selected.
Name	The setup file name (DEFAULT.SET in a Basic backup).
Verify	Data Verification option selected (on or off).
Disks	Estimated versus actual number of diskettes used.
Files	Estimated versus actual number of files backed up.
Bytes	Estimated versus actual bytes of data backed up.
Time	Estimated versus actual total backup time.

After you remove each full backup diskette, label it with the date, backup diskette number, and catalog name shown on the screen.

You can cancel the backup operation at any time by pressing Esc. When backup is complete, a dialog box informs you. Select OK from this box to exit the backup progress screen and return to the main Norton Backup menu.

Using the Norton Backup 249

Comparing Your Backup Files to the Originals

You can use the Compare choice from the Backup main menu to make sure your new backup is accurate and complete. Compare looks at the files in your backup catalog and ensures that they match the files on your hard drive. Here's the basic Compare procedure:

1. Choose **Compare** from the main Backup menu. The screen shown in Figure 12.11 appears.

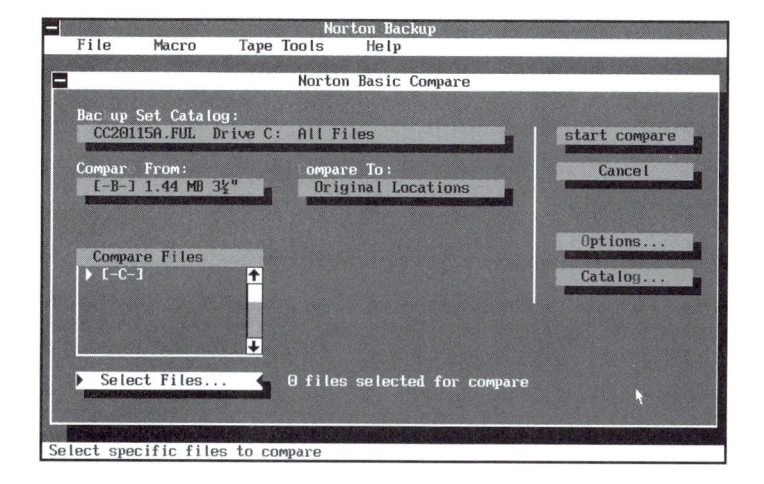

Figure 12.11

The screen you use to Compare your backup files to the files on your hard drive.

2. Load the catalog file you want to check. If you just backed up, you can skip this step. Press Alt+K or click on **Backup Set Catalog**. Double-click or use the arrow keys plus Spacebar to choose the catalog file you want to compare. Choose **Load**.

3. If needed, choose **Compare From**. Choose the location in which the catalog file is stored. Choose OK.

4. If you want to compare only a few files, choose **Select Files**. Select the directories and files to restore. When you have marked all files to be restored, select OK.

5. Choose Start Compare.

6. Insert the disk with the backup catalog file when prompted, then choose Continue.

7. If Compare finds a file that doesn't match, it displays an alert. Choose Continue to have Compare update the backup file to match the file that's on your hard disk, then resume checking files.

8. When the procedure's finished, you'll see the Compare Complete screen, which tells you how many files were compared or skipped, how many files didn't match, and how many errors were found and corrected. Choose OK to return to the main Backup menu.

The Basic Restore

The Restore operation enables you to retrieve any or all of the files you back up.

> **NOTE:** Most people never experience the kind of hard disk disaster that requires restoration of all backed up files. A more likely scenario is that you will accidentally overwrite an important file with a newer version, then discover that you need information from the older file. With Restore, you can easily retrieve that one important file.

The following quick steps give you an overview of the Restore operation. Each step is explained in greater detail in the sections that follow.

Using the Norton Backup 251

Running the Basic Level Restore *QUICK STEPS*

1. Select **Restore** from the main menu.

   The Norton Basic Restore screen appears, as shown in Figure 12.12.

2. Select the drive to Restor**e** From. The default is the floppy disk drive to which you copied your files during your last backup.

3. Select **Catalog** from the Norton Basic Restore screen.

   The Catalog screen appears.

4. Select the catalog name that matches the backup you want to restore. Select any other catalog options, and then select **Load**.

   The Norton Basic Restore screen returns (Figure 12.12).

5. Select **Options** to check or change the Basic Restore options.

   The Basic Restore Options screen appears, with a check box beside each option.

6. Turn options on or off, then select **OK**.

   The Norton Basic Restore screen returns.

7. Select the **Select Files** box.

   The Select Restore Files screen appears.

   continues

continued

8. Select the directories and files to restore. Select **D**isplay to check or change file display options, then choose OK. Select **V**ersion to display multiple versions of a file if you have selected a master catalog to restore. When you have marked all files to be restored, select OK.	The Norton Basic Restore screen returns, showing the total number of files selected for the Restore operation.
9. Select **S**tart Restore.	The Alert window appears. A prompt indicates which backup diskette to insert.
10. Insert the diskette(s) when prompted and press ⏎Enter.	The program automatically restores your selected backup files and prompts you both when you should insert other diskettes and when the restore process is complete.
11. Select OK.	The program returns you either to the main menu or to the DOS prompt, depending on the setup option you chose.

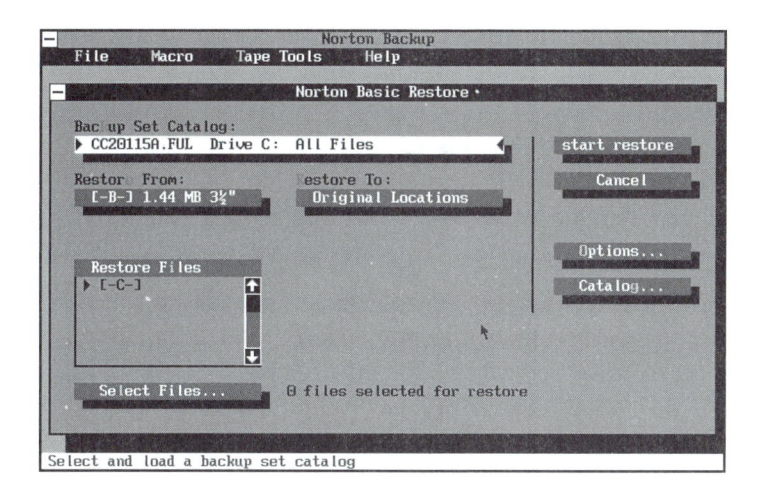

Using the Norton Backup 253

Figure 12.12
The Norton Basic Restore screen assumes that you want to restore files to the drive from which they were backed up.

Selecting the Drives to Restore to and From

You do not have to choose a drive to **R**estore To; the program knows which drive you last backed up from and automatically restores to that drive. (If you want to restore to a different drive than the one you backed up from, you must perform an Advanced restore.)

Likewise, the program sets the Restor**e** From drive as the drive to which you last backed up. You can change the Restore From drive if, for example, you wish to restore an earlier backup that was made on a different drive than your most recent backup. Select Restor**e** From on the Basic Restore screen. This gives you a list of all drives on your system. Select the desired drive, then select OK.

What Is a Catalog?

A catalog is a list of the files that are included in a particular backup, with information about each file's location on the backup diskette(s). The information contained in a backup catalog is critical to the successful restoration of backed up files. For this reason, a catalog file is created automatically during each backup and is stored in two locations: on the hard disk (in the directory containing the Norton Backup) and on the last backup diskette. Thus, if your hard disk is ever erased completely, the backup catalog can still be retrieved from the backup diskettes themselves.

There are two types of catalogs: the *individual catalog* for a particular backup and a *master catalog*. As a rule, you use an individual catalog to restore backup files.

Catalogs for individual backups each have distinctive names, but the names follow a format. Once you learn to read this format, you can tell much about a backup from its catalog name alone. Table 11.1 shows the elements in the sample catalog name CC10315A.INC.

Table 11.1
Elements in the Sample Catalog Name CC10315A.INC

Element	Description
C	First drive backed up.
C	Last drive backed up.
1	Last digit of backup year.
03	Backup month.
15	Backup day.
A	Sequence of backup (A-Z). Indicates first backup of day, B would indicate second backup of day, and so on.
INC	Type of backup (.FUL = Full; .INC = Incremental; .DIF = Differential; .CPY = Full or Incremental Copy).

The second type of catalog, the master catalog, contains all of the catalogs created with the same setup file since the last full backup. A master catalog name is the same as the name of the setup file used to create it, but it has a .CAT extension. So if you use the DEFAULT.SET setup file when you back up, the master catalog created has the name DEFAULT.CAT. If you perform many backups using the same file, the master catalog lets you see all of the individual catalogs for the different backups (and view the files they contain) to determine which catalog you need to use.

Selecting Catalog Files

When you choose the Restore operation, the program checks its own directory for catalog files and selects the most recently created catalog. You can choose a different catalog file by selecting **Catalog** from the Basic Restore screen. This brings up the Select Catalog dialog box shown in Figure 12.13.

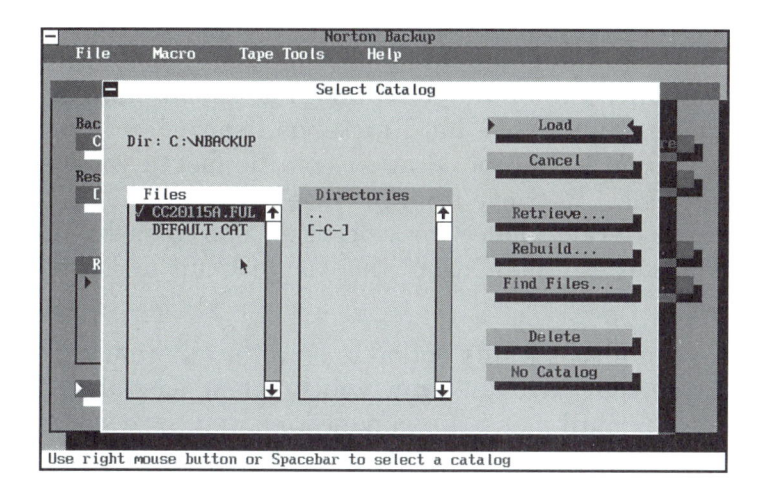

Figure 12.13
The Select Catalog dialog box includes several options.

On the right side of the screen is a list of available **D**irectories. On the left side of the screen is a list of catalogs available in the current directory, shown at the top of the dialog box. Select a different drive or catalog by highlighting your choice and pressing ↵Enter (or click on your choice with the right mouse button).

The screen also makes available several options. Two of them—**R**etrieve and Re**b**uild—are explained in the next section. **L**oad does what its name implies: loads the selected catalog and returns you to the Norton Basic Restore screen. If you change the catalog selection, you must load it before you can proceed with the Restore operation.

Find Files lets you look for certain files in a catalog. Just choose this option, type a file name (with or without wild cards), and choose OK. The **D**elete option deletes the highlighted catalog file. Use this choice to purge old catalogs. When you choose

No Catalog, you must return to the Basic Restore screen and choose Select Files. The Include/Exclude dialog box appears. Choose Edit and specify files to Include or Exclude by clicking on the appropriate button and by specifying a Drive, Path, and File.

Retrieving and Rebuilding a Catalog

If the program does not find the catalog file on your hard drive (if, for example, your entire hard disk has been erased), you can retrieve it from its second location—on the last of your backup diskettes. Select Retrieve from the Select Catalog dialog box. In the Retrieve Catalog dialog box, select the floppy disk drive for the backup diskettes, then insert the last backup diskette when prompted.

You can also use this option to select a different drive and directory on your hard disk from which to load a catalog. This is useful if your hard disk is undamaged but you have stored your catalog files in a separate directory.

If disaster has truly struck (your hard disk has been erased and the last backup diskette has been damaged), all is not lost. As long as some of your backup diskettes are readable, the program can rebuild at least a partial catalog file from special files that are stored on each backup diskette. Select Rebuild from the Select Catalog dialog box. On the Rebuild Catalog dialog box, select the floppy disk drive for your backup diskettes and insert the backup diskettes when prompted.

If your last backup was to your hard disk and the hard disk itself is undamaged but the catalog file is gone, specify the drive and path containing the backup files on the Rebuild Catalog dialog box.

When a catalog has been retrieved or rebuilt, remember to select it before you return to the Basic Restore screen.

Selecting Restore Options

When you select **O**ptions on the Norton Basic Restore screen, the Disk Restore Options dialog box appears, as shown in Figure 12.14. Following are the options you can select.

- **V**erify Restore Data (Read and Compare) verifies that the data restored to your hard disk matches the data on the backup diskettes. As in the backup operation, verification slows down the restore process somewhat.

- Perform an **U**nattended Restore will let The Norton Backup supply automatic answers to prompts and proceed with the restore if you don't have time to go through the process.

- Retry Busy **N**etwork Files should be left off so that The Norton Backup will skip locked files on a network during a restore.

- **G**enerate a Restore Report creates a report of the details of the backup, including backup date and time, the setup and catalog file names, options settings, files processed, and more. Use the **File Print** command to output a hard copy of your report.

- Prompt Before Creating **D**irectories informs you during the restore operation if the drive to which you are restoring does not contain a directory that you've selected to restore. You may then choose to Create Directory or Skip Directory.

- Prompt Before **C**reating Files similarly informs you if the drive to which you are restoring does not contain a file that you've selected to restore. You can choose whether you want to Restore the file anyway, Skip that file, or Cancel Restore.

- Prompt Before Overwriting **E**xisting Files warns you when an existing file on your hard disk is about to be overwritten (erased) by a file that you've selected to restore. You can choose from Overwrite, Do Not Restore (keep the existing file), or Cancel Restore.

- **R**estore Empty Directories lets you restore directories that contain no files—for example, a \TEMP directory that is used for temporary files.

- **A**udible Prompts (Beep) accompanies each prompt during restore with a beep.

- **Q**uit After Restore returns you to the DOS prompt, rather than to the Norton Backup main menu, when the restore is complete.

Figure 12.14

The Disk Restore Options dialog box lets you customize the way Norton Basic Restore operates.

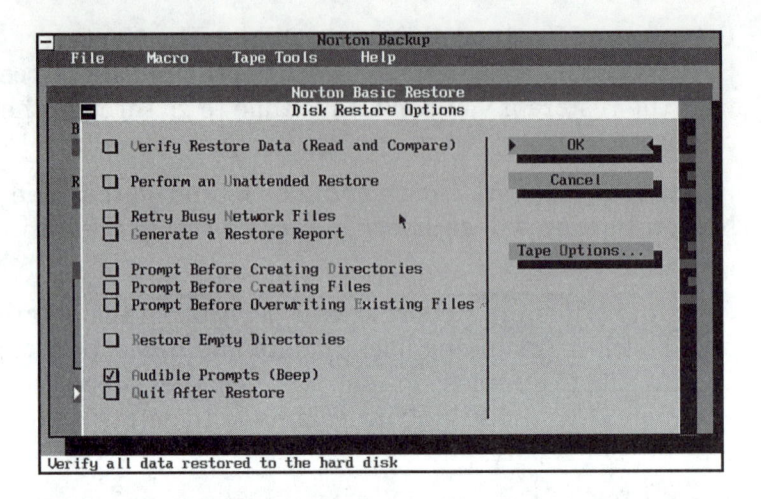

Selecting Files to Restore

You can select all files that have been backed up in the current drive by right clicking on the drive (or by pressing Spacebar) in the Restore Files list. You must do this after making any catalog selections, because exiting the Select Catalog dialog box erases any file selections.

> **CAUTION** If you select ALL files to restore, you run a greater risk of overwriting a newer version of a file with an older version. Unless you are restoring all files to a completely erased hard disk, it is better to take the time to select the files you want to restore.

Using the Norton Backup 259

If you do not want to restore all files, the Select Files option takes you to the Select Restore Files screen, shown in Figure 12.15. This is nearly identical to the Select Backup Files screen, except for the Version option at the bottom of the screen. This option works the same on the Select Restore Files screen as it does on the View Catalog screen.

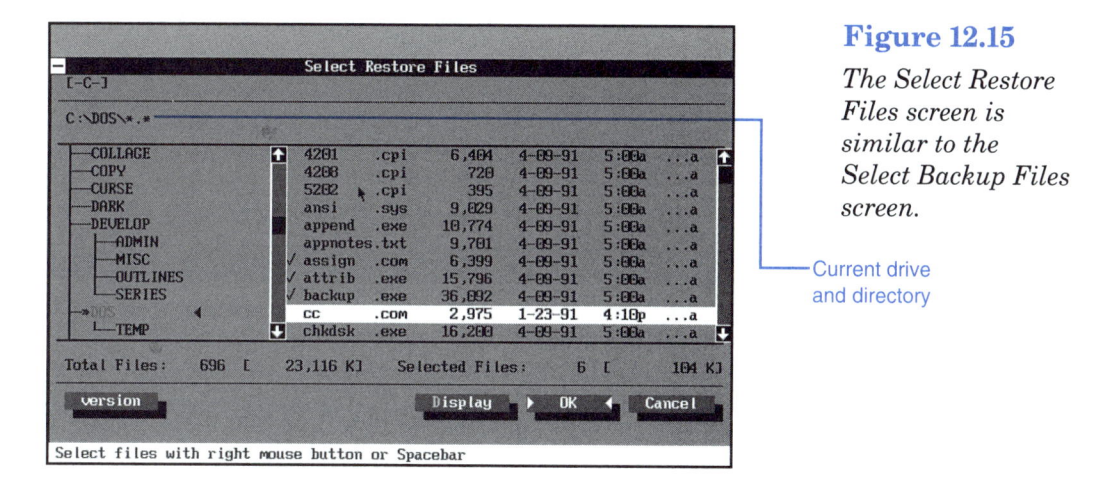

Figure 12.15

The Select Restore Files screen is similar to the Select Backup Files screen.

The directories and files shown on the screen are those listed in the selected backup catalog file. You select directories and files to be restored from this list exactly as you selected directories and files to be backed up. Highlight a file with the arrow keys or by clicking on it, then press (Spacebar). The **D**isplay option also works the same as on the Select Backup Files screen.

Starting the Basic Restore

After you have selected files to be restored and have returned to the Basic Restore screen, you start the restore operation by selecting the **S**tart Restore box. This box is not available until you load a catalog file and select files to restore.

After you start the restore operation, a message prompts you to insert a numbered backup diskette (if you backed up to a floppy disk drive). After inserting the disk, select Continue, and the progress screen shown in Figure 12.16 appears.

Figure 12.16
The basic restore progress screen provides prompts and statistical information about the restore.

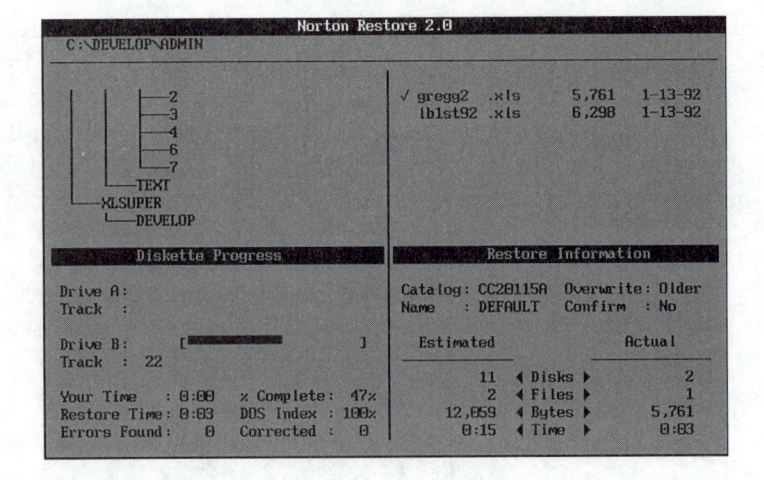

During the restore process, screen prompts let you know when to insert diskettes and when you need to make restore decisions (based on the restore options you set). Files change color as they are restored, and a moving bar in the lower left window of the screen tracks the progress of the restore operation. A prompt informs you when the restore is complete. Select OK at the prompt to return to the Norton Backup main menu or the DOS prompt (depending on whether you selected the **Q**uit After Restore option).

Using Macros with the Norton Backup

A macro is a mini-program that automates a process. The Norton Backup allows you to create such a program by recording the keystrokes you use to complete a process. Then when you run the macro (with a keystroke or two), it "replays" all of the keystrokes you recorded. The result is a significant savings in time.

Macros are stored in *setup files*. When you save a setup file, it saves not only the macro you've created, but the options you've specified for backing up and restoring.

Loading a Setup File

If you want to use an existing setup file as a starting point to create a file holding your macros, load the existing file, make your changes, then save it under a different name. The file you used as a starting point will still exist under its original name.

To load the setup file where you will store the macro, choose **File Open Setup**. With the arrow keys or the mouse, highlight the file you want to open in the **F**iles list, press [Spacebar] to select it, and press [Enter]. Return to the main menu. All macros must start from here.

> **TIP:** You can load a setup file from the Norton Basic Backup or Norton Basic Restore screens. Choose **Setup File**. From the list of existing setup files on the Setup File dialog box, select the file you want to change. Then select **O**pen. You return to the Backup or Restore screen, with the settings contained in that file displayed.

Recording a Backup Macro

Before you record a macro, it is a good idea to map out the process that you want to automate, keystroke by keystroke (you cannot use a mouse when recording a macro). Note that special keystrokes must be substituted for keystrokes that make certain types of selections. This prevents you from actually running a backup or restore operation when all you want to do is set up a macro to run a backup or restore. These special keystrokes and other keys used in macros are listed in Table 11.2.

Table 11.2
Macro Keystrokes

Keystroke	Description
[Ctrl]+[Enter]	Use instead of Enter when you don't want the recorded keystroke to activate a process during recording.

continues

Table 11.2
Continued

Keystroke	Description
[Ins]	Use instead of Spacebar to turn an option on when recording.
[Del]	Use instead of Spacebar to turn an option off when recording.
[F7]	Start\stop recording a macro.
[Alt]+[F7]	Pause during recording (inserts a pause to allow input when the macro is replayed).
[F8]	Replay a macro.

Follow these quick steps to record the macro.

QUICK STEPS — Recording a Backup Macro

1. Press [F7] or choose **Macro Record**.

   The word Recording appears in the lower right corner of the screen.

2. Perform the keystrokes needed to complete the process you want to automate. (Refer to Table 11.2 for substitute keystrokes for Enter and Spacebar.)

   You see the action resulting from each keystroke, as if you were actually completing the process, unless you use substitute keys.

3. Press [Alt]+[F7] to insert a pause in the macro, whenever you want the user to make a menu selection or enter information. Follow the message that appears at the bottom of the screen to continue recording. Select OK from the menu or press [F7] to resume recording.

   The word Waiting replaces Recording during the pause.

4. When you are finished recording, press `F7`.	The macro is saved automatically in the setup file currently loaded.
5. Choose **F**ile **S**ave Setup **A**s.	The Save Setup File dialog box appears.
6. Enter a file name.	
7. Choose **S**ave.	The new setup file is saved under the name you specified.

Playing a Macro

When you want to replay a macro, first load the setup file containing it, then press `F8`. The message Working appears in the lower left corner of the screen, unless the macro is pausing for input. Then the message is Waiting. Even though the Working message is visible, you cannot use either the keyboard or mouse because the macro is in control of the program.

Installing a Setup File for Others

If you want to share a setup file with other less experienced users, you can transfer it to the other person's NBACKUP directory using a floppy diskette. You must transfer two files for the setup file to work: the file you created with the .SET file name extension and another file that the program creates automatically with the same file name and an .SLT extension. Use the DOS COPY command to copy both files onto a floppy diskette.
Say you want to transfer setup file C-BACK, which is stored on your hard disk in C:\NBACKUP, to another user's \NBACKUP directory on the D: drive. Your floppy

continues

continued

disk drive is A:. First, make sure you are on the C: drive, then use the following commands to copy the files to a blank floppy diskette inserted in drive A:

```
copy \nbackup\c-back.set a:
copy \nbackup\c-back.slt a:
```

Insert the diskette containing the copied files into the other user's floppy disk drive and type

copy a:*.* d:\nbackup

This copies both files on A: to D: in the \NBACKUP directory.

In This Chapter

Understanding viruses

Introducing The Norton AntiVirus

Installing The Norton AntiVirus

Intercepting viruses

Scanning for and removing viruses

To start Virus Clinic, type NAV at the prompt and press [↵Enter]. In Windows, open The Norton AntiVirus program group window, then double-click The Norton AntiVirus program-item icon.

Scanning a Drive

1. If you just started Virus Clinic, skip to step 3. Otherwise, select the **Scan** menu.
2. Select **Drive**.
3. In the Scan Drive dialog box, highlight the name of the drive you want to scan in the **D**rives list.
4. Press [Alt]+[O] or click on **OK**.

Scanning a File

1. Select the **Scan** menu.
2. Select **File**.
3. In the **F**ile text box, type the full drive, directory, and file name to specify the file you want to scan.
4. Select the **OK** button.

If the scan finds viruses, you should:

1. Exit Virus Clinic and back up your system.
2. Rerun the scan.
3. Repair or delete the infected files by selecting the **Repair** button or the **Delete** button.
4. Select **Scan** to double check your system.
5. If your system is now clean, select **Exit**.

Chapter 13

Protecting Your System with The Norton AntiVirus

Chapter 7's explanation of Norton's DISKMON utility gave you a brief glimpse of computer viruses and how you can monitor your hard disk for unauthorized activity. This chapter examines a new method of protecting your system—The Norton AntiVirus.

What Are Viruses?

A *virus* is software that enters your system by attaching itself to another file. The virus will attach to the boot sectors of a hard or floppy disk, to any program on your disk, or to a system file (such as COMMAND.COM). You can get viruses from floppy disks or in files you download to your system with a modem.

Once the virus is on your system, it copies itself over and over until it is triggered to do what it's programmed to do. Often, a certain date or time or starting a certain program will trigger a virus. Once triggered, a virus may destroy data or prevent a particular program from operating correctly. Or a virus may simply display a message. But beware! Even seemingly harmless viruses can cause system crashes.

Hundreds of viruses now have been identified. Once a virus is discovered, programmers can analyze it for "signature" characteristics that can be identified on disk. Virus identification programs like The Norton AntiVirus can scan your disks for the signatures of known viruses. (Norton calls the virus signatures *virus definitions*.)

Introducing The Norton AntiVirus

The Norton AntiVirus program offers two forms of protection against viruses. The *Virus Intercept* component of The Norton AntiVirus checks any file you run or copy for viruses, and alerts you when it detects a virus. The *Virus Clinic* component of The Norton AntiVirus lets you scan a disk for viruses and repair or delete infected files. You can customize how both Virus Clinic and Virus Intercept operate to best meet your needs. In addition, Virus Clinic offers the security of password protection so unauthorized users can't alter how it's configured.

To run The Norton AntiVirus, you must have an IBM PC or compatible system with a hard drive and 448K of RAM. You can use the Install program to set up AntiVirus to run from your hard disk (described next).

> **TIP:** Before you install The Norton AntiVirus, check the READ.ME file on the program disk for specific information about how to use The Norton AntiVirus with your system.

Hard Disk Installation

Installing The Norton AntiVirus on your hard disk system is basically a two-step procedure. First, you should create a backup copy of The Norton AntiVirus disks. Then you can run the Install program.

Running Install

The Install program on The Norton AntiVirus Program Disk streamlines the hard disk installation procedure. First, it scans your system to ensure that it's virus free. It copies the program files to the specified drive and directory and modifies (or creates) your CONFIG.SYS file so Virus Intercept will automatically load when you start your system. The Install procedure also creates a Rescue Disk to store vital information about your system—copies of its File Allocation Table, and CMOS values. Use the following steps to run the Install program.

1. Put your copy of the Program Disk into drive A: or B:. Type **A:** or **B:** and press Enter to move to the prompt.

2. Type **INSTALL** and press Enter.

3. A box appears warning you not to install The Norton AntiVirus if you suspect your system has viruses. If you do, click **R**eturn to DOS or press Alt+R. Then reboot from a floppy diskette that has system files and restart the Install process. Otherwise, press Enter to continue.

> **TIP:** To create a disk with your system files, place a disk in drive A: or B:. Then type **FORMAT A:/S** or **FORMAT B:/S** and press Enter.

4. An explanation screen about the Install program appears. Click on **C**ontinue or press Enter. Install scans your system for viruses, then displays a dialog box asking you to personalize your copy of The Norton AntiVirus.

5. At the screen that appears, type your **N**ame. Press ⏎Enter. Type the name of Your **C**ompany. Press ⏎Enter twice or click **OK**.

6. At the next screen, press ⏎Enter to choose the **F**ull Install.

7. The Install screen prompts you to specify a drive and PATH (directory) on your hard disk for The Norton AntiVirus files. (It suggests a directory named \NAV.) Choose **C**ontinue to accept Norton's suggestion, or type a new drive and directory and then choose **C**ontinue.

8. Install creates the specified directory and tells you as it copies program files to the hard disk. When prompted, insert subsequent program disks and press ⏎Enter.

9. The Save Rescue Data box appears. Remove any program disks from the drive you're installing from. Choose **OK**. Use the arrow keys or click to highlight the appropriate drive letter. Choose **OK**. Place a blank formatted diskette in the drive you specified. Choose **OK**. When the procedure is completed, choose **OK** again and store your rescue data in a safe place.

10. Install displays its next screen. Press Alt+O or click **OK** to have Install automatically make changes to your startup files, CONFIG.SYS or AUTOEXEC.BAT.

11. Press Alt+S or click **S**ave Changes to continue. Press ⏎Enter twice or click **OK** twice.

12. The final screen appears (Figure 13.1). Choose **R**eboot from the final screen to restart your computer so that Virus Intercept will be active. Install reminds you to remove The Norton AntiVirus Program Disk from a drive. Do so and choose **OK**.

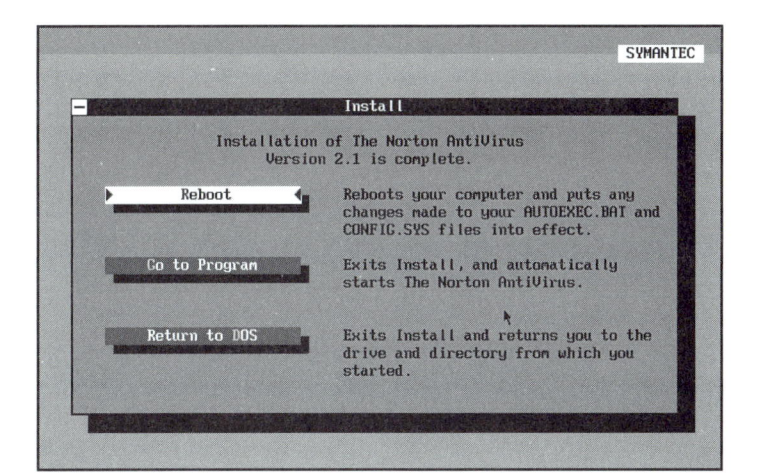

Protecting Your System with The Norton AntiVirus   271

Figure 13.1
After you install the Norton AntiVirus, you should choose Reboot.

TIP: If you want to start your system without loading Virus Intercept, hold down both ⇧Shift keys while the system boots.

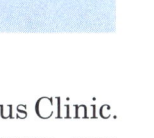

Now Virus Intercept is loaded, and you can run Virus Clinic. But before you start to use The Norton AntiVirus program, you probably will want to customize the program. To do so, see the section "Configuring The Norton AntiVirus" later in this chapter.

Running The Norton AntiVirus with Windows

If you choose, you can run The Norton AntiVirus program from Microsoft Windows version 3.0 or 3.1. The Norton AntiVirus Install program:

- Copies the files you'll need to work with Windows to the same directory as the rest of the AntiVirus program files.

- Sets up a Norton AntiVirus program group window and program-item icons.

- Installs help files you can use with Windows and sets up Norton AntiVirus Intercept to work with Windows.

All you have to do is start Windows, and you'll see the new program group, as shown in Figure 13.2.

Figure 13.2
The Norton AntiVirus program group window and program-item icon in Windows.

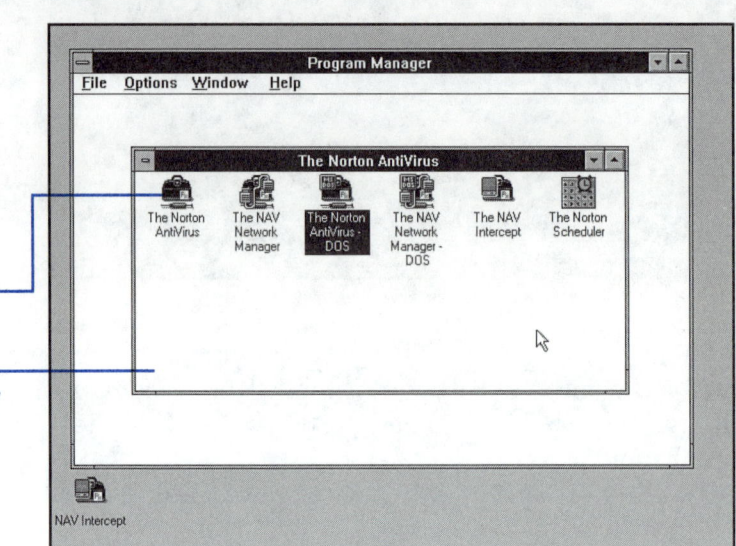

To run The Norton AntiVirus from Windows, simply move to the window containing The Norton AntiVirus icon and double-click on the icon. To get help when running The Norton AntiVirus in Windows, move to the screen you want and press F1. For Norton AntiVirus Intercept help, double-click on one of the Intercept icons, then press F1.

Running Virus Intercept

The installation procedure sets up Virus Intercept to run each time you start your system. It stays in your computer's memory and constantly checks for signs of viruses as you work. Because Virus Intercept stays in memory, it is known as a TSR program.

When you start your system, Norton loads Virus Intercept, scans your system, and displays the results, as shown in Figure 13.3.

```
The Norton AntiVirus, 2.1,
Copyright 1989-1992 by Symantec Corporation

Scanning memory...
No viruses were detected.
Begin scan on directory "C:"...
Scanning

End of scan.
Scan Summary (Scan Executables Only)
   Items Processed:   26
   Items Scanned:      6
   Items Infected:     0
C:\>
```

Figure 13.3
Virus Intercept loads when you start your system.

Virus Intercept checks for known viruses each time you run a program file or copy a file of any type. When it detects a virus, it sounds a siren-like alert and flashes an alert box that shows the full path and name of the infected file and the type of virus. At this point, you should select the Stop button to cancel running the program or copying the file. Because Virus Intercept detects only the first virus it encounters, you need to stop and scan your entire drive with Virus Clinic, as described later in this chapter.

You can customize some of the basic Virus Intercept options through Virus Clinic. You can enable or disable the alert siren sound and the alert boxes. You can have Virus Intercept remove the alert box by specifying the number of seconds the box should appear on-screen. By default, Virus Intercept keeps an *audit trail* file that records all your responses to alert messages. You can turn the audit trail off or assign a new name to the audit trail file. And you can enter a customized message for the alert box. See the section "Configuring The Norton AntiVirus" later in this chapter to learn how to choose configuration options.

TIP: Your audit trail file may become quite large. From time to time, print out the audit trail file or copy it to another disk and rename the working version. Then you won't have to examine as much material if you need to look at the audit trail file. Unless you rename it, your audit file is named AUDIT.LOG, and Norton AntiVirus places it in the root directory of drive C (C:\).

Running Virus Clinic

As described earlier, Virus Clinic enables you to scan your disks for viruses, repair infected files, add new virus definitions, and configure The Norton AntiVirus program, including Virus Intercept.

To start Virus Clinic, type **NAV** at the prompt, and press Enter. (You'll have to change to the drive and directory containing The Norton AntiVirus program before typing the startup command if you did not add The Norton AntiVirus to your AUTOEXEC.BAT PATH statement.) Or you can double-click on the Norton AntiVirus icon in the Norton AntiVirus program group if you want to start Virus Clinic from Windows. In any case, the main Virus Clinic screen appears with the Scan Drives dialog box on top, as shown in Figures 13.4 and 13.5. You can press Esc to close the dialog box now or press Enter to scan the drive highlighted in the drives box.

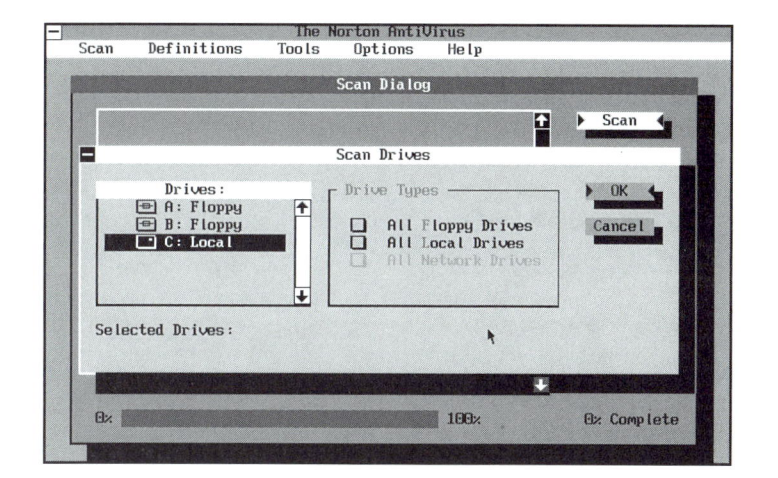

Protecting Your System with The Norton AntiVirus 275

Figure 13.4
The main Virus Clinic screen, with the Scan Drives dialog box on top.

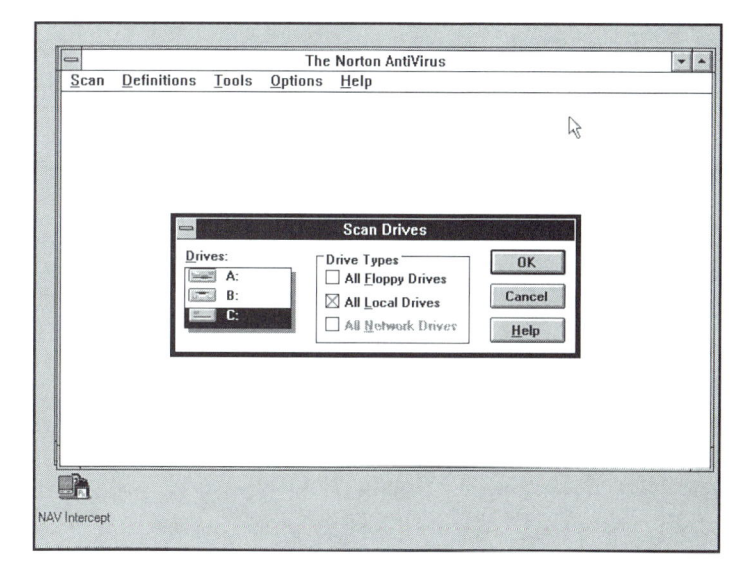

Figure 13.5
The main Virus Clinic screen in Windows.

Moving Around

Getting around in the Virus Clinic environment is easy. To select a pull-down menu from the menu bar, press **Alt** plus the highlighted letter in the menu name. Figure 13.6 shows the **S**can pull-down menu. When the menu is visible, select a command by pressing the highlighted letter in the command name. You also can select a menu command by clicking on the menu name and then clicking on the command you want.

Figure 13.6
Choose commands from pull-down menus in Virus Clinic.

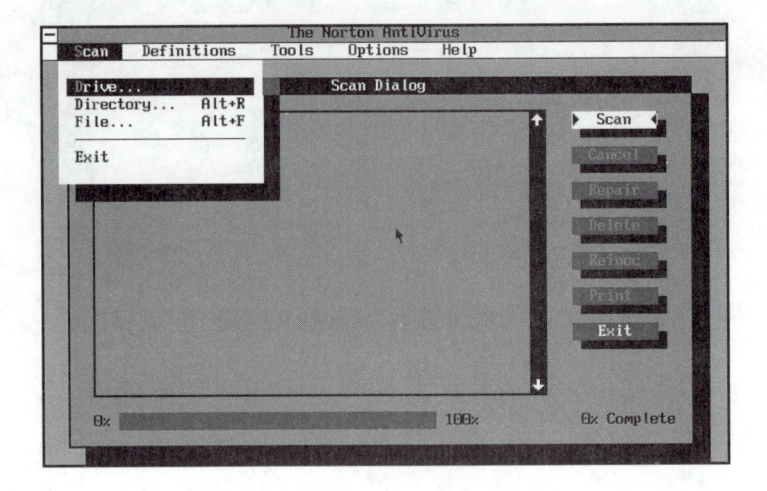

The Norton AntiVirus also has dialog boxes with check boxes, text boxes, lists, pull-down lists, and command buttons.

For lists, pull-down lists, and check boxes, you can press Alt plus the highlighted letter in the option name or click on the option, then perform a second step to finish your selection.

For check boxes and command buttons, you can select an option by pressing Alt plus the highlighted letter in its name or by clicking on it with the mouse.

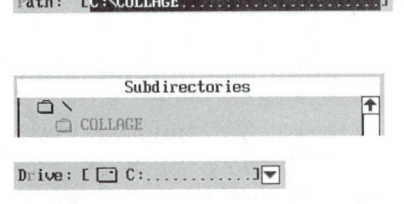

Move to a text box, and type your entry.

In a list, click or use the arrow keys to highlight your choice.

Move to a pull-down list and press Alt+↓ or click the down arrow beside the list to pull it down. Click on your choice or highlight it with the arrow keys and press Enter.

> **TIP:** Press [Esc] at any time to close a menu or dialog box.

Configuring The Norton AntiVirus

Figures 13.7 and 13.8 show the Clinic Options and Intercept Options dialog boxes. Use these dialog boxes to customize how both Virus Intercept and Virus Clinic operate. When you've specified all the options you want, select OK to save the configuration options you requested.

You access this box from the main AntiVirus screen by opening the **O**ptions menu and selecting **C**linic or **I**ntercept. Use the techniques for working with dialog boxes described in the previous section to select the options you want. Tables 13.1 and 13.2 describe the options in the dialog boxes that let you configure Virus Clinic and Virus Intercept.

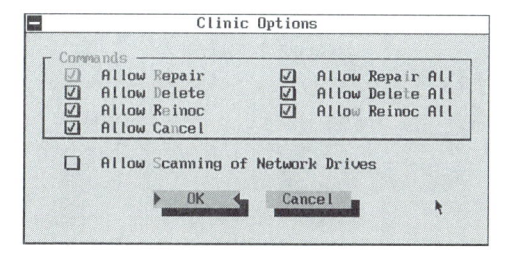

Figure 13.7
The options for Virus Clinic.

Figure 13.8
The options for Virus Intercept.

Table 13.1
Clinic Options

Option	Effect When Selected
Allow **R**epair	Turns on the option to repair infected files at the Scan Results screen.
Allow **D**elete	Turns on the option to delete infected files at the Scan Results screen.
Allow R**e**inoc	Turns on the Reinoculate option at the Scan Results screen.
Allow **C**ancel	Lets the user cancel the scan.
Allow Repa**i**r All	Turns on the option to repair all infected files at the Scan Results screen.
Allow Dele**t**e All	Turns on the option to delete all infected files at the Scan Results screen.
Allo**w** Reinoc All	Turns on the option to reinoculate all infected files at the Scan Results screen.
Allow **S**canning of Network Drives	Lets users scan the network drives.

Table 13.2
Intercept Options

Option	Effect When Selected
Enable Beep **A**lert	Sounds an alert beep when Virus Intercept detects a virus.
Enable **P**opup Alert	Turns on the Virus Intercept alert box.
Seconds to Display Alert Box [ ]	Enables you to enter a time, in seconds, that the Virus Intercept alert box will remain on-screen.
Enable **L**og to File	Makes Virus Intercept create and keep an audit trail file that records your responses to alert boxes.
File**n**ame	Enables you to enter a new PATH and file name for the audit trail file.
Write-Protect **H**ard Disk System Areas	Keeps virus files from changing data in the Hard Disk system area.
Write-Protect **F**loppy Disk System Areas	Keeps virus files from changing data on the floppy disk system area.
Scan All Floppies on **R**eboot	Scans disks in both floppy drives if you warm boot (press Ctrl+Alt+Delete); when off, only drive A: is scanned.

Protecting Your System with The Norton AntiVirus

Option	Effect When Selected
Allow Proceed	Turns on the Proceed command button which lets you continue accessing a file after a virus is intercepted.
Allow Reinoculate	Lets you choose to have Norton capture new file inoculation data.

Choose the **Options Global** command to specify whether The Norton AntiVirus should **D**etect Unknown Viruses, **A**uto-Inoculate (without your okay), or **S**can Executables Only (that is, scan only program files such as .COM, .EXE, .BAT, and .OVL files). Also use the Global Options dialog box to enter a **N**etwork Inoculation Directory or a **V**irus Alert Custom Message.

You can password-protect your configuration settings so they can't be changed by unauthorized users. Preventing unauthorized configuration changes is particularly useful if you're using Norton AntiVirus on a network.

To assign a password to your configuration settings, pull down the **O**ptions menu and select **Set Password**. Enter a password of up to 16 characters in the **N**ew Password field and press `Enter`, then retype the password in the Con**f**irm New Password field and press `Enter`.

To change the password later, type the old password and the new password, pressing `Enter` after each. Confirm the password, then press `Enter` again to activate the new password. To specify no new password, simply press `Enter` at the new password and verification fields.

Use the **Options Video and Mouse Options** command to choose new settings for these hardware options. (These options are similar to those for The Norton Backup. See Chapter 12 for more details about Video and Mouse settings.)

Scanning

You can scan your hard or floppy drives any time you think you need to check for viruses. If you've already started The Norton AntiVirus, begin by pulling down the **S**can menu. It offers you the choice to scan by **D**rive, Di**r**ectory, or **F**ile. At the end of each type of scan, the Scan Results screen summarizes the findings of the scan. See the section entitled "Working with the Scan Results Screen" to find out how to proceed. The following sets of Quick Steps summarize each of the scan procedures.

Quick Steps: Scanning a Drive

1. Select the **S**can menu. — The Scan pull-down menu appears (see Figure 13.6).

2. Select **D**rive. — The Scan Drives dialog box appears, as shown in Figure 13.4 or 13.5.

3. Use the up and down arrow keys or click with the mouse to highlight the name of the drive you want to scan in the **D**rives list.

4. Press Alt+O or click on **OK**. — Virus Clinic begins the scan and displays the Scan Results screen. When the scan is complete, a summary appears. See Figure 13.9 for an example.

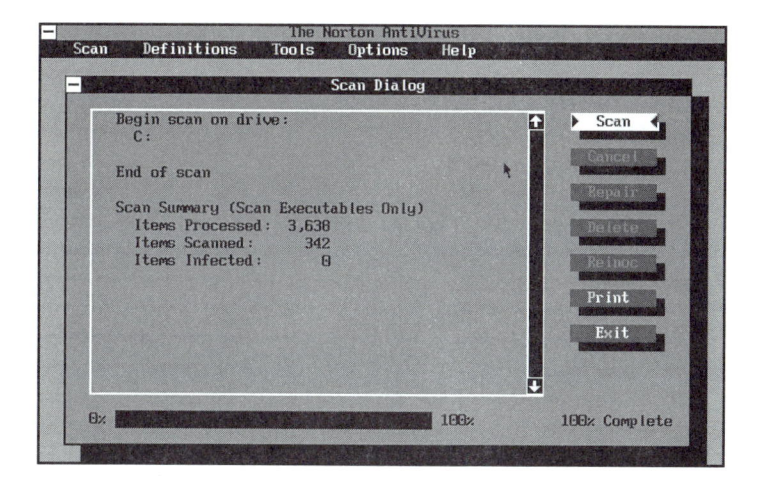

Figure 13.9
The results of scanning a drive.

TIP: In step 3 of the preceding procedure, you can press [Alt]+[F] or click to scan All **F**loppy Drives, or press [Alt]+[L] or click to scan All **L**ocal Drives (hard drives).

Scanning a Directory

QUICK STEPS

1. Select the **S**can menu.

The Scan pull-down menu appears (see Figure 13.6).

2. Select Di**r**ectory.

The Scan Directory dialog box appears, as shown in Figure 13.10.

3. Type the drive and name of the directory you want to scan in the **P**ath text box and press [Enter]. Or use the **D**rive and **S**ubdirectories lists to make your selection.

continues

Chapter 13

continued

4. Press Alt+O, or click on the **OK** button.

Virus Clinic begins the scan and displays the Scan Results screen when the scan is complete.

Figure 13.10
The Scan Directory dialog box.

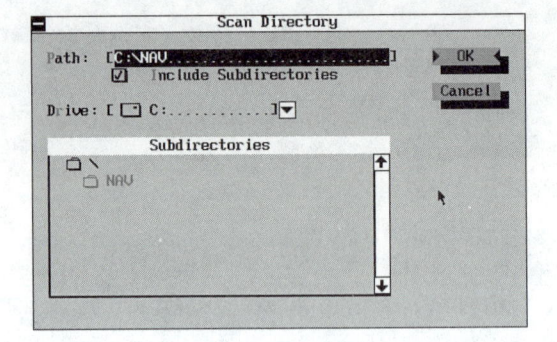

TIP: In step 3 of the preceding procedure, double-clicking the top directory name in the **S**ubdirectories list displays all the subdirectories it contains.

Quick Steps

Scanning a File

1. Select the **S**can menu.

   The Scan pull-down menu appears (see Figure 13.6).

2. Select **F**ile.

   The Scan File dialog box appears, as shown in Figure 13.11.

Protecting Your System with The Norton AntiVirus 283

> 3. Type the full drive, directory, and file name in the **F**ile text box to specify the file you want to scan. Or use the **D**rive, **D**irectories, and **F**iles lists to make your selection.
>
> 4. Select the **OK** button.   Virus Clinic begins the scan and displays the Scan Results screen when the scan is complete.

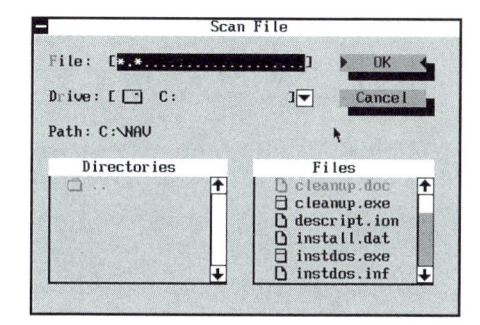

Figure 13.11
The Scan File dialog box.

What to Do with the Scan Results

Whether you scan a drive, directory, or file, you have several options at the Scan Results screen when the scan is complete.

If the scan finds no viruses, you can:

- Select the **Print** button to print the scan results.
- Select the **Exit** button to return to the DOS prompt.

If the scan finds viruses, you should:

1. Exit Virus Clinic and back up your system. Repairing files can damage them, so you'll want up-to-date backup copies of your files, even if infected. (If you can't completely repair the file, you may be able to retrieve the needed data from a backup in another way.)

2. Rerun the scan. Print the scan summary, if you choose.

3. Repair or delete the infected files by selecting the Repair button or the Delete button.

4. Select Scan to double check your system.

5. If your system is now clean, select Exit.

Virus Definitions

As new viruses are identified, you can get the definitions for the viruses and add them to The Norton AntiVirus program so you can scan for the new viruses on your system. Symantec Corporation, the makers of The Norton AntiVirus, will keep registered users informed about new viruses and provide new virus definitions. You can also get new definitions by calling the 24-hour Virus Newsline or through their bulletin board system.

For information about getting and adding virus definitions, see your User's Manual. To see what virus definitions are currently on your system, you can print a list. The following Quick Steps explain how.

Protecting Your System with The Norton AntiVirus   285

Printing the List of Virus Definitions *QUICK STEPS*

1. Pull down the Definitions menu.

2. Select Modify List.   The Modify List dialog box appears, as shown in Figure 13.12.

3. Press Alt + P or click on the Print command button.   The list prints.

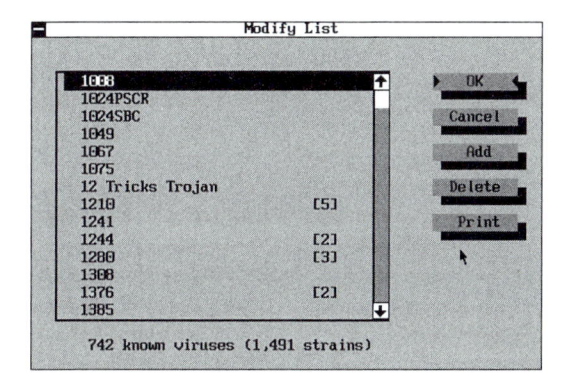

Figure 13.12
The List virus names dialog box.

Leaving the Virus Clinic

After you've completed working with the Virus Clinic, you'll want to leave the program. At the Scan Result screen, press Alt + X or click on Exit. Otherwise, press Esc or double-click the Control menu box at the upper left corner of the Virus Clinic window.

Appendix

Installation and Configuration

The Norton Utilities come with an Installation program that automates the installation process. It decompresses the program files and places them in the disk drive and directory that you specify. During or after the installation procedure, you can use the NUCONFIG program to configure The Norton Utilities to run most effectively with your system.

Using the Emergency Disks

If you accidentally erase files on your hard drive or format your hard drive and you have not yet installed Norton, *do not install The Norton Utilities*. Installing The Norton Utilities could overwrite the data you want to retrieve. You can perform these three rescue operations with the Emergency Disk(s) that came with The Norton Utilities: unformat a hard drive, recover erased files, and diagnose a disk with Norton Disk Doctor.

Appendix A

- To unformat your hard drive, insert Emergency Disk #1 in drive A and reboot your system. At the screen that appears, use the arrow keys to highlight Unformat. Press Enter twice. Highlight the drive you want with the arrow keys and press Enter. Then follow the on-screen prompts.

- If you've accidentally erased files, don't copy or save any files to your disk. Instead, insert Emergency Disk 1 in drive A. Type A:UNERASE and press Enter to activate the UnErase utility. Use the arrow keys to highlight a file to undelete and press U. Type the first letter for the file name.

- When your computer won't start from the hard drive, reboot it with Emergency Disk 1 in drive A. Highlight Norton Disk Doctor and press Enter. Run Norton Disk Doctor by pressing Enter when it appears highlighted on-screen. If your computer does start, insert Emergency Disk #1 (5 1/4") or Emergency Disk #2 (3 1/2") in drive A. Type A:NDD and press Enter. In either case, once Disk Doctor starts, use the arrow keys to highlight the drive. Press Enter and follow the screen prompts.

Installing The Norton Utilities

NOTE: In earlier versions of The Norton Utilities (before version 5.0), you could use DOS's COPY command to place the utilities on your hard disk. Many of the utilities in version 7.0 are in a special compressed format on the distribution disks, so you must use the Install program to decompress them on your hard disk. The Install program also performs several extra useful operations such as creating a directory for The Norton Utilities and tailoring the utilities for your system.

Installation and Configuration

The Install program is very easy to use, because it provides helpful explanations throughout the process. The program displays a series of screens and dialog boxes with many options and command buttons. To select an option or command button, use the arrow keys or [Tab⇆] to highlight the option you want, then press [Spacebar] or [⏎Enter]. You can also click on your choice with the mouse. A typical installation takes about 10 minutes.

During Install, you'll create a Rescue Disk you can use to boot in emergencies. Have a blank disk ready to go when you start Install. To exit the Installation program at any time, point to the icon that looks like a minus sign in the upper left corner of the dialog box, and double-click with the mouse.

Following are the general steps for installing The Norton Utilities on your hard disk.

1. The Norton Utilities distribution diskettes are labeled for identification. Make a backup copy of your distribution disks using DOS's DISKCOPY command, and store the originals in a safe place. Run the Install program from the backup copies.

2. Find the Install Disk #1, insert it in drive A: (or B:), type **A:INSTALL** (or **B:INSTALL**), and press [⏎Enter]. This command starts the Installation program and displays the opening screen, as shown in Figure A.1.

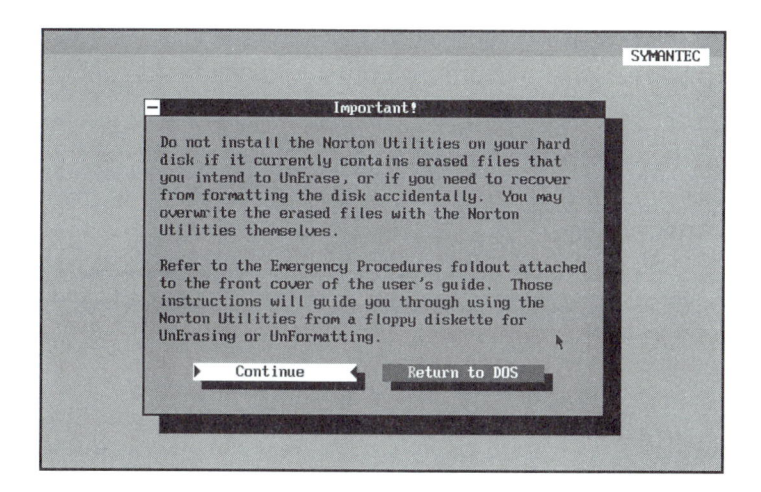

Figure A.1

This is the first screen you'll see when you start the installation program.

3. The Installation program displays an information screen that warns you that installation may overwrite erased files on your hard drive. Choose **Return to DOS** if you want to retrieve erased files. Otherwise, choose **Continue**.

4. Another information screen appears. Read it, then choose **Continue**.

5. Next, you must enter your name at the Install program prompt so you can complete the installation procedure. Type your name, then press `Tab`. Also enter your company name, then press `Enter` or click **OK**.

6. At the next screen, press `F` to choose a **F**ull Install, which copies all the utilities to your hard drive. (Choose **C**ustom Install only if you have limited disk space.)

7. The next screen lets you specify the drive and directory where Install should place the utility files. The program tells you if you have an earlier version on your system and suggests the drive and directory where it's located as the drive and directory for version 7.0. Press `Enter` or click the **Continue** button to accept Norton's suggestion, or type another drive and directory name and press `Enter`.

8. If you do have a previous version of The Norton Utilities on your system, you can choose to **D**elete the files or **S**kip the deletion. Press `D` or `S`, or click the option you want.

9. The Install program begins copying files to your hard drive. Follow the prompts to insert disks as the installation continues. (See Figure A.2.) Press `Enter`.

10. The Installation program next displays a Save System Files screen (see Figure A.3). Choose **Make Changes to Startup Files** to add The Norton Utilities to your system's AUTOEXEC.BAT and CONFIG.SYS files, unless you are experienced enough to understand why you don't want the changes to be made.

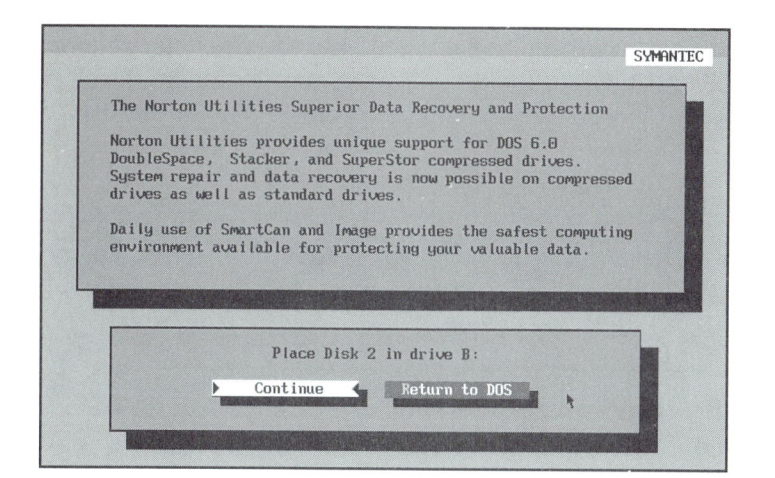

Installation and Configuration

Figure A.2
Install prompts you for other disks.

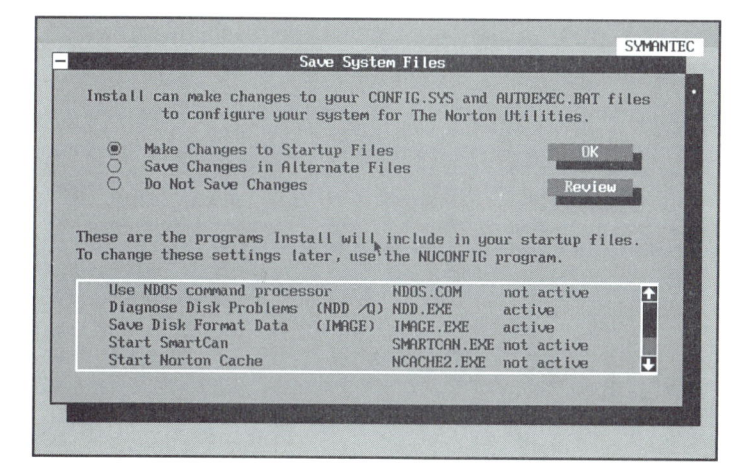

Figure A.3
The Install program asks whether you want to save changes to your system files.

11. If prompted, remove the install disk and press ⏎Enter or click **OK**.

12. A screen appears asking you to create a Rescue Disk. Place a blank disk in the drive (specify another drive to **S**ave Rescue Information To and a Rescue **D**iskette Type if needed). Choose **Create**.

13. When you return to the Install program, you have the option to **R**eboot your system, **G**o to Program, or **R**eturn to DOS. Choose the appropriate option to complete the installation.

> **CAUTION** If you chose Make Changes to Startup Files in step 10, you should choose Reboot your system in step 13 so the changes will take effect.

After you've installed The Norton Utilities, be sure to read the READ.ME file in the utilities directory. The READ.ME file contains important information that doesn't appear in The Norton Utilities documentation. Use DOS's TYPE command to list the READ.ME file and pause for each screenful of information. To do so, enter the following line at the DOS prompt and press ⏎Enter:

```
TYPE READ.ME | MORE
```

If you have a printer connected to your PC, you can use the command COPY READ.ME PRN: to print a copy of READ.ME.

Configuration

You can control many aspects of how The Norton Utilities work with your system. Specifying these options is called *configuring* The Norton Utilities. You can start the Configuration program using one of the following methods:

- At the DOS prompt, type **NUCONFIG** and press ⏎Enter.
- Start the main Norton program by typing **NORTON** and pressing ⏎Enter. Select the NUCONFIG command from the list at the left side of The Norton Utilities Integration (main) screen by highlighting it with the down arrow key then pressing ⏎Enter or by clicking on it with the mouse.

Installation and Configuration 293

When you start the Configuration program, the main Configuration screen appears, as shown in Figure A.4. The screen has buttons with the names of the features you can alter, along with a brief description of each option.

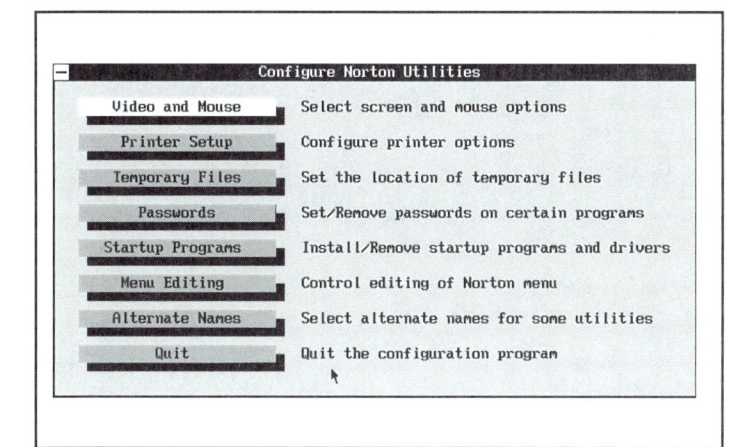

```
┌─ Configure Norton Utilities ──────────────────────┐
│                                                   │
│   Video and Mouse    Select screen and mouse options      │
│   Printer Setup      Configure printer options            │
│   Temporary Files    Set the location of temporary files  │
│   Passwords          Set/Remove passwords on certain programs │
│   Startup Programs   Install/Remove startup programs and drivers │
│   Menu Editing       Control editing of Norton menu       │
│   Alternate Names    Select alternate names for some utilities │
│   Quit               Quit the configuration program       │
│                              ▸                            │
└───────────────────────────────────────────────────┘
```

Figure A.4
The Norton Utilities Configuration screen, with buttons for the aspects of the program you can configure.

TIP: You can choose options quickly at the main Configuration screen by pressing the highlighted letter in the button name.

Choosing an option button displays a dialog box with the choices for the option (for example, Figure A.5). Use the arrow keys or the mouse to move among the *check boxes* and other dialog box choices. Here are some pointers for selecting items:

- Press (Spacebar) or click with the mouse to select a check box.

- Pressing (Alt) plus the highlighted letter moves you to a text box, list, or pull-down list choice.

- Type your entry in a text box or use the arrow keys to highlight choices in a list or pull-down list. You may have to press (Alt)+(↓) to display the list, and you may have to press (Spacebar) to select highlighted items.

- If you prefer, you can make most of your choices by simply clicking with the mouse.

Figure A.5
The Video and Mouse Options dialog box.

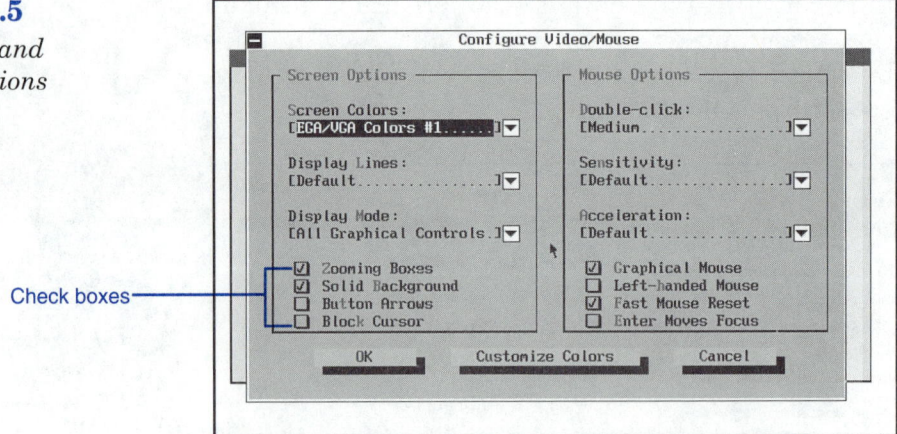

Check boxes

```
┌─────────────────────────────────────────────────┐
│ ─              Configure Video/Mouse            │
│  ┌─ Screen Options ──────┐ ┌─ Mouse Options ──┐ │
│  │ Screen Colors:        │ │ Double-click:    │ │
│  │ [EGA/VGA Colors #1..]▼│ │ [Medium........]▼│ │
│  │                       │ │                  │ │
│  │ Display Lines:        │ │ Sensitivity:     │ │
│  │ [Default...........]▼ │ │ [Default.......]▼│ │
│  │                       │ │                  │ │
│  │ Display Mode:         │ │ Acceleration:    │ │
│  │ [All Graphical Ctrls]▼│ │ [Default.......]▼│ │
│  │                       │ │                  │ │
│  │ ☑ Zooming Boxes       │ │ ☑ Graphical Mouse│ │
│  │ ☑ Solid Background    │ │ ☐ Left-handed Mse│ │
│  │ ☐ Button Arrows       │ │ ☑ Fast Mouse Rset│ │
│  │ ☐ Block Cursor        │ │ ☐ Enter Moves Foc│ │
│  └───────────────────────┘ └──────────────────┘ │
│        OK        Customize Colors     Cancel    │
└─────────────────────────────────────────────────┘
```

Let's take a moment to look at the buttons shown in Figure A.4 and learn what each one does.

The **V**ideo and Mouse button displays the dialog box shown in Figure A.5, which lets you specify screen colors and set graphical, mouse, and screen options.

If you select the **S**creen Colors list, you can choose from several color sets. You also can choose the C**u**stomize Colors button at the bottom of the dialog box to specify the custom colors. Choose a screen area in the box at the left, then select the C**o**lor button to display a Select New Color screen, from which you can choose a color.

You can specify whether to display the Norton screens with standard (text) or graphical characters. The graphical options are only supported if your system has an EGA (Enhanced Graphics Adapter) or VGA (Video Graphics Array) adapter. And you can set the number of **L**ines displayed on-screen.

You can set dialog boxes to zoom when they open, choose a solid screen background, display arrows on command buttons, and display the cursor as a Bloc**k**.

The Mouse options area lets you set the mouse for left-handed use. You can adjust **D**ouble-click speed, Se**n**sitivity, and other mouse options.

Installation and Configuration

Click on the **P**rinter Setup button to display a dialog box that lets you add, select, and delete printers to use with The Norton Utilities.

Use the **T**emporary Files button to specify the location of Windows temporary files.

The **P**asswords button displays the Password Protection screen shown in Figure A.6, which lists the utilities to which you can assign a password. Highlight a utility name, then press (Spacebar) or double-click on the utility name to select it. Select **OK**. Configuration displays the Password box. Enter a password of up to 16 letters and press (↵Enter). Con**f**irm the new password and choose **OK**.

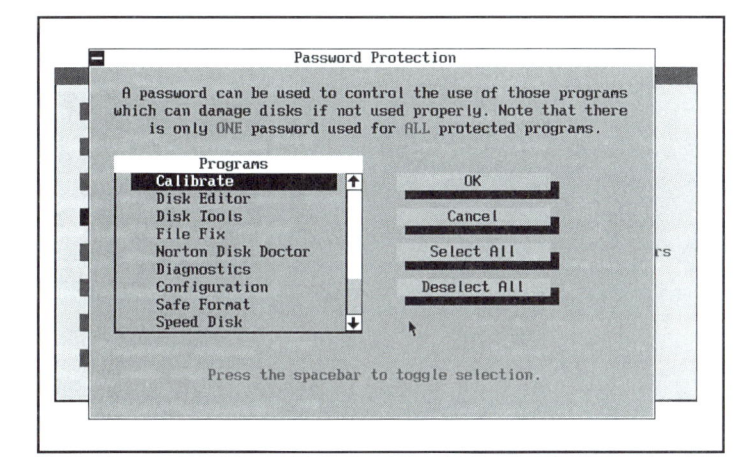

Figure A.6
The Password Protection screen.

TIP: To be able to access a utility without a password again, deselect it at the Password Protection screen and choose **OK**.

Use the **S**tartup Programs button to adjust your DOS startup files, AUTOEXEC.BAT and CONFIG.SYS. If you declined to have the installation program change these files, you can change them from here.

Clicking on the **M**enu Editing button displays a dialog box that lets you enable or disable the ability to add or delete programs from the menu in The Norton Utilities Integration (main screen) program. Click on it or use Spacebar to enable or disable menu editing, then select **OK**.

The **A**lternate Names button displays the screen shown in Figure A.7. You can select abbreviated, two-letter names for several of the utilities. If you do so, you can type the two-letter name (rather than the full name) at the DOS prompt to start the utility. You can also rename the Safe Format (SFORMAT.EXE) program to FORMAT (in place of DOS's FORMAT.EXE, which will be renamed XXFORMAT.EXE). Choose **OK** after you've made your selections. You can also pick the All **S**hort button to give all the Utilities short names.

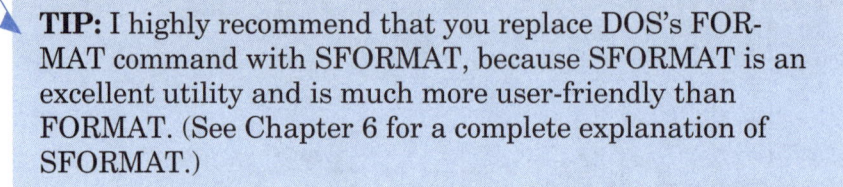

> **TIP:** I highly recommend that you replace DOS's FORMAT command with SFORMAT, because SFORMAT is an excellent utility and is much more user-friendly than FORMAT. (See Chapter 6 for a complete explanation of SFORMAT.)

Figure A.7
The Alternate Program Names dialog box.

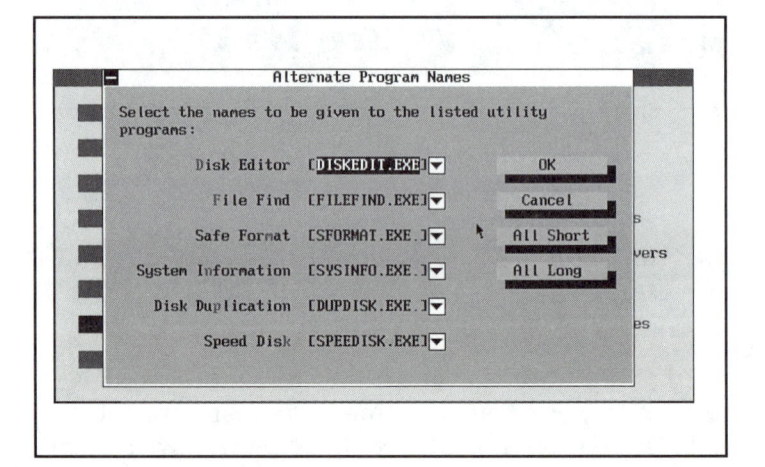

Installation and Configuration   297

The final button on the Configuration screen, **Q**uit, lets you leave the Configuration program and return to the Installation program, the DOS prompt, or The Norton Utilities Integration (main) screen.

After you've installed and configured The Norton Utilities, you're ready to begin using its handy programs.

Setting Up The Norton Utilities to Run with Windows

If you choose, you can run The Norton Utilities from Microsoft Windows version 3.0 or 3.1. Norton's Installation program copies the icon files (with .ICO extensions) for various utilities to the same directory as the rest of Norton's program files. The following Quick Steps describe how to use Windows' Program Manager to set up The Norton Utilities to run with Windows.

Creating a Program Icon for The Norton Utilities

1. At the Program Manager, click on **File** or press Alt + F.

   The File menu appears.

2. Click on **New** or press Enter.

   The New Program Object dialog box appears.

3. Press G or click on Program **G**roup. Press Enter or click OK.

   The Program Group Properties dialog box appears.

continues

continued

4. Type **The Norton Utilities** or another short name in the Description: text box and select **OK**. — Windows displays a new window called The Norton Utilities, as shown in Figure A.8. Next, you'll need to place the utilities in the window, one by one.

5. Click on **File** again or press Alt+F. — The File menu appears.

6. Click on **New** or press Enter. — The New Program Object dialog box appears.

7. Press I or click on **Program Item**. Press Enter or click **OK**. — The Program Item Properties dialog box appears.

8. Type a Description: for the utility you're installing (for example, type **Norton** for the main Norton utility) in the text box and press Tab. — The cursor moves to the Command Line: text box.

9. Type the drive and directory where your Norton program files are located, followed by the file name of the startup file for the utility you're setting up. For example, type **C:\NU\NORTON.EXE**.

10. Press Alt+I or click the **Change Icon...** button. Choose **OK**. — The Change Icon dialog box appears, with the default icon name in the File Name: text box.

Installation and Configuration   299

11. Type the drive and directory where your program files for The Norton Utilities are located, followed by the name of the .ICO file for the utility you're setting up. For example, type `C:\NU\NORTON.ICO`. Press ↵Enter or click OK.

12. Press ↵Enter or click OK. The Program Item Properties dialog box closes. An icon for the utility you specified appears in the Norton window. Figure 1.12 shows the Norton Utilities icon installed in the Norton Window.

13. Repeat steps 5 through 12 for each utility you would like to install in the Norton window.

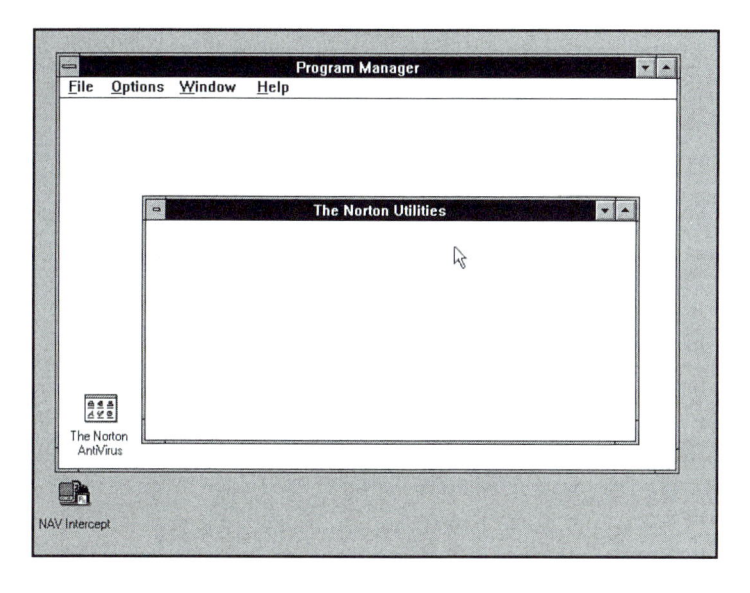

Figure A.8
The new Norton window.

Appendix A

To run a utility from the Norton window, simply double-click on its icon, or highlight the icon name and press ⏎Enter.

> **CAUTION** There are certain utilities that you can't run from Windows. When you try to run one of them, you'll see an error message. Running SpeeDisk and Norton Disk Doctor from Windows can damage your files, so don't even attempt to run either of those utilities from Windows.

Appendix **B**

Command Line Utilities

You can start all the programs that come with The Norton Utilities either through the main Norton menu program or by typing a command at the DOS prompt. Several of the utilities, in particular, are especially easy to use from DOS. These are known as the *command line utilities*.

Using the command line utilities from the DOS prompt rather than the main Norton screen offers the convenience of bypassing the menu. You can also include command line utilities in the batch files you create. You start each of the command line utilities by typing its name at the DOS prompt. Specify special conditions for an operation, called *parameters*, by typing *startup switches* (special codes) along with the command that starts the utility.

> **NOTE:** If you did not add The Norton Utilities to your PATH statement when you installed the program, you need to return to the directory containing The Norton Utilities program files before typing the command to run a command line utility.

Appendix B

This appendix describes Norton's command line utilities and explains the parameters and switches you can use with each.

Directory Sort (DS.EXE)

Organizing files in a more coherent order makes it easier for you to find and retrieve the files you need. As described in Chapter 5, the Directory Sort utility places one or more directories in order according to date, extension, name, size, or time. If the directory you sort contains subdirectories, they are grouped first, followed by files.

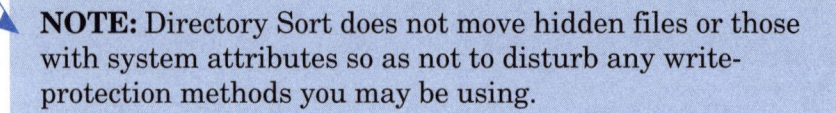

> **NOTE:** Directory Sort does not move hidden files or those with system attributes so as not to disturb any write-protection methods you may be using.

Unless you specify otherwise, Directory Sort sorts files in ascending alphabetical order when sorting by name or extension, smallest to largest when sorting by size, or least recent to most recent when sorting by date or time.

Chapter 5 describes how to use Directory Sort in its full-screen version. To use Directory Sort from the command line, type *sort-keys* along with the command name when you start the utility. Table B.1 lists the sort-keys and other parameters you can specify when using Directory Sort.

Table B.1
Directory Sort Command Line Sort-Keys

Use	By Entering	To Sort
D	DS D	By file creation date
E	DS E	By extension
N	DS N	By file name
S	DS S	By file size
T	DS T	By file creation time

Use	By Entering	To Sort
–	DS *(sort-key)*–	In reverse order
drive:\directory	DS *(sort-keys) drive:\directory*	A drive or directory other than the current drive and directory
/S	DS /S	Files in subdirectories of the current directory

You can enter more than one sort-key per operation by typing all sort-keys you wish after the command. Directory Sort first orders the files according to the first sort-key you enter (the *primary sort*), then by the second sort-key, and so on. For example, typing **DS ND** at the DOS prompt would sort the files in the current directory by file name, then by creation date.

File Attributes (FA.EXE)

As explained in Chapter 3, DOS tracks specific *attributes* for each file stored on disk: archive, hidden, read-only, and system. (See Table 3.1 for an explanation of each attribute.)

Attributes protect a file from being accidentally overwritten and remind you to back up certain files. However, on occasion you may need to change a file's attributes to update it, or you may need to change a file to read-only to protect it. In addition to using the FILEFIND utility (see Chapter 3) or the Norton Commander (see Chapter 10) to change a file's attributes, you can use the File Attributes command line utility.

Type **FA** at the DOS prompt to list all the current directory's files and their attributes. Including + with an attribute switch turns that attribute on, while including – with an attribute switch turns that attribute off. Table B.2 summarizes the switches you can use with the FA command.

Table B.2
File Attributes Command Line Switches

Switch	Function
/A	Sets the archive attribute.
/CLEAR	Removes all file attributes.
/DIR (+ or –)	Assigns or removes the hidden attribute to a directory.
/HID	Sets the hidden attribute.
/P	Pauses after each screenful of files is displayed.
/R	Sets the read-only attribute.
/S	Makes the command line act on subdirectories of the current directory.
/SYS	Sets the system attribute.
/T	Displays the file and directory totals.
/U	Lists any files with an attribute set.

You may also specify a certain drive, directory, and file name (including the wild-card characters * and ?) with the File Attributes command. For example, typing `FA D:\WORD5\*.DOC /R+` would assign read-only status to all the files with the .DOC extension in the WORD5 directory of drive D:.

File Date (FD.EXE)

The File Date command line utility does just what you'd expect. It enables you to assign a different date and/or time to a file or group of files. (In Chapter 3, you learned how to use FILEFIND to do the same thing.) Simply type `FD` at the DOS prompt to assign the current system date and time to all the files in the current directory. You may also specify a file or group of files in the command line, as in typing `FD A:\JOEB\TEST1.TIF`. Table B.3 summarizes the switches you can enter with the FD command.

Table B.3
File Date Command Line Switches

Use	To
/D:*month-day-year*	Assign the given date to the specified file(s).
/P	Pause after displaying each screenful of files.
/S	Assign the new date/time to files in the current directory's subdirectories.
/T:*hour:minute:second*	Assigns the given time to the specified file(s).

File Locate (FL.EXE)

If you've ever forgotten an exact file name or where you've stored a particular file, you know that searching disks and directories can be a frustrating and time-consuming process. The File Locate command line utility offers a simple, faster way to find lost files—even system or hidden files that DOS's DIR command won't list—and print a catalog of files.

- Type **FL** at the prompt to locate (and display) all files on the current disk. (Pressing Spacebar will pause and resume the file names scrolling on your screen.)

- You can include a drive letter, file name, or partial file name with wild cards in the command line. For example, typing FL S* will locate all files starting with S on the current drive. Typing **FL D:\STEVE.DOC** would locate any file named STEVE.DOC on drive D.

- Typing **FL > PRN** at the DOS prompt prints a catalog of all files on the current disk.

Table B.4 summarizes the switches you can include with the File Locate command line.

Table B.4
File Locate Command Line Switches

Switch	Function
/A	Searches all drives.
/F[n]	Lists only the first *n* matching files located instead of all the files located.
/P	Pauses after each screenful of file names is displayed.
/T	Searches the directories listed in the AUTOEXEC.BAT PATH statement only.
/W	Lists the files in wide format on-screen.

File Size (FS.EXE)

Rather than using the FILEFIND utility (see Chapter 3) to check file sizes, you can use the File Size command line utility to check the size of a single file or a group of files. If you want to copy the specified files to another disk, the File Size utility lets you check to see if there's enough room.

In addition, the File Size utility reports the *slack* in the amount of space occupied by the specified file(s). That is, when a computer stores a file on disk, the smallest storage area it uses is called a *cluster*. When a file is not large enough to fill out a cluster, the remaining space is the slack. So, if one disk uses larger cluster sizes than another, the files stored on the disk with the larger cluster sizes could appear to occupy more disk space than they would occupy on the disk using smaller cluster sizes if you simply checked the file sizes using DOS's DIR command.

Typing **FS** at the DOS prompt lists the sizes of files in the current directory, the amount of disk space occupied by the files, the amount of slack space created, and the amounts of used and unused space on the drive. Table B.5 summarizes the other options for using the File Size command line utility.

Table B.5
File Size Command Line Options

Include	To	Command Example
drive\directory*filename*	List the size of the specified file(s).	FS C:\JEN*.TXT
drive\directory*filename*	Determine whether there is room to copy the file(s) indicated to the target drive.	FS C:\STEVE*.TXT A:
/P	Pause after each screenful displayed.	FS /P
/S	Also list sizes for files in subdirectories of current directory.	FS /S
/T	Display directory and disktotals only.	FS /T

Line Print (LP.EXE)

Rather than pulling up a word processing program or other text editor to print a text file, you can print directly from the DOS prompt using the Line Print command line utility. Line Print can print to any printer (such as LPT1) or device (such as COM1). By default, Line Print divides the file into pages headed with the file name, current time and date, and page number.

If you don't want to use the default printing format and have embedded printer setup strings in the file you want to print, use the /SET switch with the LP command. To simply print the specified document to the default printer attached to your system, type `LP drive\directory\filename`. Table B.6 explains the additional switches you can use with the Line Print command line utility.

Table B.6
Line Print Command Line Switches

Include	To
output	Specify a device or printer other than the default (such as LPT2).
/132	Print in 132-column width.
/80	Print in 80-column width.
/A	Add data to another output file.
/Bn	Specify a bottom margin of n lines (3 is the default).
/EBCDIC	Print EBCDIC encrypted files.
/HIn	Specify a page height of n lines (66 is the default).
/HEADER0	Print the file without page headers.
/HEADER1	Print with the default headers.
/HEADER2	In addition to the current date and time, print the file date and time on the second header line.
/Ln	Specify a left margin of n characters (5 is the default).
/N	Print line numbers.
/PAn	Specify n as the starting page number (1 is the default).
/PR:xx	Specify a printer to print to in place of the xx variable. Choose *TT*y, *GE*neric, *EP*son, *PR*oprinter, *QU*ietwriter, *TO*shiba, *LA*serjet, or *PO*stscript.
/Rn	Specify a right margin of n characters (5 is the default).
/SPn	Specify line spacing of n lines (1 is the default).
/Tn	Specify a top margin of n lines (3 is the default).
/WS	Print WordStar files.

Text Search (TS.EXE)

The Text Search command line utility is useful for finding text contained in a file. This utility also searches for text on areas of a disk containing only erased files. (You can then copy the found data to a new file.) Include the text you want to search for in quotation marks when you enter the Text Search command, as in

TS "Find me". By entering a drive, directory, and file name (complete or using wild cards) with the TS command, you can search only the specified file(s) for the text string you enter. For example, typing

```
TS C:\PHYLLIS\*.DOC "Series Ideas"
```

at the DOS prompt would search for the words "Series Ideas" in all files with the .DOC extension in the PHYLLIS directory of drive C.

Each time Text Search finds the string of characters it's looking for, it displays several lines of the text around the located string and the full path name of the file containing the located text, and asks whether you'd like to continue the search. Table B.7 summarizes the Text Search options.

Table B.7
Text Search Command Line

Include	To
/A	Make the search automatic (assumes a "Yes" answer to all prompts).
/C*n*	Begin the search at cluster *n* of the disk.
/CS	Make the search case-sensitive.
/D	Search the whole disk.
/E	Look for the text string on only the erased portion of the disk.
/EBCDIC	Searches EBCDIC encoded files.
/F:*filename*	Lets you store each occurrence of the found text in a file on a separate disk.
/LOG	Output results in a log format you can print or save in a file.
/S	Search all subdirectories of the current directory.
/T	Give only summary information of the search.
/WS	Omit characters in the IBM PC extended character set from the search.

Index

Symbols

! (exclamation point) wild-card character in NDOS, 146
* (asterisk) wild-card character, 58
   in NDOS, 146
   searching for files, 69
/? switch, 20-21
/4 switch, DIR command, 144
? (NDOS) command, 147
? (question mark) wild-card character, 58
   in NDOS, 146
   searching for files, 69
[] (brackets) wild-card character in NDOS, 146
^ (caret) character in NDOS, 145
… (ellipsis), 15
1st FAT (DISKEDIT Object menu) command, 188-189

A

/A switch, FILEFIND command, 74
Alert window, 252
ALIAS (NDOS) command, 147-148
AntiVirus, see Norton AntiVirus
archive attribute, 72
.ASC file extension, 58
ASCII (American Standard Code for Information Interchange) character set, 110
   viewing disk contents in, 187
ASK (Batch Enhancer) subcommand, 168
asterisk (*) wild-card character, 58
   in NDOS, 146
   searching for files, 69
ATTRIB (DOS) command, 202
attributes
   files, 303-304
      as file filters, 75
      clearing all, 75
      command line identifier switches, 74
      setting/clearing, 72-73
      types, 72
   screen, setting, 164-166
audit trail files, 273-274
AUTOEXEC.BAT file, viewing, 33

B

background screen colors, 46-47, 165-166
Backup (NBACKUP main menu) command, 236-238
Backup Files screen, 237

Backup Options window, 237
Basic Restore Options screen, 251
Backup, see Norton Backup
backups
    backing up, 246-248
    Basic, 236-248
    canceling operations, 248
    catalogs, 253-254
    comparing to originals, 249-250
    configuring, 241-243
    differential, 240
    drives, choosing, 238-239
    flagging files for, 239, 244-245
    full, 239
    full copy, 240
    incremental, 240
    incremental copy, 241
    levels, 226
    macros for, 260-264
    of system area, 124-126
    restoring, 250-260
    selecting files for, 243-246
Bad command or file name
    message, 11, 145
base memory, 27
base names, files, 57
Basic backups, 236-248
    configuring, 241-243
Batch Enhancer (BE) utility, 4
    ASK subcommand, 168
    BEEP subcommand, 170
    BOX subcommand, 169
    CLS subcommand, 164
    creating interactive batch files, 161-164
    DELAY subcommand, 170-171
    ERRORLEVEL variable, 168-169
    ROWCOL subcommand, 167
    SA subcommand, 164-166
    script files, 171-174
    subcommands, 174-175
    WINDOW subcommand, 166-167
batch files
    copying individual files without
        overwriting, 158-160
    creating, 152-155
    interacting with users, 160-175
    looping within, 157-158
    parameters, 155-157
    pausing execution, 155
BEEP (Batch Enhancer)
    subcommand, 170
BEEP (NDOS) command, 147
bits (binary digits), 26, 110
boot records, 113
bootable disks, creating, 178-179
borders, screens, customizing
    colors, 46-47
BOX (Batch Enhancer)
    subcommand, 169
brackets ([]) wild-card character in
    NDOS, 146
branching, 158-160
bus sizes, microprocessors, 25-26
bytes, 26, 110

C

/C switch, NDOS command, 144-145
CALIBRAT command, 221
Calibrate (CALIBRAT) utility, 5, 219-222
Calibrate information dialog box, 221-222
canceling backup operations, 248
caret (^) character in NDOS, 145
.CAT file extension, 254
Catalog screen, 251
catalogs, 253-254
    files, selecting, 255-256
    retrieving and rebuilding, 256
CD (DOS) command, 60
Central Processing Units (CPUs), 25-26
Change Attributes dialog box, 72-73
Change Directory dialog box, 104
Change Disk (NCD Disk menu)
    command, 95-96
Change Icon dialog box, 298-299
character sets, ASCII, 110
check boxes, 16-17
chips, 25-26

Index

/CLEAR switch, FILEFIND
   command, 75
clearing
   file attributes, 72-73
      all, 75
   screens, 164
clicking, 15
Clinic (NAV Options menu)
   command, 277-279
Clinic Options dialog box, 277-279
close box, quitting utilities, 21
CLS (Batch Enhancer)
   subcommand, 164
CLS (DOS) command, 164
clusters, 110
   bad, marking, 181-182
   slack, 306
CMOS (Complementary Metal-
   Oxide Semiconductor), 37
CMOS Values screen, 36-37
CMOS Status (SYSINFO System
   menu) command, 36-37
colors
   palettes, setting, 48
   screens, 46-47, 165-166
   text, placing on-screen, 167
command buttons, 16-17
command line utilities, 301-302
   Directory Sort (DS), 302-303
   File Attributes (FA), 303-304
   File Date (FD), 304-305
   File Locate (FL), 305-306
   File Size (FS), 306-307
   Line Print (LP), 307-308
   Text Search (TS), 308-309
command processors, 23
   NDOS.COM, 141-142
COMMAND.COM command
   processor, 23
commands
   Batch Enhancer (BE)
      subcommands, 174-175
         ASK, 168
         BEEP, 170
         BOX, 169
         CLS, 164

DELAY, 170-171
ROWCOL, 167
SA, 164-166
WINDOW, 166-167
CALIBRAT, 221
Disk Editor
   1st FAT (Object menu),
      188-189
   Configuration (Tools
      menu), 186
   Hex (View menu), 186
   Memory Dump (Object
      menu), 189
   Print Object As (Tools menu),
      190-191
   Text (View menu), 186, 188
DISKEDIT, 184
DISKMON, 198, 200-202
DISKREET, 203
DISKTOOL, 178
DOS
   ATTRIB, 202
   CD, 60
   CLS, 164
   COPY, 240
   DIR, 103
   DISKCOPY, 130
   ECHO, 154
   FDISK, 30-31
   FOR, 157-158
   FORMAT, 119
   GOTO, 158-160
   IF, 158-160
   LABEL, 97
   MD, 59
   PAUSE, 155, 160-161
   PROMPT, 60
   RD, 59
   RECOVER, 179-180
   REM, 154
   SYS, 178
   TYPE, 184
   UNFORMAT, 126
   VER, 24
DS, 104, 302-303
DUPDISK, 130

EP, 85
FA, 303-304
FD, 304-305
File Exit, 21
File Find
   Set Attributes (Commands menu), 72-73
   Set Date/Time (Commands menu), 77
FILEFIND, 66, 71-72, 78
FILEFIX, 88
FL, 305-306
FS, 306-307
Help The Norton Advisor, 18-19
IMAGE, 125
LP, 307-308
NAV, 274
NBACKUP, 233
NCC, 45
NCD, 61, 92
NDD, 132
NDIAGS, 42
NDOS, 142
NDOS command processor, 146-148
   DIR, 144
   entering multiple, 145
   executing on multiple files, 141, 146
   EXIT, 142
   NDOSHELP, 143-144
   repeating, 145-146
   syntax, 144-145
NORTON, 10
Norton AntiVirus
   Clinic (Options menu), 277-279
   Directory (Scan menu), 281-282
   Drive (Scan menu), 280
   File (Scan menu), 282-283
   Global (Options menu), 279
   Intercept (Options menu), 277-279
   Modify List (Definitions menu), 285

Set Password (Options menu), 279
Video and Mouse Options (Options menu), 279
Norton Backup
   Backup (main menu), 236-238
   Compare (main menu), 249-250
   Configure (main menu), 231-233
   Exit (File pull-down menu), 235-236
   Open Setup (File pull-down menu), 261
   Quit (main menu), 235-236
   Restore (main menu), 251-253, 255, 257
Norton Change Directory
   Change Disk (Disk menu), 95-96
   Configure (Directory menu), 98
   Delete (Directory menu), 63, 96-97
   Make (Directory menu), 62-63, 96-97
   Prune & Graft (Directory menu), 99
   Rename (Directory menu), 96
   Rescan Disk (Disk menu), 94-95
   Volume Label (Disk menu), 97
Norton Change Directory, 62
NUCONFIG, 218, 292
RESCUE, 182
selecting, 14-15, 17
SFORMAT, 120
SMARTCAN, 83
SPEEDISK, 216
syntax help, 20-21
SYSINFO, 32
System Information
   CMOS Status (System menu), 36-37
   CPU Speed (Benchmarks menu), 40-41

Index

Device Drivers (Memory menu), 40
Disk Characteristics (Disks menu), 118
Disk Summary (Disks menu), 116-117
Expanded Memory (EMS) (Memory menu), 39
Extended Memory (XMS) (Memory menu), 39
Hard Disk Speed (Benchmarks menu), 41
Hardware Interrupts (System menu), 36
Memory Block List (Memory menu), 39
Memory Usage Summary (Memory menu), 37-39
Network Information (System menu), 36
Network Performance Speed (Benchmarks menu), 42
Overall Performance Index (Benchmarks menu), 41
Partition Tables (Disks menu), 118-119
Print Report (File menu), 34
Software Interrupts (System menu), 36
System Summary (System menu), 35
TSR Programs (Memory menu), 39-40
Video Summary (System menu), 35
View AUTOEXEC.BAT (File menu), 33
View CONFIG.SYS (File menu), 33
View NDOS.INI (File menu), 33
View SYSTEM.INI (File menu), 34
View WIN.INI (File menu), 34
TS, 309
UNERASE, 80
UnErase, Manual UnErase (File menu), 192-194
UNFORMAT, 127
WIPEINFO, 208
comments, 154
Common Solutions, Norton Disk Doctor, 177-178
Compare (NBACKUP main menu) command, 249-250
computers
    configuring for foreign countries, 55
    rebooting with Emergency Disks, 288
CONFIG.SYS file, viewing, 33
Configuration (DISKEDIT Tools menu) command, 186
Configuration program, 292-297
Configuration screen, 293-297
Configuration Tests, Norton Backup, 232-233
Configure command
    NBACKUP main menu, 231-233
    NCD Directory menu, 98
configuring
    Basic backups, 241-243
    Norton AntiVirus, 277-279
    Norton Backup, 231-233
    Norton Utilities, 292-297
    PCs for foreign countries, 55
    serial ports, 52-53
    surface tests, 135-137
    Wipe Information, 208-210
COPY (DOS) command, 240
copying
    disks, 130-131
    files
        individually without overwriting, 158-160
        multiple at one time, 141
corrupted files, repairing, 87-89
CPU Speed (SYSINFO Benchmarks menu) command, 40-41
CPU Speed screen, 40-41
CPUs (Central Processing Units), 25-26

Create Rescue Disk screen, 182
cursor, 19
   resizing, 46
Cursor Size window, 46
cylinders, 112

D

/D switch, FILEFIND command, 78
data area, 115
data bus sizes, microprocessors, 25-26
Data Encryption Standard (DES), 205
data storage
   disks, 29-31
   memory, 26-29
dates
   assigning to files, 304-305
   sorting files by, 103-106
   stamps, 76-78
   system, setting, 55
decrypting files, 206-207
default date/time, setting date/time stamps to, 78
defragmenting hard disks, 215-217
DELAY (Batch Enhancer) subcommand, 170-171
delay before auto repeat, keyboards, 49-50
Delete (NCD Directory menu) command, 63, 96-97
deleting
   directories, 59, 62-63, 96-97
      recovering, 100-103
   disk contents, wiping permanently, 210-212
   files
      recovering, 79-82, 85-86, 191-194, 288
      wiping permanently, 207-208
DES (Data Encryption Standard), 205
DESCRIBE (NDOS) command, 147
device drivers, 33

Device Drivers (SYSINFO Memory menu) command, 40
Device Drivers screen, 40
diagnostic tests for hardware, 42-44
dialog boxes, 15-17
   Calibrate information, 221-222
   Change Attributes, 72-73
   Change Directory, 104
   Change Icon, 298-299
   Clinic Options, 277-279
   Directory Sort, 104-106
   Disk Monitor, 199-201
   Disk Park, 201-202
   Disk Restore Options, 257-258
   IMAGE, 127
   Intercept Options, 277-279
   Modify List, 285
   NCD Configuration, 98
   New Program Object, 297-298
   Print As, 190
   Program Group Properties, 297-298
   Program Item Properties, 298
   Save Setup File, 263
   Scan Directory, 281-282
   Scan Drives, 274, 280
   Scan File, 282-283
   Select Catalog, 255-256
   Select Drives to Diagnose, 132
   selecting items in Norton Backup, 227
   Set Date/Time, 77
   Volume Label, 97
differential backups, 240
DIR (DOS) command, 103
   /4 switch in NDOS, 144
directories
   changing, 92-93
   creating, 62-63, 96-97
   deleting, 62-63, 96-97
   pruning and grafting, 98-99
   recovering deleted, 100-103
   renaming, 62, 96
   root, 59, 113
   scanning for viruses, 281-282

Index

searching for, 61-62
   speed search, 93
SMARTCAN, 85
sorting files, 103-106, 302-303
subdirectories, 59
tree structures, 58-60
   updating, 62, 94-95
Directory (NAV Scan menu) command, 281-282
Directory Sort (DS) utility, 103-106
   as command line utility, 302-303
Directory Sort dialog box, 104-106
disk caches, 218-219
Disk Characteristics (SYSINFO Disks menu) command, 118
Disk Characteristics screen, 116, 118
Disk Doctor Options screen, 135
Disk Editor (DISKEDIT) utility, 5
   browsing file contents, 184-186
   hexadecimal notation, 186
   views
      hexadecimal/ASCII, 187
      types, 188-190
Disk Monitor (DISKMON) utility, 5
   displaying disk read/write activity messages, 201
   parking hard disks, 201-202
   preventing viruses from writing to disks, 198-200
   protecting specified areas, 200-201
Disk Monitor dialog box, 199-201
Disk Monitor screen, 198
Disk Park dialog box, 201-202
Disk Protect screen, 198, 200-201
Disk Restore Options dialog box, 257-258
Disk Summary (SYSINFO Disks menu) command, 116-117
Disk Summary screen, 116-117
Disk Tools (DISKTOOL) utility, 5, 177-178
   creating bootable disks, 178-179
   formatting diskettes without destroying contents, 181

marking bad clusters, 181-182
undoing disk recoveries, 179-181
Disk Tools screen, 178
DISKCOPY (DOS) command, 130
DISKEDIT command, 184
DISKEDIT screen, 184
DISKMON command, 198
   /LIGHT switch, 201
   /PARK switch, 202
   /PROTECT switch, 200
Diskreet (DISKREET) utility, 5, 202-207
DISKREET command, 203
Diskreet screen, 203
disks
   as data storage devices, 29
   boot record, 113
   bootable, creating, 178-179
   copying, 130-131
   data area, 115
   data divisions, 110
   displaying read/write activity messages, 201
   Emergency, 287-288
   FAT (file allocation table), 113-115
   formatting, 119-124
   help, 18-19
   information about, 116-119
   preventing viruses from writing to, 198-200
   printing on-screen contents, 190-191
   protecting specified areas, 200-201
   recovering from accidental formatting, 126-130
      undoing recovery, 179-181
   root directory, 113
   testing, 132-139
   viewing contents, 184-186
      hexadecimal/ASCII view of contents, 187
      types of views/data, 188-190
   volume labels, 97

wiping permanently
  deleting contents, 210-212
  files from, 207-208
  see also floppy diskettes; hard disks
DISKTOOL command, 178
display, *see* video
.DOC file extension, 58
DOS (Disk Operating System), 23-24
  versions, 24
DOS Memory Blocks screen, 39
DOS mode, Safe Format utility, 123
DOS prompt, customizing, 60
Drive (NAV Scan menu) command, 280
drives
  backup, choosing, 238-239
  changing, 95-96
  logical, 30-31
  restore, selecting, 253
  scanning for viruses, 280-281
DS command, 104, 302-303
dummy parameters, 158
dumping memory on-screen, 189
DUPDISK command, 130
Duplicate Disk (DUPDISK) utility, 6, 130-131

E

ECHO (DOS) command, 154
ellipsis (...), 15
Emergency Disks, 287-288
Encrypt a File screen, 203
encrypting files, 202-207
EP command, 85
ERASE PROTECT utility, 85
error messages, *see* messages
ERRORLEVEL variable, 168-169
Esc key, 21
exclamation point (!) wild-card character in NDOS, 146
EXIT (Batch Enhancer) subcommand, 175

Exit (NBACKUP File pull-down menu) command, 235-236
EXIT (NDOS) command, 142
exiting
  NDOS, 142
  Norton Backup, 235-236
  Norton Change Directory, 62
  utilities, 21
  Virus Clinic, 285
expanded memory, 27
  information about, 39
Expanded Memory (EMS) (SYSINFO Memory menu) command, 39
Expanded Memory Summary screen, 39
extended memory, 27
  information about, 39
Extended Memory (XMS) (SYSINFO Memory menu) command, 39
Extended Memory Summary screen, 39
extensions, 57
  .ASC, 58
  .CAT, 254
  .DOC, 58
  .SAV, 86
  sorting files by, 103-106
  .TXT, 58
extra memory, information about, 39

F

FA command, 303-304
FAT (file allocation table), 113-115
  viewing contents, 188-189
FD command, 304-305
FDISK (DOS) command, 30-31
File (NAV Scan menu) command, 282-283
File Attributes (FA) command line utility, 303-304
File Date (FD) command line utility, 304-305

Index

File Encryption Options screen, 205-206
File Exit command, 21
File Find (FILEFIND) utility, 6
   date/time stamps, 76-78
   displaying files, 66, 67
   file attributes, 72-75
   searching for
      files, 68-69
      text strings, 69-72
File Find screen, 66
File Fix (FILEFIX) utility, 6
   repairing corrupted files, 87-89
File Locate (FL) command line utility, 305-306
File Size (FS) command line utility, 306-307
FILEFIND command, 66
   /A switch, 74
   /CLEAR switch, 75
   /CS switch, 71
   /D switch, 78
   /HID switch, 74
   /NOW switch, 78
   /R switch, 74
   /S switch, 71-72
   /SYS switch, 74
   /T switch, 78
FILEFIX command, 88
files
   attributes, 303-304
      as file filters, 75
      clearing all, 75
      command line identifier switches, 74
      setting/clearing, 72-73
      types, 72
   audit trail, 273-274
   AUTOEXEC.BAT, viewing, 33
   backup
      comparing to originals, 249-250
      flagging for, 239, 244-245
      restoring, 250-260
      selecting for, 243-246
   batch
      copying individual files without overwriting, 158-160
      creating, 152-155
      interacting with users, 160-175
      looping within, 157-158
      parameters, 155-157
      pausing execution, 155
   catalog, selecting, 255-256
   CONFIG.SYS, viewing, 33
   copying multiple at one time, 141
   dates/times
      assigning, 304-305
      stamps, 76-78
   decrypting, 206-207
   displaying, 66-67
   encrypting, 202-207
   extensions, 57
      .ASC, 58
      .CAT, 254
      .DOC, 58
      .SAV, 86
      sorting files by, 103-106
      .TXT, 58
   fragmented, 114-115
   IMAGE.DAT, 124
   lost, causes for, 225
   multiple, executing NDOS commands on, 141, 146
   naming, 57-58
   NDOS.INI, viewing, 33
   printing, 307-308
      on-screen contents, 190-191
   protecting specified, 200-201
   purging from SMARTCAN directory, 86-87
   READ.ME, 292
   recovering deleted, 79-82, 85-86
      manually, 191-194
      with Emergency Disks, 288
   repairing corrupt, 87-89, 132-138
      undoing repairs, 138-139
   scanning for viruses, 282-283
   script, 171-174

searching for, 68-69, 305-306
  text, 308-309
setup, 260
  installing for other users, 263-264
  loading, 261
sizes, checking, 306-307
SMARTCAN.INI, 85
SMARTCAN.MAP, 86
sorting in directories, 103-106, 302-303
SYSTEM.INI, viewing, 34
TREEINFO.NCD, 94-95
viewing contents, 184-186
  hexadecimal/ASCII view of contents, 187
  types of views/data, 188-190
WIN.INI, viewing, 34
wiping permanently, 207-208
filters, file attributes as, 75
FL command, 305-306
flagging files for backup, 239, 244-245
floppy diskettes, 29-30
  formatting without destroying contents, 181
  rescue, creating, 182-183
FOR (DOS) command, 157-158
foreground screen colors, setting, 165-166
foreign countries, configuring PCs for, 55
FORMAT (DOS) command, 119
formatting
  diskettes without destroying contents, 181
  disks, 119-124
    recovering, 126-130
fragmented files, 114-115
FREE (NDOS) command, 147
freezing screens, 170-171
FS command, 306-307
full backups, 239
full copy backups, 240

G

Global (NAV Options menu) command, 279
GOTO (Batch Enhancer) subcommand, 175
GOTO (DOS) command, 158-160
grafting directories, 98-99

H

Hard Disk Speed (SYSINFO Benchmarks menu) command, 41
Hard Disk Speed screen, 41
hard disks, 30-31
  causes for lost files, 225
  defragmenting, 215-217
  optimizing interleave factor, 219-222
  parking, 201-202
  speed information, 41
  unformatting with Emergency Disks, 288
hardware
  interrupts, information about, 36
  Norton AntiVirus requirements, 268
  Norton Utilities requirements, 4
  testing for problems, 42-44
Hardware Interrupts (SYSINFO System menu) command, 36
Hardware Interrupts screen, 36
help
  disk problems and error messages, 18-19
  NDOS, 143-144
  Norton Backup, 234-235
  utility information, 19
  utility syntax, 20-21
Help The Norton Advisor command, 18-19
Hex (DISKEDIT View menu) command, 186
hexadecimal notation, 186
  viewing disk contents in, 187

Index

/HID switch, FILEFIND command, 74
hidden attribute, 72
hiding command line display, 154
HISTORY (NDOS) command, 147
home position, 164
hot keys, 28

I

icons, program, creating for Norton Utilities, 297-300
IF (DOS) command, 158-160
Image (IMAGE) utility, 6, 124-126
IMAGE command, 125
IMAGE dialog box, 127
IMAGE.DAT file, 124
incremental backups, 240
incremental copy backups, 241
individual catalogs, 254
Install program, 289-292
installing
    Norton AntiVirus, 269-272
    Norton Backup, 227-230
    Norton Utilities, 288-292
    setup files for other users, 263-264
Intercept (NAV Options menu) command, 277-279
Intercept Options dialog box, 277-279
interleave factor, optimizing, 219-222
interrupts, hardware and software, information about, 36

J

JUMP (Batch Enhancer) subcommand, 175

K

keyboard
    repeat rate, 49-50

shortcuts
    Help (F1), 19
    in Norton Change Directory (NCD) utility, 94-97
    Menu (F10), 14
    speed, setting, 49-50
keys
    Esc, 21
    hot, 28
    sort, 103
kilobytes (K), 26

L

LABEL (DOS) command, 97
labels, 160
/LIGHT switch, DISKMON command, 201
Line Print (LP) command line utility, 307-308
LIST (NDOS) command, 147
listings
    8.1 ONE.BAT Batch File Listing, 153
    8.2 TWO.BAT with a Parameter, 155
    8.3 THREE.BAT with Two Parameters, 156
    8.4 FOUR.BAT with a Looping Construct, 157
    8.5 C.BAT—An Individual File Copy Utility, 159
    8.6 The MENU.BAT Batch File, 161-163
    8.7 The SCREEN.SCR Script File, 171-172
    8.8 The Revised MENU.BAT File, 172-174
lists, 17
logical drives, 30-31
looping within batch files, 157-158
lost files, causes for, 225
LP command, 307-308

M

macros for backing up, 260
   loading setup files, 261
   playing, 263-264
   recording, 261-263
main memory, information about, 38
Make (NCD Directory menu) command, 62-63, 96-97
Manual UnErase (UNERASE File menu) command, 192-194
manually recovering files, 191-194
marking bad clusters, 181-182
master catalogs, 254
MD (DOS) command, 59
megabytes (MB), 26
megahertz (MHz), 25-26
memory
   base, 27
   disk caches, 218-219
   expanded, 27
      information about, 39
   extended, 27
      information about, 39
   extra, information about, 39
   main, information about, 38
   RAM (Random-Access Memory)
      comparing with ROM, 26-27
      usage amounts, 27-28
   ROM (Read-Only Memory), 26-27
   screen dumps, 189
   TSR (Terminate-and-Stay-Resident) programs, 28-29
   units of measurement, 26
   video, information about, 38
   volatile, 27
Memory Block List (SYSINFO Memory menu) command, 39
Memory Dump (DISKEDIT Object menu) command, 189
Memory Summary screen, 37-39
Memory Usage Summary (SYSINFO Memory menu) command, 37-39
menus, 14-15
messages
   Bad command or file name, 11, 145
   disk read/write activity, 201
   during disk-testing, customizing, 137
   help, 18-19
microprocessors, 25-26
   speed information, 40-41
Microsoft Windows, *see* Windows
modes
   DOS, Safe Format utility, 123
   Quick, Safe Format utility, 123
   Safe, Safe Format utility, 122
   video, selecting, 48
Modify List (NAV Definitions menu) command, 285
Modify List dialog box, 285
MONTHDAY (Batch Enhancer) subcommand, 175
mouse
   configuring for Norton Backup, 231-232
   operations, 15
   speed, setting, 51
MOVE (NDOS) command, 148

N

naming
   files, 57-58
   renaming directories, 62, 96
NAV command, 274
NBACKUP command, 233
NCC command, 45
NCD command, 61, 92
NCD Configuration dialog box, 98
NDD command, 132
NDD operation screen, 132-134
NDIAGS command, 42
NDOS command processor, 23
   commands, 146-148
      entering multiple, 145
      executing on multiple files, 141, 146

Index

repeating, 145-146
syntax, 144-145
help, 143-144
starting, 141-142
temporarily loading from DOS, 144-145
wild-card characters, 146
NDOS command, 142
/C switch, 144-145
NDOS.INI file, viewing, 33
NDOSHELP command, 143-144
Network Information (SYSINFO System menu) command, 36
Network Information screen, 36
Network Performance Speed (SYSINFO Benchmarks menu) command, 42
Network Performance Speed screen, 42
New Program Object dialog box, 297, 298
Norton AntiVirus (NAV) (Symantec)
  configuring, 277-279
  hardware and software requirements, 268
  installing, 269-272
  printing virus definition lists, 284-285
  scan results, guidelines for, 283-284
  scanning with, 280-283
  Virus Clinic, 268
    exiting, 285
    navigating, 275-277
    starting, 274
  Virus Intercept, 268, 272-274
Norton Backup (Symantec)
  Basic backups, 236-248
  comparing backup files to originals, 249-250
  configuring, 231-233
  exiting, 235-236
  help, 234-235
  installing, 227-230
  levels of backups, 226

macros, 260-264
restoring backup files, 250-260
selecting items, 227
Norton Backup screen, 237
Norton Backup Configuration screen, 231-233
Norton Backup Install screen, 227-230
Norton Basic Backup screen, 236
Norton Basic Restore screen, 251-253, 255, 257
Norton Cache (NCACHE) utility, 7, 218-219
Norton Change Directory (NCD) utility, 7
  directories
    changing, 92-93
    creating, 62-63
    deleting, 62-63
    pruning and grafting, 98-99
    searching for, 61-62
    tree structures, 60
  function keys, 94-97
  menu commands, 62
  speed search, 93
  volume labels, 97
NORTON command, 10
Norton Control Center (NCC) utility, 7
  cursor, resizing, 46
  foreign countries, configuring PCs for, 55
  keyboard speed, setting, 49-50
  mouse speed, setting, 51
  palette colors, setting, 48
  screen colors, customizing, 46-47
  serial ports, configuring, 52-53
  starting, 45-46
  stopwatches, 53-54
  system time and date, setting, 55
  video modes, selecting, 48
Norton Control Center screen, 45
Norton Disk Doctor (NDD) utility, 7
  configuring surface tests, 135-137
  testing disks, 132-134
  undoing repairs, 138-139

Norton program utility, 8
   accessing utilities from, 10-14
Norton program utility screen, 11-14
Norton Utilities
   configuring, 292-297
   hardware and software
      requirements, 4
   installing, 288-292
   running with Windows, 297-300
/NOW switch, FILEFIND
   command, 78
NUCONFIG command, 218, 292
numbers, hexadecimal notation, 186

O

offsets, 187
Open Setup (NBACKUP File pull-
   down menu) command, 261
Overall Performance Index
   (SYSINFO Benchmarks menu)
   command, 41
Overall Performance Index
   screen, 41

P

palettes, setting colors, 48
parameters, 144
   dummy, 158
   in batch files, 155-157
   see also switches
/PARK switch, DISKMON
   command, 202
Partition Tables (SYSINFO Disks
   menu) command, 118-119
Partition Tables screen, 116,
   118-119
partitions, information about,
   118-119
passwords
   for encrypting files, 206
   Norton AntiVirus
      configurations, 279
PAUSE (DOS) command, 155,
   160-161

pausing file/program execution, 155
PCs
   configuring for foreign
      countries, 55
   rebooting with Emergency
      Disks, 288
platters, 111
playing backup macros, 263-264
pointing, 15
ports, serial, configuring, 52-53
primary sort, 303
Print As dialog box, 190
Print Object As (DISKEDIT Tools
   menu) command, 190-191
Print Report (SYSINFO File menu)
   command, 34
PRINTCHAR (Batch Enhancer)
   subcommand, 175
printing
   files, 307-308
   on-screen disk contents, 190-191
   System Information reports, 34
   virus definition lists, 284-285
Program Group Properties dialog
   box, 297-298
program icons, creating for Norton
   Utilities, 297-300
Program Item Properties dialog
   box, 298
programs
   Configuration, 292-297
   Install, 289-292
   TSR (Terminate-and-Stay-
      Resident), 28-29
   see also software; utilities
PROMPT (DOS) command, 60
prompts
   DOS, customizing, 60
   for user interaction, 168
/PROTECT switch, DISKMON
   command, 200
protecting
   by checking for viruses, 272-274
   disks
      preventing viruses from
         writing to, 198-200

Index

specified areas, 200-201
   wiping permanently, 210-212
files
   encrypting, 202-207
   specified, 200-201
   wiping permanently, 207-208
   hard disks, by parking, 201-202
Prune & Graft (NCD Directory menu) command, 99
pruning directories, 98-99
pull-down lists, 17
Purge Deleted Files screen, 87
purging files from SMARTCAN directory, 86-87

Q

question mark (?) wild-card character, 58
   in NDOS, 146
   searching for files, 69
Quick mode, Safe Format utility, 123
Quit (NBACKUP main menu) command, 235-236
quitting, *see* exiting

R

/R switch, FILEFIND command, 74
radio buttons, 16-17
RAM (Random-Access Memory)
   comparing with ROM, 26-27
   disk caches, 218-219
   usage amounts, 27-28
RD (DOS) command, 59
read-only attribute, 72
READ.ME file, 292
REBOOT (Batch Enhancer) subcommand, 175
rebooting with Emergency Disks, 288
recording backup macros, 261-263
RECOVER (DOS) command, 179-180

recovering
   deleted directories, 100-103
   deleted files, 79-82, 85-86
      manually, 191-194
   disk data, 181
   formatted disks, 126-130
      undoing recovery, 179-181
   system information with rescue diskettes, 182-183
   with bootable disks, 178-179
   with Emergency Disks, 287-288
REM (DOS) command, 154
Rename (NCD Directory menu) command, 96
renaming directories, 62, 96
Repair Excel File screen, 88
repairing corrupted files, 87-89, 132-138
   undoing repairs, 138-139
repeating NDOS commands, 145-146
Report Topics screen, 34
reports, System Information, printing, 34
Rescan Disk (NCD Disk menu) command, 94-95
rescanning directories to update tree structures, 94-95
RESCUE command, 182
Rescue Disk (RESCUE) utility, 8, 182-183
Rescue Disk screen, 182
Rescue Diskettes, creating, 182-183
resizing cursor, 46
Restore (NBACKUP main menu) command, 251-253, 255, 257
restoring backup files, 250-252, 259-260
   retrieving and rebuilding catalogs, 256
   selecting catalog files, 255-256
   selecting drives for, 253
   selecting files for, 258-259
   setting options for, 257-258
ROM (Read-Only Memory), 26-27

root directory, 59, 113
ROWCOL (Batch Enhancer) subcommand, 167

S

SA (Batch Enhancer) subcommand, 164-166
Safe Format (SFORMAT) utility, 8, 120-124
Safe Format screen, 120
Safe mode, Safe Format utility, 122
.SAV file extension, 86
Save Setup File dialog box, 263
Save System Files screen, 290
Scan Directory dialog box, 281-282
Scan Drives dialog box, 274, 280
Scan File dialog box, 282-283
Scan Result screen, 285
scanning for viruses
    directories, 281-282
    drives, 280-281
    files, 282-283
    results, guidelines for, 283-284
screens
    attributes, setting, 164-166
    Backup Files, 237
    Basic Restore Options, 251
    building quickly, 171-174
    Catalog, 251
    clearing, 164
    CMOS Values, 36-37
    Configuration, 293-297
    CPU Speed, 40-41
    Create Rescue Disk, 182
    customizing colors, 46-47
    Device Drivers, 40
    Disk Characteristics, 116, 118
    Disk Doctor Options, 135
    Disk Monitor, 198
    Disk Protect, 198, 200-201
    Disk Summary, 116-117
    Disk Tools, 178
    DISKEDIT, 184
    Diskreet, 203
    displays, configuring for Norton Backup, 231-232
    DOS Memory Blocks, 39
    Encrypt a File, 203
    encryption file selection, 203
    Expanded Memory Summary, 39
    Extended Memory Summary, 39
    File Encryption Options, 205-206
    File Find, 66
    freezing, 170-171
    Hard Disk Speed, 41
    Hardware Interrupts, 36
    memory dumps, 189
    Memory Summary, 37-39
    NDD operation, 132-134
    Network Information, 36
    Network Performance Speed, 42
    Norton Backup, 237
    Norton Backup Configuration, 231-233
    Norton Backup Install, 227-230
    Norton Basic Backup, 236
    Norton Basic Restore, 251-253, 255, 257
    Norton Control Center, 45
    Norton program utility, 11-14
    Overall Performance Index, 41
    Partition Tables, 116, 118-119
    Purge Deleted Files, 87
    Repair Excel File, 88
    Report Topics, 34
    Rescue Disk, 182
    Safe Format, 120
    Save System Files, 290
    Scan Result, 285
    Select Backup Files, 243-246
    Select Drives to Wipe, 211
    Select Restore Files, 251, 259
    Set Custom Message, 137
    Software Interrupts, 36
    Surface Test, 133
    Surface Test Options, 135-137
    System Summary, 32, 35
    Tests to Skip, 138
    TSR Programs, 39-40
    Video Summary, 35

Index

Virus Clinic, 274
Wipe Configuration, 209-210
Wipe Files, 208
WIPEINFO, 211
see also windows
script files, Batch Enhancer (BE) utility, 171-174
scroll bars, 12
searching
   for directories, 61-62
      speed search, 93
   for files, 68-69, 305-306
   for text, 308-309
   for text strings, 69-72
sectors, 110
   boot, 113
SELECT (NDOS) command, 148
Select Backup Files screen, 243-246
Select Catalog dialog box, 255-256
Select Drives to Diagnose dialog box, 132
Select Drives to Wipe screen, 211
Select Item window, 46
Select Restore Files screen, 251, 259
serial ports, configuring, 52-53
Set Attributes (FILEFIND Commands menu) command, 72-73
Set Custom Message screen, 137
Set Date/Time (FILEFIND Commands menu) command, 77
Set Date/Time dialog box, 77
Set Password (NAV Options menu) command, 279
setup files, 260
   installing for others, 263-264
   loading, 261
SETUP utility, 37
SFORMAT command, 120
SHIFTSTATE (Batch Enhancer) subcommand, 175
sizes
   files, checking, 306-307
   sorting files by, 103-106
slack, 306

SmartCan (SMARTCAN) utility, 9, 83-87
SMARTCAN command, 83
SMARTCAN directory, 85
   purging files from, 86-87
SMARTCAN.INI file, 85
SMARTCAN.MAP files, 86
software
   interrupts, information about, 36
   Norton AntiVirus requirements, 268
   Norton Utilities requirements, 4
   see also programs; utilities
Software Interrupts (SYSINFO System menu) command, 36
Software Interrupts screen, 36
sort-keys, 103
sorting
   files in directories, 103-106, 302-303
   primary, 303
sounds, beeps, 147, 170
speed
   hard disks, 41
   increasing
      by defragmenting hard disks, 215-217
      by optimizing interleave factor, 219-222
      with disk caches, 218-219
   keyboard, setting, 49-50
   microprocessors, 25-26, 40-41
   mouse, setting, 51
   network connections, 42
Speed Disk (SPEEDISK) utility, 9, 215-217
speed search, 93
SPEEDISK command, 216
stamps, date/time, 76-78
starting
   NDOS, 141-142
   Norton Control Center, 45-46
   System Information, 31-33
   Virus Clinic, 274
/STATUS switch, EP command, 85
stopwatches, 53-54

storing data
  disks, 29-31
  memory, 26-29
subdirectories, 59
Surface Test Options screen, 135-137
Surface Test screen, 133
surface tests, configuring, 135-137
switches, 144
  /?, 20-21
  /4, DIR command, 144
  /A, FILEFIND command, 74
  batch files, 155-157
  /C switch, NDOS command, 144-145
  /CLEAR, FILEFIND command, 75
  /D, FILEFIND command, 78
  Directory Sort command line utility, 302-303
  dummy, 158
  File Attributes command line utility, 303-304
  File Date command line utility, 304-305
  File Locate command line utility, 305-306
  File Size command line utility, 306-307
  /HID, FILEFIND command, 74
  /LIGHT, DISKMON command, 201
  Line Print command line utility, 307-308
  /NOW, FILEFIND command, 78
  /PARK, DISKMON command, 202
  /PROTECT, DISKMON command, 200
  /R, FILEFIND command, 74
  /STATUS, EP command, 85
  /SYS, FILEFIND command, 74
  /T, FILEFIND command, 78
  Text Search command line utility, 308-309
  /TSR, SYSINFO command, 13

syntax
  NDOS commands, 144-145
  utilities, help, 20-21
SYS (DOS) command, 178
/SYS switch, FILEFIND command, 74
SYSINFO command, 32
/TSR switch, 13
system
  date/time
    setting, 55
    setting date/time stamps to, 78
  information
    displaying, 31-42, 116-119
    restoring with rescue diskettes, 182-183
  read/write patterns, testing, 219-222
system area
  boot record, 113
  FAT (file allocation table), 113-115
  root directory, 113
  saving copies in hidden files, 124-126
system attribute, 72
System Information (SYSINFO) utility, 9
  Benchmarks menu, 40-42
  Disks menu, 115-119
  File menu, 33-34
  Memory menu, 37-40
  starting, 31-33
  System menu, 35-37
System Summary (SYSINFO System menu) command, 35
System Summary screen, 32, 35
SYSTEM.INI file, viewing, 34

T

/T switch, FILEFIND command, 78
temporarily loading NDOS from DOS, 144-145
testing
  Configuration Tests, Norton Backup, 232-233

Index

disks, 132-139
  hardware, 42-44
  system read/write patterns, 219-222
Tests to Skip screen, 138
text
  colored, placing on-screen, 46-47, 167
  searching for, 308-309
    strings, 69-72
Text (DISKEDIT View menu) command, 186, 188
text boxes, 16-17
text editors for batch files, 152
Text Search (TS) command line utility, 308-309
times
  assigning to files, 304-305
  sorting files by, 103-106
  stamps, File Find (FILEFIND), 76-78
  stopwatches, 53-54
  system, setting, 55
tracks, 111-112
TREEINFO.NCD file, 94-95
TRIGGER (Batch Enhancer) subcommand, 175
TS command, 309
TSR (Terminate-and-Stay-Resident) programs, 28-29
TSR Programs (SYSINFO Memory menu) command, 39-40
TSR Programs screen, 39-40
/TSR switch, SYSINFO command, 13
.TXT file extension, 58
TYPE (DOS) command, 184

U

UNALIAS (NDOS) command, 147
undoing
  disk recovery, 179-181
  file repairs, 138-139
UnErase (UNERASE) utility, 9
  recovering deleted directories, 100-103

recovering deleted files, 79-82, 85-86
recovering files manually, 191-194
UNERASE command, 80
UnFormat (UNFORMAT) utility, 10, 126-130
UNFORMAT (DOS) command, 126-127
unformatting with Emergency Disks, 288
updating directory tree structures, 62, 94-95
utilities
  accessing from Norton program utility, 10-14
  Batch Enhancer (BE), 4, 161-175
  Calibrate (CALIBRAT), 5, 219-222
  command line, 301-302
  Directory Sort (DS), 103-106, 302-303
  Disk Editor (DISKEDIT), 5, 184-191
  Disk Monitor (DISKMON), 5, 198-202
  Disk Tools (DISKTOOL), 5, 177-182
  Diskreet (DISKREET), 5, 202-207
  Duplicate Disk (DUPDISK), 6, 130-131
  ERASE PROTECT (EP), 85
  File Attributes (FA), 303-304
  File Date (FD), 304-305
  File Find (FILEFIND), 6, 66-78
  File Fix (FILEFIX), 6, 87-89
  File Locate (FL), 305-306
  File Size (FS), 306-307
  help information, 19
  Image (IMAGE), 6, 124-126
  Line Print (LP), 307-308
  Norton AntiVirus (NAV) (Symantec), 268-285
  Norton Backup (NBACKUP) (Symantec), 226-264

Norton Cache (NCACHE), 7, 218-219
Norton Change Directory (NCD), 7, 60-63, 92-99
Norton Control Center (NCC), 7, 45-55
Norton Diagnostics (NDIAGS), 8, 42-44
Norton Disk Doctor (NDD), 7, 132-139
Norton program, 8, 10-14
quitting, 21
Rescue Disk (RESCUE), 8, 182-183
Safe Format (SFORMAT), 8, 120-124
SETUP, 37
SmartCan (SMARTCAN), 9, 83-87
Speed Disk (SPEEDISK), 9, 215-217
syntax help, 20-21
System Information (SYSINFO), 9, 31-42, 115-119
Text Search (TS), 308-309
UnErase (UNERASE), 9, 79-82, 85-86, 100-103, 191-194
UnFormat (UNFORMAT), 10, 126-130
Wipe Information (WIPEINFO), 10, 207-212
see also programs; software

V

variables, ERRORLEVEL, 168-169
VER (DOS) command, 24
video
    configuration information, 35
    displays, configuring for Norton Backup, 231-232
    memory, information about, 38
    modes, selecting, 48
Video and Mouse Options (NAV Options menu) command, 279

Video Summary (SYSINFO System menu) command, 35
Video Summary screen, 35
View AUTOEXEC.BAT (SYSINFO File menu) command, 33
View CONFIG.SYS (SYSINFO File menu) command, 33
View NDOS.INI (SYSINFO File menu) command, 33
View SYSTEM.INI (SYSINFO File menu) command, 34
View WIN.INI (SYSINFO File menu) command, 34
Virus Clinic, 268
    configuring, 277-279
    exiting, 285
    navigating, 275-277
    scan results, guidelines for, 283-284
    scanning with, 280-283
    starting, 274
    virus definitions, printing lists of, 284-285
Virus Clinic screen, 274
virus definitions, 268
    printing lists of, 284-285
Virus Intercept, 268, 272-274
    configuring, 277-279
virus signatures, 268
viruses, 197-198, 267-268
    checking for, 272-274
    preventing from writing to disks, 198-200
    scanning for, 280-283
        results, guidelines for, 283-284
volatile memory, 27
Volume Label dialog box, 97
volume labels, 97
Volume Labels (NCD Disk menu) command, 97

W-Z

WEEKDAY (Batch Enhancer) subcommand, 175

Index

wild card characters, 58
   in NDOS, 146
   searching for files, 69
WIN.INI file, viewing, 34
WINDOW (Batch Enhancer)
  subcommand, 166-167
Windows
   with Norton AntiVirus, 271-272
   with Norton Cache, 219
   with Norton Utilities, 297-300
windows
   Alert, 252
   Backup Options, 237
   creating, 166-167
   Cursor Size, 46
   Select Item, 46
   see also screens
Wipe Configuration screen, 209-210
Wipe Files screen, 208
Wipe Information (WIPEINFO)
  utility, 10
   configuring, 208-210
   wiping
     disks, 210-212
     files from disks, 207-208
WIPEINFO command, 208
WIPEINFO screen, 211